The Game Is Never Over

This book is dedicated
with love
to
Jeremy and Joshua Langford.

The Game Is Never Over

An Appreciative History of the Chicago Cubs

Jim Langford

Icarus Press
South Bend, Indiana

THE GAME IS NEVER OVER
Copyright © 1980, 1982 , by Jim Langford

photo credits
composite photo: courtesy, Donald Steinbach,
The Sports Collector's Store
Ernie Banks photo: United Press International
Jack Brickhouse photo: courtesy, WGN Continental
Broadcasting Company
all other photos: Wide World Photo

Icarus Press, Inc.
Post Office Box 1225
South Bend, Indiana 46624
12 3 4 5 6 7 86 85 84 83 82
Library of Congress Cataloging in Publication Data

Langford, Jim, 1937 -
  The game is never over.
  Enl. ed. of the book published in 1980.
  Includes index.
  1. Chicago Cubs (Baseball team) — History.   I. Title.
GV875.C6L36   1982   796.357'64'0977311   82-3033
ISBN 0-89651-266-5 (pbk.)   AACR2

Contents

Acknowledgments

It was fun to research and write this book. After more than three decades of being a devoted Cub fan, I confess that it was enjoyable to relive the high and low points of the Cub story during those years. I trust that the reader will understand that devotion does not exclude the recognition of humor.

I owe a great debt to people in the broadcast and print media in Chicago over the years: Bert Wilson, Jack Quinlan, Jack Brickhouse, Vince Lloyd, Lou Boudreau, Milo Hamilton, Jerome Holtzman, Ed Burns, Edgar Munzel, Warren Brown, Jim Enright, Dave Condon, Richard Dozer, Joe Goddard, and George Langford, to name a few. I was deeply influenced by the way they told the Cub story at the time and also as it formed part of my research.

For many kindnesses, I am indebted to the staff of the microtext reading room at the University of Notre Dame Library and particularly to Herb Juliano, curator of the excellent International Sports and Games Research Collection there. I am additionally grateful to Donald Steinbach of the Sports Collector's Store (Chicago), who provided valuable research materials from his extensive collection of Chicago Cub memorabilia. Photo assistance was also generously provided by William Wills of station WGN's publicity department.

More than a usual tip of the cap is due to Bruce Fingerhut, president of Icarus Press, for his willingness to take a chance on a rookie. To my colleagues at the University of Notre Dame Press, I owe thanks for their constant encouragement and support.

By far the largest share of gratitude goes to two very special friends, Jeanne and Bill Krier. They helped immensely in the research and revision phases, and their enthusiasm and encouragement inspired whatever merits the book may have. Any and all defects in the book belong solely to me. Though I tried to do careful research and to critique with fairness, the reader is asked to remember that this is a book about the Cubs — perhaps a few errors can be forgiven.

Finally, to all Cub players during this period, "Thanks for the Memories."

JRL

Chapter One:
On Being a Cub Fan

WE ARE DEALING HERE WITH A MYSTERY: WHY WOULD anyone of sound mind continue to love a team that has not only not won a pennant for thirty-four years, but which has done more depth-diving than the German U-boat force in World War II. Rooting for the Cubs is like continuing to fly on Disaster Airlines, Inc., with a record of at least one major crash every year; you have to be an incredible optimist, a complete pessimist, or a candidate for *The Guinness Book of World Records* in the category of stoicism in the face of interminable adversity.

I cannot solve the mystery. The best I can do is to make public a memo I wrote my two boys on what baseball means to me, then to invent a conversation with a psychiatrist on what led me to be a Cub fan, and finally to share with you letters I have written over the past thirty years to P. K. Wrigley and his son William Wrigley.

I

Memo to: Jeremy and Joshua
From: Dad
Subject: Baseball

Dear Sons:
    As you know, the snow is melting and before
long we will again experience spring. Little pieces
are beginning to appear in the back of the sports
page notifying us that spring training camps are
open; the next breeze that comes from the south
will bring with it the crisp crack of baseballs
against leather and wood. It is time for us to oil our
own gloves. Soon we'll be tossing the ball, playing
hotbox, and I'll be throwing you my split-fingered
fast ball with the house as our catcher-backstop.
Since we use a tennis ball and since the neighbors
have a picture window in straightaway center
field, I will again attempt to make you pull the ball
to the blue spruce in left. Remember, the pin oak
in right is an automatic out. I should warn you that
I intend to mix up my pitches this year. I am a year
older now and my legs and arm are not as strong as
they were last year.
    The onset of spring will require a few
adjustments in our routine and priorities. While I
really did enjoy playing Nerf football and
basketball with you, from now until October if
that is what you want to play you'll have to do
without me. I cannot be Roger Staubach and Bruce
Sutter at the same time. What I am trying to say is
that baseball will take precedence over other
activities in the months ahead. I will be needing
more time to study the sports page. In the
evenings when the Cubs are on the road, the

television is hereby reserved. Besides, you
probably watch too much television anyway.

I hope that you will want to watch a lot of
games with me. I will get you to Wrigley Field in
person as often as I can. It pleases me very much
that you like baseball. Let me tell you why.

Baseball is very much like life. Watch it
closely, and you will learn a great deal about
things like courage, beauty, strength, finesse,
chance, fallibility, and loyalty. Study baseball and
you will have a head start in understanding life.
Even at your ages, you've rallied in the late
innings and turned defeat into victory. You also
know what it is like to lose suddenly with one
mistake what it had taken time and energy to
build. You have schoolmates whose scrappiness
lifts them above their ordinary talents. And you
know others who could do a lot better than they
are doing but who don't seem to care. There are a
lot of baseball players of both types. And there are
many who are very talented and who develop their
skills to the full by giving all they have all the time.
You will see rookies whose agility allows them to
challenge established players for a regular spot in
the lineup. But note how cagey veterans use
experience and know-how to fend off such a
challenge, at least for another year. It is right that
Young Turks attempt to take over from their
elders, but strength alone cannot displace wisdom.

Let your imagination run free. Fantasize
yourself into games. Be the left fielder who makes a
spectacular leaping catch at the wall to save the
game . . . but sometimes imagine yourself as the
hitter who gave it all he had only to be denied by
that catch. Like some players, you will have days
in your life when you make two errors on the same

play; remember, there is always a chance for redemption. I've seen lots of players change boos to cheers with one swing of the bat.

In baseball as in life, there are advances and setbacks. Even in the midst of a losing streak, there is assurance that, if we keep working at it, someday soon there will again be cause for joy. And winning streaks too must end.

Baseball is not as simple as it looks. Every game presents a huge variety of possibilities that have to be weighed by the manager and coaches. At the heart of it all is the ability to take calculated risks. On every pitch there is strategy in operation: the guessing game between pitcher and hitter, where the fielders position themselves, who will cover which base, how the wind is blowing, who is next in the batting order, who to warm up in the bullpen and when to bring him in. All of this goes on simultaneously, almost instinctively, and the fan is challenged to capture all or even part of it in one eyebite.

It is good to learn that even the best laid plans can run afoul of chance and circumstance. You'll see easy grounders elude fielders by hitting a pebble in the infield, you'll watch home runs blown into long foul balls by a sudden gust of wind, and you will see games won or lost because of a checked-swing hit or the mistaken call of an umpire. There are things in life that happen like that too. The best we can do is to rebound from them with grace.

Baseball is a game of exquisite moves, of subtlety no less demanding than that of a concert orchestra. It is a thrilling sight to watch the pitching motion of a Steve Carlton, the swing of a Billy Williams or Rod Carew, the incredible fielding of a Brooks Robinson or Graig Nettles, the strong beautiful throw from a rightfielder like Roberto Clemente that cuts down a runner at the plate. Beauty is where you find it. You can even find it at Wrigley Field.

Courage, anger, exhaustion, and exuberance are part of every game, as they are of every life. If you study the records, you will discover that individual stars may dominate a team, but team play as a whole is the crucial factor in the final standings. No team has ever won a pennant without good utility players.

Finally, be gentle in your judgment of the Cubs. It does us no credit to complain about our players because they are not as good as those fielded by other teams. Our protest must be directed toward the management, which either thinks that these guys are really good or that we won't care if they're not.

At your age, Jeremy, I became addicted to baseball and to the Cubs. I used to race home from school at 2:45 so that I could listen to the last few innings of the Cubs. As soon as the radio warmed up, there would be Bert Wilson describing the scene and I could tell by the tone of his voice after only a few words whether we were ahead or behind. For my eleventh birthday in June, my father gave me the *Complete Encyclopedia of Baseball*, a book I still treasure despite its vintage. There I studied and learned the past glories of the Cubs, though they now floundered at the bottom of the League. If you think Cub fans have it bad now, you should have followed the 1948 version. We had an infield like a fishnet. Roy Smalley at shortstop and Andy Pafko — who was made to play at third though he was a fine outfielder — led

the league in errors at their respective positions.
And somebody named Dutch McCall was 4-13 on
the mound that year. But from that season on I
have never wavered even momentarily in my
devotion to the Cubs. As Bert Wilson used to
repeat time and again with two outs in the ninth
and the Cubs trailing by half-a-dozen runs, "The
game is never over until the last man is out." The
game has never been over for me. It goes on
through the winter until it takes up where it left
off the previous season. Baseball is a celebration of
hope. Maybe that's why the season begins in the
spring.

II

Not even my psychiatrist questions my love for
baseball. The last time I saw him I used some analogies
from the game to explain how optimism is so important to
my outlook on life. The next thing I knew, he wanted to go
into specifics.

"What team do you follow?" he asks.

"The Cubs," I say with no hint of apology or
embarrassment.

"Umhummm," he responds, "And how do you feel
about liking the Cubs?"

"How do I feel about it? Well, great, I guess."

"Great?"

"WHY do you like the CUBS?"

"You mean 'Why do I LOVE the Cubs?' "

"All right."

"Well, they might be a little weak at second, and they
need two starting pitchers and another outfielder,
but . . ."

"No, that's not what I'm asking you. I want to know how anyone, particularly someone with at least a modicum of intelligence, can give this kind of devotion to a team that hasn't won a pennant for thirty-four years. And that's putting it as gently as I can."

"O.K., I see. I'll tell you why. It's because of Bert Wilson, Jack Quinlan, Milo Hamilton, Jack Brickhouse, Vince Lloyd, Lou Boudreau . . ."

"Were these childhood friends of yours?"

"In a way. They were the voices I grew up with. They were the people who were on the scene; they taught me to love the Cubs no matter what."

"You heard voices . . . where were these voices coming from?"

"WIND, WGN, from all the cities in the National League and especially from Beautiful Wrigley Field."

"And what did these voices say?"

"I'll tell you what they said. Bert Wilson said that the Cubs were a wonderful team, beleaguered by bad luck, victims of circumstances, but always ready for more, always building, always about to reach their full potential, always trying. Bert taught me to believe that even if you're behind 16-0 with two outs in the ninth, there is still a chance. He was right, you know, the game isn't over until the last man is out. Jack Quinlan, Milo Hamilton, and Vince Lloyd were cut from the same cloth. They make Tug McGraw look like a plagiarist. And Jack Brickhouse taught me how to survive defeat. I mean even if we got drubbed, Jack would appear in the post-game show completely unshaken. He'd tell us not to worry, that every team has a bad day and now that we have that out of our system we can look forward to tomorrow. If it was a narrow loss, Jack would point out how close it was and how with a minor change of wind velocity at the right moment we could have won it. If we won, Jack would remind us how well our boys played, how good they are looking now, and he'd get us ready for a winning streak. The thing is, you could believe

Jack Brickhouse; you could tell he meant what he said. And Jack had been doing this for twenty-five years, so he knew what he was talking about. And from Lou Boudreau I learned how easy it is to mispronounce names. For example, he always called Len Gabrielson 'Len Gableson.' But so what? Lou's in the Hall of Fame. He knows a lot about baseball.

"I mean I was raised on these voices. I remember days in the summer when my Dad had the radio tuned to Bob Elson reciting the woes of the White Sox, and I'd stay for a laugh or two and then go outside where the sky was perfectly blue and the leaves were blowing gently on the trees that lined our street. Our neighbor would be washing his car, and he'd have the Cubs game playing on his radio, and I'd sit on his steps and pet his dog 'Boots' and root for the Cubs."

The psychiatrist took off his glasses and rubbed his eyes. He interrupted me, "That's all very nice. But surely as you grew older, you realized that there were better teams to follow."

"Hey, wait a minute! Sure there were better teams; but not worth giving up the Cubs for. Listen, it doesn't take any courage to be a Yankee or Dodger fan."

"I know, but I assume you know that of the sixteen teams in existence in 1948, all of them have won at least one pennant since then except for the Cubs. Do you regard yourself as a pessimist? Do you like pain?"

"A pessimist! I'm a fanatic optimist. If Bert, Jack, Vince, Milo, Jack, Lou, and I were locked in a stable piled to the roof with horse droppings, we'd all start digging to find the pony. No! I don't LIKE pain. Being a Cubs fan has helped me see past pain. Look. Suppose the Cubs are leading three to nothing in the ninth inning. Let's say that our pitcher slips off the mound as he is warming up and sprains his ankle. So we bring in, oh, say, Paul Reuschel. The Phillies get three hits in a row, and now it's 3-1 with runners on first and third. We bring in Willie Hernandez, and he strikes out two batters. But the next one singles, and it's 3-2. Then Ontiveros drops a foul fly, and Schmidt hits Willie's next pitch into Waveland Avenue and we lose 5-3. I'm not going to slam the television and storm around like some Yankee fan. Jack Brickhouse's "oh, brother" when Schmidt swings and connects is all the comment that's needed. If Ontiveros catches that pop foul, we win. So Ontiveros makes a mistake. Do you want me to hold that against him? We all make mistakes."

"Well, maybe the explanation is that you just have very low expectations for the Cubs, and that's why it doesn't bother you when they lose."

"Wrong again, Doc. How can I have low expectations? Every game is different. There is always a chance. Season averages don't always tell the whole story. I've seen .300 hitters strike out in crucial situations and .167 hitters win games. It's like Vince Lloyd always says, "Anyone with a bat in his hands is dangerous."

"All right. But be honest with me. Haven't you ever been tempted way down inside to abandon the Cubs for a more exciting team . . . Look at the Cardinals, you could have been cheering for Musial, Slaughter, Gibson . . ."

The passion with which he spoke alerted me to the fact that beneath the horned rim glasses and the cool, calm exterior, my shrink was a Cardinal fan. I decided to take him on. "Well," I said aggressively, "if the Cardinals are so great, why have the Cubs whipped them in a majority of series over the past twenty years?"

His eyes lit up with a fiendish flash that betrayed his loss of professional composure. "Well," he asked with a banzai tone in his voice, "THEN HOW THE HELL DO YOU FEEL ABOUT THE BROCK-FOR-BROGLIO TRADE?"

Then I knew I had him. He'd gone for the jugular. He thought he had me with two outs in the ninth and nobody on. I paused. Bert's words came back, "The game is never over until the last man is out." I looked at him calmly, like Jack Brickhouse would. "You know something, Doc? The same team that traded Brock for Broglio went on to trade Larry Jackson and Bob Buhl at the end of their careers to the Phillies for Fergie Jenkins, Adolfo Phillips, and John Herrnstein, and after getting six straight 20-game years out of Jenkins, traded him to Texas for Bill Madlock who won two straight batting titles. Besides, Billy Williams was a better left fielder than Brock anyway!"

He was stunned. We both knew that a shift has taken place. Shaken, he said that we will do a little word association and call it a day.

"Mediocrity," he said nastily.

"Improvement," I replied suavely.

"Last place," he spat.

"Mets," I retorted quickly.

"Error," he snorted.

"Smalley," I said before thinking, but, recovering quickly, I added, "Forgive."

"Hopeless," he snapped.

"Never."

"Losers."

"Wait till next year," I said.

"My bill," he cried in resignation.

"Wait till next year."

III

September 1, 1948

Mr. P. K. Wrigley
Wrigley Field
Chicago, Ill.

Dear Mr. Wrigley:

I read your ad in the paper apologizing for the 1948 Cubs. I am just eleven years old and I don't know what the answer is, but don't blame the players. Bert Wilson said that they are trying as hard as they can. Maybe we need new players. Why don't you hire Branch Rickey away from the Dodgers and give him the money he needs to build a better team? (Well, what do I know? I'm just a kid.)

> Your friend,
> Jim Langford

January 15, 1950

Mr. P. K. Wrigley
Wrigley Field
Chicago, Ill.

Dear Mr. Wrigley:

Remember me? I'm thirteen now and two years ago I wrote you and suggested that you hire Branch Rickey. I saw in the paper that you hired Mr. Wid Matthews who worked for Mr. Rickey. I still wish you'd gotten Mr. Rickey himself but maybe Mr. Matthews will be good. I wrote to Frankie Frisch applying for a job as bat boy but he never answered. I wrote to Hank Sauer and told him how glad I am that he is a Cub. He wrote me back a real nice letter. Why don't you make Hank Sauer manager?

> Sincerely,
> Jim Langford

October 13, 1951

Mr. P. K. Wrigley
Wrigley Field
Chicago, Illinois

Dear Mr. Wrigley:
      Do you think there is any possibility that Wid
Matthews is getting a kickback from Branch
Rickey? Trading Andy Pafko to the Dodgers makes
Roy Smalley look flawless by comparison. And
since you probably sign the checks, you've
probably noticed how much he is spending to buy
up leftovers from the Dodger system.
      I'm glad that Frankie Frisch has been fired and
that you're going to keep Phil Cavarretta for
another year as manager. Old number 44 is great
and if he can't do it I don't know who can.
                              As Always,
                              Jim Langford

April 3, 1956

Mr. P. K. Wrigley
Wrigley Field
Chicago, Illinois

Dear Mr. Wrigley:
      How are you? I want you to know that I think
you're getting a bum rap from the press. They say
you care more about gum than you do about the
Cubs. That isn't true. Surely you've suffered even
more than we have. You impress me as a highly
principled man. I mean, anyone who refuses to
yield to the lure of increased attendance that comes
with night baseball because you don't want to
disturb the neighborhood around your park is

somebody special. I'll bet you're even tempted to feel guilty about taking our money at the box office. Don't. We love the Cubs.

I do want to share a few thoughts with you, and since I have been writing to you for eight years, I hope you won't mind if I say what I really think.

The thing is, we are now in the seventh year of Wid Matthews' Five-Year Plan, and things look pretty bad. The fact that he just traded Hank Sauer for Pete Whisenant and $10,000 is not redeemed even by his success in getting rid of Roy Smalley.

Like you, I hoped it would work to trade a lot and to have Cubs from the last pennant team come back as managers. I think you made a big mistake in firing Phil Cavarretta, though I'm sure that Stan Hack is a nice guy. But it wouldn't be a mistake to fire Matthews. Let him go back to work for Branch Rickey; Rickey owes him one (or maybe fifteen!). Meanwhile, maybe you could see if Frank Lane would be interested in the job. What do you think?

> Devotedly,
> Jim

October 11, 1962

Mr. P. K. Wrigley
Wrigley Field
Chicago, Illinois

Dear Mr. Wrigley:

I've written you, off and on, for fourteen years. While I applaud many of the innovations you have hatched during that time to strengthen the Cubs, I'm afraid that the latest one is proving to be a disaster of rather major proportions. The Cubs have been like the Spanish army on San Juan

Hill trying to find their leaders to fend off Teddy Roosevelt's attack.

Years ago, you suggested installing a punching bag in the dressing room so that the players could work off their tensions and be relaxed at game time. How were you to know that they would take the field in such a placid manner? Then you paid for a deluxe pitching machine to help the boys in spring training. Too bad you couldn't have dressed the machine and started it on opening day. A few seasons ago you ordered an oxygen bottle for the dugout. It was not your fault that the only person who used it was Pat Peiper, the field announcer. But your idea of revolving managers is a bust. In two seasons we've won 123 and lost 193, and not one of the revolvers has a winning record. It's bad enough when the players don't know whether or where they might play on any given day; it's worse when the manager pro tempore has to be concerned about whether he'll be able to get to O'Hare in time to catch the 4:45 flight to San Antonio. Why don't you take this occasion to set a new record by firing the whole bunch at once? I've been with you up to this point, but now you're pushing it a bit. For the next month, I'm going to chew Dentyne.

Sincerely,

Jim Langford

February 6, 1966

Mr. P. K. Wrigley
Wrigley Field
Chicago, Illinois

Dear Mr. Wrigley:

I am sure you are painfully aware that in the four years since the league expanded to ten teams, the Cubs have finished ninth once, seventh once, and eighth twice. Now you've hired Leo Durocher. Putting aside for a moment the fact that I don't like Durocher's style, I think I should warn you lest you put credence in his statements and make yourself vulnerable to further hurts. I remember back in 1951 when Durocher predicted big things for the Cubs. You will recall that they finished last. The next year he made a wisecrack about Hank Sauer. Hank, you will recall, won the Most Valuable Player in the league award that year. Now Durocher is quoted as saying that the Cubs are not an eighth place ballclub. Look out, Mr. Wrigley. Remember, there are ten places in the league now.

Yours,
Jim

August 3, 1969

Mr. P. K. Wrigley
Wrigley Field
Chicago, Illinois

Dear Mr. Wrigley:

You've done it! I'll have to admit that I didn't like Durocher and still don't. I think even I could have managed this team to the pennant. This has to be one of the greatest Cubs teams ever. We have power, fielding, good catching, and fine pitching. Wow! And a majority of the roster grew up in our farm system. Those who didn't came to us in fabulous trades: Jenkins, Phillips, and Herrnstein for Jackson and Buhl; Hands and Hundley for almost nothing! Sheer genius!

I'm not a season ticket-holder because I live in South Bend. Is there any way you can see that I get series tickets? Now that we are ten games ahead of the league, I'm sure the lines are already long. Wow! Finally! Let the Yankees eat their hearts out!

Congratulations,
Jim

August 21, 1972

Mr. P. K. Wrigley
Wrigley Field
Chicago, Illinois

Dear Mr. Wrigley:

It's been nearly a quarter of a century since I first wrote you and about three years since my last letter. I decided to wait a while after what happened in 1969; I know that you were even more disappointed than I was. If we didn't know the meaning of "swoon" before then, we sure learned it that September. What rotten luck! Maybe we need to look into exorcism as a possibility.

I'm glad Durocher is gone. But it looks to me like the Cubs of '69 are over the hill. Banks, Beckert, Kessinger, Santo, Williams, Hickman, Hundley, Jenkins, Hands . . . What a team! What a shame!

About twenty years ago you said that if one system doesn't work, we'll try another. By now we

must be on system number eighteen. Let me offer
you a suggestion. Why don't we break the mold of
slow-footed sluggers, of pitching staffs built
around one bona fide starter? Let's go after some
guys who can scratch out hits and run like hell,
guys who rob hitters with astonishing speed
afield, and who show the kind of scrappiness that
slides in head first. And let's get some thin, stylish
pitchers. How about Maury Wills as manager?
We've been at it for a long time, Mr. Wrigley, but
speed's the one thing we haven't tried. If things
don't improve, I may try some myself.

All best,

Jim

November 3, 1977

Mr. William Wrigley
Wrigley Field
Chicago, Illinois

Dear Mr. Wrigley:

I was genuinely grieved by your father's
death. Although I never met him in person, I
corresponded with him for many years, and I
admired him very much. I don't think many
people have done as much for baseball as your
father did. Among many other things, it was
largely through his efforts and initiative that major
league baseball made it to the West Coast.
Moreover, he always stood high as a man of
fairness and principle. I only wish that the Cubs
could have won a championship for him.

Now that you have taken over, I hope that
they win a title for you. To be quite honest with
you, I hope they win one for me before I die.

If you go through the files, you may come
across letters I have written since 1948. I hope you

won't mind if I continue to offer a suggestion now
and then. I've spent a great deal of time trying to
figure out what possible course of action could
help us win.

Do we need more and better scouts?

Do we need to be more astute in our trades?

Do we need to concentrate on pitching,
fielding, and speed?

Should we get into the free-agent market?

☒ All of the above.

Yours sincerely,
James R. Langford

March 26, 1980

Mr. William Wrigley
Wrigley Field
Chicago, Illinois

Dear Mr. Wrigley:

I've got it! Eureka! I know how we can turn
the Cubs into winners! You are no doubt aware
that various minor leagues use a system whereby
the season is divided into two equal halves. The
team in first place after half the games are played is
declared winner of the first half. The league starts
even for the second half of the season. If a different
team comes out on top in the second half, the
winner of the first half and the winner of the
second half play off for the championship.

Mr. Wrigley, lobby, fight, scratch, and cajole
to get that system adopted in the major leagues.
Tell Bowie Kuhn he'll have a chance to play major
domo at all kinds of playoff games. He'll love it. So
will Howard Cosell.

You see, don't you, that we've got an instant
dynasty on this system? What team is always at or

near the top in late June? Right, the Cubs. July,
August, and September swoons won't matter
anymore! We can do our thing — play over our
heads for three months and then rest the next three
months, giving rookies a chance to play until the
playoffs begin. This will work! We're in!

> Go get 'em,
> Your friend,
> Jim

April 1, 1982

Mr. R. Stanton Cook, Tribune Co.
Mr. Andy McKenna, Chairman of the Cubs' Board
Mr. Dallas Green, General Manager
Mr. Lee Elia, Manager
Wrigley Field,
Chicago, Illinois

Gentlemen:

If you go through the files at Wrigley Field you may
find a bunch of old letters from someone named Langford.
Those letters never seemed to do any good. As you know,
my theory about the split season guaranteeing the Cubs a
pennant was exploded last year. I'm out of theories,
explanations, and suggestions. But for no reason at all I am
full of confidence. I really think that you are going to build a
new tradition by giving us a fighting team. In time, the
Cubs will be known as "The Green Machine." Remember
you read it first here and not in the *Chicago Tribune*.

> Devotedly,
> Langford

Chapter Two:
"Beautiful Wrigley Field"

IN THIS ERA OF DOMED STADIA, EXPANSIVE WATERFRONT parks, artificial turf, and heavy night schedules, Wrigley Field is a splendid anomaly. It sits, uncovered, in the midst of an old neighborhood in north Chicago. Both its grass and its lighting system are natural. Its exterior and interior each betray the fact that it has been here for sixty-six years and counting. No doubt it has seen happier days in more ways than one. Yet despite its lack of spatial largesse and bright colors, it looks more like a baseball park than do those giant structures built to house football as conveniently as baseball.

Inside, one feels pleasure at the beauty of the green grass, the vines covering the outfield walls, the symmetry of the left and right field bleachers as they sweep away from the large scoreboard in center. There is also a strong sense that your presence is part of what will take place here today. The seats are close enough to the field that shouts of encouragement or dismay will be heard and, if at all possible, heeded.

For Wrigley Field is more than a park with a charm all its own; it is more than a functional antique. Wrigley Field is a shrine to the endurance and resilience of hope. It is a witness to the fact that teams do not necessarily have to win pennants to inspire and keep allegiance. The Cubs have never had to be an itinerant team moving from city to city, staying only until the novelty of winning has worn off. The Cubs have been in Chicago since 1876, the year the National League was founded. And Wrigley Field has been their home since 1916, through good times and bad. There is something uniquely familial, American, traditional about Wrigley Field, something shared by no other ballpark in the country, save perhaps Fenway Park in Boston and Comiskey Park on the south side of Chicago.

Its distinction as the only major league stadium without lights indicates not merely the traditional wisdom that baseball was meant to be played in the sun, but also reflects an admirable sense of responsibility to one's neighbors. Night baseball would bring with it crowds and cars, shouts and sirens, denying the neighboring families their right to evenings of peace and quiet. As Philip K. Wrigley put it: "It's just self-protection, as I see it, to maintain good relations with our neighbors. Imagine night games in that residential neighborhood and with the noise, confusion, traffic and late hours, we'd soon lose our rating as a good neighbor." Pressured in the early sixties to install lights as a way of combatting declining attendance, Mr. Wrigley answered with true insight, "It's not night baseball we need, it's winning baseball." Record attendance in the near-pennant years of the late sixties bore out the truth of what he said.

But it is not only the neighbors of Wrigley Field who appreciate the absence of lights at the park. Scores of Cub players have said how much they prefer to play in the daylight. None has said it better than longtime Cub player, manager, and executive, Charlie Grimm: "In my time you could tell a ballplayer by his clear, sharp eyes and his ruddy skin. If things keep going in the night ball trend the modern ballplayer can be identified by the thick-lensed glasses he wears and his squint when he ventures out into the sun."

Wrigley Field is, in fact, a sign of continuity to the way baseball was played even before Charlie Grimm's time. The park was built in the teen years of this century and is now in seventh decade of continuous service. Its early contemporaries in National League cities — Forbes Field in Pittsburgh, Crosley Field in Cincinnati, Shibe Park in Philadelphia, Braves Field in Boston, the Polo Grounds in New York, Ebbets Field in Brooklyn, and Sportsman's Park in St. Louis — are all gone or retired now. Only Wrigley Field remains. So what? Nothing, except that there is a special sense of history in this field that you cannot find elsewhere. You cannot see the Reds play today in the same park where Johnny Vander Meer pitched successive no-hitters on June 11 and June 15, 1938. The Polo Grounds and Ebbets Field are parking lots now, and there is no way to see for oneself where Bobby Thomson hit his dramatic homer off Ralph Branca to win the pennant for the Giants in 1951, or where Willie Mays made his spectacular catch of Vic Wertz's long drive in the 1954 World Series, or where Jackie Robinson first took up his station at second base and broke the color line that had kept black players out of the big leagues. And so on through hundreds of memorable moments in baseball now deprived of their historical settings.

But you can still come to Wrigley Field and be in a park where all of the greatest stars in the National League since 1916 have played and where the American League champions met the Cubs in five World Series. Sample a few of the names: Grover Cleveland Alexander, Rogers Hornsby, Honus Wagner, Frankie Frisch, Mel Ott, the Waner brothers, Dizzy Dean, Bill Terry, Gabby Hartnett,

Kiki Cuyler. Or, for that matter, Babe Ruth, Lou Gehrig, Bill Dickey, Mickey Cochrane, Joe DiMaggio, Red Ruffing, Jimmy Foxx, and Hank Greenberg. In fact, a majority of those honored in the Baseball Hall of Fame came to this park, walked through its gates, dressed in its innards, leaned on its bricks, and played the game as only they could.

It was in this very park that the greatest pitching duel of all time took place. On May 2, 1917, Fred Toney, a right-hander for the Cincinnati Reds, went against Cub southpaw Jim "Hippo" Vaughn. There was not a single hit on either side for nine innings. In the tenth frame, with one out, Cincinnati's Larry Kopf singled between Fred Merkle and Larry Doyle for the game's first hit. Cy Williams of the Cubs then proceeded to muff Hal Chase's pop fly (yes, Virginia, it was happening even back then), and Kopf raced to third. Up came the fabled Jim Thorpe. He hit a high bounder in front of the plate. Hippo Vaughn came pounding in to get it and threw to the plate, but catcher Art Wilson was looking elsewhere, missed the ball, and a run scored. Toney retired the Cubs in order in the tenth to preserve his no-hitter and take the 1-0 win.

Wrigley Field was the home of Hack Wilson in 1930 when he hit 56 home runs and drove in 190 runs. It was at Wrigley Field in 1932 that Babe Ruth is supposed to have pointed to the spot where he would hit Charlie Root's next pitch and then did so. And it was here in 1938 that Gabby Hartnett hit his famous "homer in the gloaming" with two outs in the ninth to take the pennant from the Pirates and give it to the Cubs. The list of thrills could go on and on to include a perfect game by Sandy Koufax, a near perfect game by Milt Pappas, and another by Don Cardwell, a dramatic no-hitter by Sam Jones, innumerable homers by Ernie Banks, and hundreds of those late-inning rallies for which the Cubs are justly famous.

And there are other memories too, less pleasant ones.

Long-suffering Cub fans still exist who can point you to the approximate section of brick behind first base that served as a backstop for erratic throws from Roy Smalley, Andre Rogers, and Roberto Pena. Some can still see the ghosts of Cub outfielders dropping flyballs and of Cub catchers racking up passed balls, dodging wild pitches, or trying in vain to nail Maury Wills or Lou Brock at second, even on a pitchout.

But Wrigley Field has another kind of history about it too. It is a stage on which thousands of dramas have played. Even if a majority of the games were not dramatic, tension-filled battles, each one meant something in the lives of the players, managers, coaches, and umpires who participated. In the ebb and flow of careers, every game was a benchmark of sorts. Hundreds of rookies played their first major league game here. One can only imagine the emotions experienced by a young athlete the first time he puts on a major-league uniform and walks down the passageway to the field. As a newcomer, he is self-conscious. He is anxious to look good even in the way he walks and jogs and plays catch. He looks for signs of acceptance from the veterans, hoping that they have not forgotten what their first day was like. And hundreds of players put on the uniform for the last time here, experiencing that special kind of pain inflicted by the knowledge that their bodies can no longer compete against those more youthful and that not even cunning can compensate for tired muscles and slowed reflexes. Their turn is up; their names will not again be penciled into the starting lineup.

Dreams have been realized and dashed in this park. Some players were here only long enough to taste what it is like and then, judged to be in need of more seasoning, were sent away never to make it back. Others came to stay. Of these, some never lost the thrill of coming onto this field to play before its fans. Listen to Ernie Banks: "Look at those people. It's just like Ebbets Field. I think baseball is meant for small parks like this. It's a personal game. You've got to feel close, get involved. These people would sleep here if they could. So would I."

As Ernie suggests, Wrigley Field not only holds a special place in the lives of those who played here, it is also a locus of personal memories for the millions of people who have been here as fans. It is not simply a matter of recalling record-breaking performances witnessed here. The game itself is only part of the experience. The rest is a whole array of memories: recollections of being at Wrigley Field years ago with a now-deceased parent or loved one or of sharing the experience with one's own children for the first time. Few who have been to Wrigley Field forget the sights and sounds of the park, the players and the fans. The simple fact is that the park itself has an important role in the creation of that awesome steadfastness of Cub fans. It is a personal park, a vital link to the glory days of the past and to traditions that find new manifestations with each decade.

In the forties, fans had several years to follow the strange career of Lou Novikoff, the "Mad Russian," who, though the most fearsome hitter in minor-league history, never came to stay in four tries with the Cubs. As sportswriter Warren Brown describes Novikoff, no one ever claimed that he was a fielding genius. According to Brown, "The vines which decorated the walls of Wrigley Field were a constant source of worry to him. When a ball was hit over his head, the Mad Russian would back up so far, and no farther. More often than not, the ball recoiling from the wall bounded past him and in toward the infield with the Mad Russian in hot pursuit." Manager Charlie Grimm tried everything he could think of to cure Novikoff's fear of the vines. Grimm brought in samples of goldenrod to prove that the vines were not goldenrod and not likely to give Lou a case of hay fever. But that didn't work. Next Grimm demonstrated that the vines weren't poison ivy either. He pulled some off the wall, rubbed it over his face and hands and even chewed on a couple of leaves. But to no avail: the Mad Russian still stopped cold whenever he moved near the wall. Perhaps Lou's real allergy was to the solid bricks that were cleverly concealed by the vines. We may never know. The fact remains that Lou was a colorful character, and Cub fans adopted him, warts and all.

But the fans had later favorites who did better for them. In the fifties, the "bleacher bums" showered Hank Sauer with packages of Beech-Nut, his favorite chewing tobacco, as a way of saying thanks for the homers he hit into their midst. In the sixties, their shouts of "ole!" transformed Adolfo Phillips, if only briefly, into a stellar outfielder. Their favorite for 1980: Dave Kingman.

Cub players and members of opposing teams as well have often marveled at the devotion of Wrigley Field's patrons. And no one has ever accused Cub fans of being unknowing or uncritical. You can ask anyone in the bleachers what the Cubs need to become a winner, and he will tell you as astutely as any seasoned scout or general manager could. At least part of the explanation of the Cub phenomenon is the fact that the Wrigleys have always maintained the park with the comfort of the fans as a high priority. Over the years many interesting experiments have been made with the fans in mind. In 1955, a small section of the left-field grandstand was equipped with loud speakers to provide the fans with the audio portion of Jack Brickhouse's telecast of the games. A year later a "speed-walk" was installed to move thousands of fans from the ground floor to the upper deck. And a flag-signaling system was invented to accommodate those fans who hadn't been able to make it to the game; the blue "W" flag or white "L" flag gave them the day's result as they drove past the park.

Of course, the very mention of flags calls to mind for all Cub fans the wonderful aspect of chance which plays into every game at Wrigley Field. The park's proximity to Lake Michigan invites the winds that can determine to a large extent whether the game today will be a home run derby or a pitcher's duel. When the wind is blowing out, no lead is safe. When it is blowing in, powerful drives are harnessed and fall harmlessly into outfielder's gloves. Still, Wrigley Field's wind is not the gale of San Francisco's Candlestick Park; it can turn a flyball into a home run or a home run into a fly out, but it does not threaten to blow the players off the field.

Wrigley Field is regarded as a hitter's park but not because there are short fences down the line. No "cheap" home runs are hit here. It is 355 feet from home plate to the wall in left field, and 353 feet to the wall in right. But unlike the newer parks, the wall here deepens only gradually and at its furthest extension it reaches 400 feet in dead center field. The power alleys in left center and right center are more reachable here than in most parks around the league. One other factor helps the batter. The stands are so close to the field that foul flies caught in other parks are out of play in Wrigley Field, thus giving the hitter another chance to get on base. Still, Ferguson Jenkins won twenty or more games six seasons in succession as a Cub, proving that a pitcher with good stuff can win here with consistency.

This hitter's dream of a park, however, was not always the home of the Cubs. In fact, it was built in 1914 with a seating capacity of 14,000 to house the Chicago Whales of the newly formed Federal League. Begun with the idea of luring players from the National and American leagues and to compete as a third major league, the Federal League lasted only two years and folded for financial reasons. The Chicago entry, renamed the "Chifeds," was the property of Charles H. Weeghman, a wealthy restaurant-chain owner. The Chifeds, managed by ex-Cub star, Joe Tinker, finished second in 1914 and won the pennant in 1915. Weeghman had invested a quarter of a million dollars in building the park at Clark and Addison. Now he found himself without a team.

The Cubs at this time were still playing their games at West Side Park, located in the block bounded by Lincoln, Wood, Polk, and Taylor Streets. West Side Park had been the home of the Chicago National League team since 1893. There Cap Anson, Bill Lange, Joe Tinker, Johnny Evers, Frank Chance, Mordecai "Three-fingered" Brown, Heinie Zimmerman, and other legendary Cub heroes wrote their names in the record books. Weeghman, wanting desperately to stay in baseball, organized a ten-man syndicate to buy the Cubs who were then owned by the Taft family in Cincinnati. Weeghman became the president of the Cubs and Weeghman Park became their new home. In the very first National League game played here, on April 20, 1916, Joe Tinker, now the Cubs' manager, led his charges to a 7-6 win over Cincinnati. The Cubs finished the year in fifth place. When they won the pennant in 1918, it was decided to hold the Chicago portion of the World Series against the Red Sox in Comiskey Park, which had been constructed in 1910 and could hold 30,000 people. It mattered little; the Red Sox won, four games to two. Babe Ruth, pitching for the Red Sox, beat the Cubs twice in the series. He would achieve his later victories over the Cubs with a bat and wearing a Yankee uniform.

In December of 1918, William Wrigley, Jr., increased his holdings in the Cubs and Weeghman had to resign as president in favor of Wrigley's choice, Bill Veeck, Sr. Now the stadium became known simply as "Cubs Park." In 1922, Wrigley hired architect Zachary Davis, who had designed the park in 1915, to oversee a $300,000 renovation and expansion project. Four years later, with William Wrigley now in solid control of Cubs stock, the park was renamed "Wrigley Field." Before opening day, 1928,

Wrigley had added the upper deck to accommodate the fans who were flocking to see the Cubs climb to contention under manager Joe McCarthy. And in 1937, now under P. K. Wrigley's direction, the outfield area was renovated to provide improved bleacher seating and a modernized scoreboard. In 1938, the box and grandstand areas received wider seats, increasing fans' comfort but decreasing the park's total capacity.

In many ways, radio announcer Bert Wilson's effulgent praise of Wrigley Field as "the world's most beautiful ballpark" rings true. But Bert was even more on the mark in emphasizing that this is "the Home of the Cubs." He might have added, "and of Cub fans too." Since the Cubs first moved to Wrigley Field in 1916, more than 56 million people have been there to cheer, to plead, and above all, to be loyal. In stiff collars and straw hats, baggy pants and bobby sox, bermuda shorts and polo-shirts, generations of fans have come to Wrigley Field to root for the Cubs. And they are still there. The fashions change, but the fans remain. Come to the field on a day when the Cubs are losing and, with two outs in the ninth, look around. There they sit. Complaining, but alert. Frustrated, but attentive. Dejected, yet happy. For Cub fans know, together, sitting there in that wonderful green field, the game is never over. Never.

Chapter Three:
The Glorious Tradition

SEARCH THE RECORDS ALL THE WAY BACK TO THE EARLIEST days of professional baseball, and you will see that the Chicago Cubs are older even than the National League. Count the pennants brought home to Chicago since the league began, and you will come up with a total of sixteen. Check the major-league record for the number of games won in a season, and wonder at the astonishing Cubs of 1906 racking up an unparalleled total of 116 wins. Believe.

Begin in 1871. Charter teams from nine cities met that year to form the National Association of Professional Baseball Players, with the Chicago club dubbing itself "the Chicago White Stockings." (Despite the name, the White Stockings were the antecedents of the present-day Cubs, not of the White Sox. There are scholarly ways of proving this, but perhaps the fate of the White Stockings in their very first season will be enough to make the point.) In the historic opening season, the White Stockings won their first seven games but then lost a tough one to the New York Mutuals, owned by the notorious Boss Tweed. New York quickly took over first place. But midway through the thirty-game season, the White Stockings worked their way back into first and held the lead into the last week of the season. A pennant? Not quite. On October 8, Mrs. O'Leary's cow started the Chicago Fire, and the Chicago White Stockings went from hot to cold. The fire burned out their Lake Street ball park, and they had to play their remaining games on the road. Result? Three straight losses and a season finish in second. Does the strange bad luck seem familiar? Hold on — there's more.

Due to the aftereffects of the fire, Chicago had to drop out of the association for the next two years. But Mr. William A. Hulbert, a man who loved Chicago and baseball, accepted the presidency of the White Stockings in 1875 and set about not only to bring a winning team to Chicago but also to put baseball on a sound and honest footing. The National Association was being overwhelmed by problems of gambling and game fixing.

Hulbert wasted no time accomplishing his goals. Even before accepting the presidency, he had contacted star pitcher A. G. Spaulding of the Boston club and convinced him to come back to the "west" and help build a winner. Three other stars of the Boston team also signed on. Then Hulbert signed Adrian "Cap" Anson and Ezra Sutton from the Philadelphia team. Signing another team's players was against the rules of the league, but the eastern owners had been doing it for years. Hulbert intended to beat them at their own game. Anticipating the anger of the easterners, Hulbert and Spaulding laid plans for a new league to be called the National League of Professional Baseball Clubs. By a series of skillful presentations, Hulbert managed to carry the day, and the National League opened for business in the spring of 1876. The National Association was out of business after five years.

Guess which team brought home the very first pennant in the National League? That's right — Chicago. Hulbert, who said that he would rather be a lamppost in Chicago than a millionaire in any other city, had brought a winner to the city he loved. Spaulding, the club's manager, was also its ace pitcher, with a 47-13 record. He played only one more year with the club, but his memory lingers on: his name appears to this day on every official National League baseball.

In 1879, Cap Anson took over as manager. Anson, a graduate of Notre Dame, was, until Ernie Banks, the greatest of all Cubs. His record was genuinely impressive. He played twenty-two seasons for Chicago, hitting over .300 in twenty and serving as manager in nineteen. Additionally, he racked up 3,041 National League hits while compiling a .333 lifetime average in the league. From 1880 to 1882 Anson and his boys dominated the league, winning three pennants in a row. The White Stockings definitely had the razzle-dazzle of champions. They dressed in expensive uniforms and could be seen riding to the park at 22nd and State Streets in an open carriage drawn by white horses. Ah, those were the days!

Chicago added two more pennants to its collection in 1885 and 1886. The White Stockings featured the incredible battery of John Clarkson and Mike "King" Kelly. In those two pennant seasons, pitcher Clarkson won 92 and lost 30, while Kelly averaged .340. But the Chicago brass let go of each of these players. Enticed by the highest cash offer ever made up to that time, Hulbert sold Kelly to Boston for $10,000 in 1887, and a year later, did it again, letting Clarkson also go to Boston for the same price. *The Chicago News,* reacting to the sale of stars, urged a reduction in ticket prices, claiming that if Chicago was to have cheap players it ought to have cheap admission too.

Salary disputes throughout the season led to the formation of a new league called the Player's League in 1890, and many veterans jumped from the National League, lured by the promise of bigger paychecks. The new league lasted only a year, but the White Stockings had been hit so hard by defections that Anson was forced to break in a group of rookies. The White Stockings' name was discarded in favor of "Anson's Colts."

But the Colts didn't exactly race to dramatic finishes. There were no more pennants won under Anson and, after the 1897 season, he was fired. The Colts, now without their leader, became known as the "Orphans." Just one year later a young man joined the team as a catcher, and it was he who as manager and first baseman would lead them back to the heights. He was Frank Chance, the Peerless Leader. Chance wasted no time in proving his value to the team. A player of extraordinary ability, Chance could field, hit, and run bases with great skill. He was switched from catcher to first base, where he earned his greatest fame. Chance kept alive the tradition of star first baseman/ managers that looked back to Anson and in years ahead would feature Charlie Grimm and Phil Cavarretta.

Meanwhile, action was developing on the south side. In 1900 the American League was founded and a second Chicago baseball-club franchise was formed for the team belonging to Charles A. Comiskey. Since the name "White Stockings" was no longer being used by the Chicago National League team, Comiskey appropriated it for his club, and it was not long before sportswriters shortened it to "White Sox."

In 1902 the Chicago National League team became known as the "Cubs," taking the name from a Chicago sportswriter's reference to the number of young players signed to fill gaps from defections to the American League. President James A. Hart and manager Frank Selee began to assemble a cast that year that would make the Cubs the most feared team in baseball. Trades, purchases from minor league teams, and some splendid signings by Cub scouts brought to Chicago catcher Johnny Kling, infielders Johnny Evers and Joe Tinker, outfielder Jimmy Slagle, and

pitchers Mordecai "Three-Fingered" Brown and Ed Reulbach, who, like Anson before him, came off the campus of
Notre Dame. The 1902 team, with potential but little
experience, finished the season in fifth place. Sometimes
inexperience leads to interesting experiments. Nineteen-
year-old-pitcher Jimmy St. Vrain, for example, was a
terrible right-handed hitter. He decided to have a go at
batting left-handed in a game against the Pirates. On the
first pitch he actually hit the ball, a slow low grounder to
shortstop Honus Wagner. Immediately, St. Vrain dashed
across the plate with his head down and elbows pumping.
Across the plate? Yes. Directly to third base. Wagner, along
with everyone else at the park, was stunned: "I'm standing
there with the ball in my hand looking at this guy running
from home to third, and for an instant I swear I don't know
where to throw the damn thing. And when I finally did
throw to first I wasn't at all sure it was the right thing to
do."

Well, it took this club a few years to mature. In 1905
manager Selee resigned because of illness, and Frank
Chance was named to succeed him. The Cubs were moving
up, however, and finished second that year to John
McGraw's Giants. At the end of the season, Hart sold the
Cubs to Charles Murphy, who was backed by Charles P.
Taft of Cincinnati. Hart should have waited a bit longer.
The team that he had been building became a baseball
dynasty.

In 1906, the Cubs ended a nineteen-year-pennant
drought with a vengeance. They won 116 games and lost
only 36, still a major-league record. It was an awesome club
with Steinfeldt, Tinkers, Evers, and Chance around the
infield; Sheckard, Slagle, and Schulte in the outfield; and
Kling behind the plate. On the mound, Brown as 26-6,
Reulbach 20-4, Pfeister 19-9, and Lundgren 17-6. The Cubs
finished twenty games ahead of the Giants and looked
forward to their first World Series. Their opponents were

none other than the Chicago White Sox. The Cubs seemed a cinch. The had outscored their regular-season opponents 704-381, while leading the league in hitting, fielding, and pitching. The White Sox had outscored their opponents only 570-460, with a team batting average of .230, thus earning the nickname "The Hitless Wonders."

The Windy City was in turmoil for weeks before the Series. Partisans backed their favorites with bets and fists. It seemed almost to be a civil war between the south side and the west side. Newspaper reports told of company foremen having to send Sox fans to one department and Cub fans to another to preserve the peace. When the Series opened on October 9, it was bitterly cold and snowing in Chicago. The White Sox won the first game, 2-1. But Cub confidence returned the next day as Reulbach hurled a one-hitter for a 7-1 victory. The third game: back to the Sox, winning behind Ed Walsh's two-hitter, 3-0. Never mind. The Cubs evened the Series on a 1-0 two-hitter by Brown. What happened next is still hard for Cub fans to swallow. The White Sox, the Hitless Wonders, won 8-6 and 8-3 to become World Champions.

But this Cub team was too good to be denied for long. The next year, 1907, they again won the pennant, this time by sixteen games over Pittsburgh. They went on to sweep the Series from the Detroit Tigers, four games to none. Ty Cobb hit exactly .200 against Cub pitching. And why not? The Cub staff had a combined ERA of 1.73 during the regular season. The World Champion Chicago Cubs! Encore!

The road to a third straight pennant was made rough the following year by the New York Giants. In late September with these two bitter rivals meeting at the Polo Grounds, fate smiled on the Cubs. The game was tied 1-1 in the bottom of the ninth, and the Giants had runners on first and third with two out. Al Bridwell then lined a hit to center, and the runner came home from third with what seemed to be the winning run. The fans began to pour out on the field, and nineteen-year-old Fred Merkle, playing his first full game with the Giants, did what most players did in those days. With the winning run coming across the plate and the game seemingly over, he didn't bother to finish his trip from first to second. In fact, avoiding the Polo Grounds fans, he ran to the clubhouse. Fiery Johnny Evers, however, knew he could call for a force-out at second. Just weeks earlier he had successfully worked the same play. But as the throw came in from the outfield, Giant player Joe McGinnity intercepted the ball and threw it into the stands. Undaunted, Evers ended up on second base with a ball in his glove and claimed a force-out. Umpire Hank O'Dea concurred. Where did he get the ball? Years later he claimed it was the original ball: "I can still see the guy who caught McGinnity's throw. A tall, stringy middle-aged gent with a brown bowler hat on. Steinfeldt and Floyd Kroh, a young pitcher of ours, raced after him. . . . The guy wouldn't let go of the ball. But suddenly Kroh solved the problem. He hit the customer right on top of the stiff hat and drove it down over his eyes. As the gent folded up, the ball fell free." Original ball or not, Merkle had been ruled out. A near riot ensued, and the game could not be resumed. It was decided that if necessary it would be replayed the day after the regular season ended. It was necessary. The Giants blew a five-game lead over the Cubs, and both teams finished with identical records of ninety-eight wins and fifty-five losses. The replay of this game would decide the league championship.

Of course the Cubs took advantage of their controversial opportunity and won the game 4-2, beating the Giants' ace Christy Mathewson (37-10 for the season). On to the World Series. Again it was the Tigers, and again the Cubs beat them handily. This time, though, the Tigers did manage to win one game. Two straight World Championships!

Nineteen hundred and eight was the last season for Cub

outfielder Jimmy Slagle. Though not of Hall of Fame calibre, Slagle was a good centerfielder and more than once showed he was a true Cub. In *Touching Second*, Johnny Evers recounted an incident that illustrates Slagle's inimitable style. In the eighteenth inning (yes, eighteenth) of a game with Philadelphia that the Cubs finally won 2-1 in the twentieth, Slagle had shoved his hand into his hip pocket to get his chewing tobacco when the batter cracked a drive to left center. Slagle started after it and discovered to his horror that his right hand would not come out. He raced on, leaped up, and made a fine glove-hand catch, saving the game for the Cubs. Then he pulled out his tobacco, bit off a piece, and grinned as the crowd cheered.

The 1909 Cubs won 104 games but finished six games behind the amazing Pittsburgh Pirates. In 1910, the Cubs again won 104 times, but it was good enough for first place, a full thirteen games ahead of the Giants. Four pennants in five years! This time, however, they came up against the Philadelphia Athletics in the Series, and the result left no doubt that the Cub dynasty had come to an end. The Athletics won easily, four games to one. In the process they hit Brown, Reulbach, Overall, and Pfeister for thirty-five runs in five games.

The decline set in, slowly at first and then more rapidly. In 1911 the Cubs finished second to the Giants. In 1912 they were third, unable to capitalize on Heine Zimmerman's Triple Crown season. After the 1912 season, Cub owner Charles Murphy fired Frank Chance and denounced the players for laxity. Chance countered that the players were sober enough, but there just were not enough good ones on the team to win pennants. And he offered a reason why: Murphy was a skinflint who wouldn't pay to get the necessary players. Tinker, Brown, and Reulbach were promptly traded away. As if to salve the feelings of Cub fans, Johnny Evers was appointed manager, but when all he could manage was a third-place finish in 1913, he too

was fired. Murphy offered to trade him to Boston, but
Evers threatened to join the outlaw Federal League, which
was now forming. The National League office decided to
step in. A meeting was held, and Murphy ended up selling
out his interest in the Cubs to his partner Charles Taft.
Evers went to Boston and helped them win the pennant in
1914. In that same year, following a series of successful
player raids on the National and American leagues, the
upstart Federal League declared itself a major league. Its
Chicago franchise, the Whales, was owned by Charles
Weeghman who tried desperately to compete for Chicago
baseball fans. Weeghman built a handsome park at Clark
and Addison Streets to house his team, but despite a
second-place finish in 1914 and a pennant in 1915, the
Whales and their league were short-lived.

Weeghman survived the failure of the Federal League,
however, and formed a syndicate that bought the Cubs
from Taft. He installed them in his ball park and hired
ex-Whale manager Joe Tinker to lead the team for the 1916
season. Unfortunately, most of Tinker's regulars were
senior veterans, and the best they could do was struggle to
a fifth-place finish. Tinker was blamed and was fired in
favor of Fred Mitchell. There was no noticeable improvement in 1917, and again the Cubs settled for fifth place.
That season was distinguished, however, by a double
no-hit game on May 2 at Cubs Park. After ten innings of
play, Cub pitcher Jim "Hippo" Vaughn lost what has been
dubbed "the greatest pitching duel in history" to
Cincinnati's Fred Toney. (See Chapter 2: "Beautiful
Wrigley Field.")

During the off-season, the Cubs made one of the greatest
deals in their history. One of the best batteries in the major
leagues, pitcher Grover Cleveland Alexander and catcher
Bill Killefer came to the Cubs for two irregulars and a sum
of cash estimated at $60,000. Alexander did not stay around
long that year, for it was 1918 and able bodies were needed

to end "the war to end all wars." Virtually all the ball clubs relied on veterans, minor leaguers, and the physically impaired to get through the season, which was curtailed right after Labor Day by a "work or fight" order. At that point the Cubs were 84-45, in first place, ten-and-a-half games ahead of the Giants. Score one more pennant for the Cubs. It seemed right and just to award the National League flag to Chicago, since with that large a lead they probably would have won even if the season hadn't been shortened. Fifty-one years later such logic would be challenged by the 1969 New York Mets.

Even though World War I curtailed the 1918 season, permission was granted for a World Series. The Cubs and the Boston Red Sox squared off. The Cubs were led by pitcher Hippo Vaughn and Boston by a pitcher-outfielder named Babe Ruth. In the opening game, Ruth shut out the Cubs for a 1-0 win, despite the fact that Vaughn allowed only two hits and the Cubs managed six off Ruth. The Cubs won the second game, 3-1. The next day, Vaughn lost 2-1 when Cub second baseman Charlie Pick tried to steal home with two out in the ninth. The Red Sox's third victory was Ruth's second, 3-2. But Vaughn came back in the fifth game to pitch a five-hit shutout. Not enough. The Red Sox finished off the Cubs with a 2-1 win on two unearned runs. Hippo Vaughn had done yeoman's service, giving up exactly three runs in twenty-seven innings and finishing with a 1-2 record. Babe Ruth? Well, at least he only batted .200 in the series.

In December of 1918, William Wrigley, Jr., acquired enough of Weeghman's stock in the Cubs to become the team's new owner. He took an active hand in the direction of the club, having Weeghman resign as president in favor of Cub manager Fred Mitchell. But the National League office nixed this appointment by ruling that a person could not be field manager and president at the same time. Thus came to the presidency a former Chicago sportswriter who used the pen name "Bill Bailey." His criticism of the Cubs had intrigued Mr. Wrigley to the point of offering him a chance to do better. The writer's real name? William L. Veeck.

It would be pleasant to recall how the Wrigley-Veeck duo built a winner quickly, but the fact is that they didn't. Over the next five years, the Cubs won a total of four more games than they lost and hung around fifth place as though it belonged to them. Managers were changed — Mitchell yielding to Evers and Evers yielding to Bill Killefer after less than a year. But no period in Cub history was without Cub heroes and team heroics. Pitching for the fifth-place Cubs in 1920 was Grover Cleveland Alexander, who won twenty-seven, lost fourteen, and saved five, while compiling a 2.91 ERA. On August 25, 1922, the fifth-place Cubs knocked off the seventh-place Phillies, 26-23. The Cubs racked up fourteen runs in the fourth inning alone. That is the stuff dreams are made of!

In preparation for the 1922 season, the Cubs trained for the first time at Catalina Island, Mr. Wrigley's private haven off the coast of California. Scenic it was, but fun in the sun it wasn't. Sportswriter Warren Brown relates how manager Killefer used the hills on the island as part of a concerted program of road work. Day after day the players ran up and down and around those hills until rookie catcher Gabby Hartnett anguished, "I hope they've got those turns banked in the National League infields, because one of my legs is shorter than the other from trying to navigate those damned hills."

But Catalina failed to make a difference. Fifth in 1922, fourth in 1923, and fifth again in 1924, the Cubs of 1925 hustled to make some deals. By giving up pitcher Vic Aldridge and first baseman Al Niehaus, Veeck acquired two talented and fun-loving baseball players named Rabbit Maranville and Charlie Grimm. Halfway through the 1925 season, Killefer was fired as manager and

Maranville selected to replace him. Rabbit lasted for a total of fifty-three games, during which a good time was had by all until Veeck decided that enough was enough, and he replaced Maranville with George Gibson for the last twenty-six games of the season. The year of the three managers was a disaster. For the first time in their history, the Cubs finished in last place.

Wrigley and Veeck were humiliated by their cellar club. What they did about it was typical of the glorious tradition of Cub history. Taking a series of calculated risks that were, at the very least, unorthodox, they hired, for openers, a manager who had never played, managed, or even coached in the major leagues: Joe McCarthy. Next, as a result of a clerical error the Giants had made, the Cubs snatched away a 5'6", 195-pound outfielder named Hack Wilson for a few thousand dollars. Wilson had played for Toledo, a Giant farm team. McCarthy, who had managed for Louisville in the American Association, then pointed Veeck in the direction of other minor-league players — outfielder Riggs Stephenson and pitcher Pat Malone among them. From the Cubs' Los Angeles team came pitcher Charlie Root. It was as though the cast was simply waiting to be assembled and rehearsed under McCarthy's master direction. In 1926, the first year of rehearsal, the Cubs rose from eighth to fourth place. And they did it without the services of Grover Cleveland Alexander, their top pitcher in the previous seven years. Alexander had his own way of staying in shape, and it didn't always work. McCarthy promptly sold him to the Cardinals, thereby letting the Cubs know that he meant business and that they had better come to the park ready to play.

In 1927, the Cubs were fourth again, this time with another new member of the cast, shortstop Woody English, who was acquired from Toledo. In 1928, with the addition of outfielder Kiki Cuyler, the Cubs moved up to third. Slowly and surely the Cubs were building a winner.

It seemed that only one more ingredient was needed and that was a quality second baseman. Why not get the best? Veeck went to Boston, giving up five players and the then astronomical sum of $120,000. He came home with Rogers Hornsby.

Nineteen twenty-nine. The Cubs infield was Grimm, Hornsby, English, and McMillan; the outfield was Cuyler, Wilson, and Stephenson; and the catchers were Hartnett and Zack Taylor catching a starting four of Root, Bush, Malone, and Blake. Despite an injury that incapacitated Hartnett, the Cubs won the pennant by ten-and-a-half games over the Pirates. Hornsby hit .380, Stephenson batted .362, Root was 19-6, Wilson hit .345 with thirty-nine homers and 159 RBIs. Cub fans, 1,485,166 of them, packed Wrigley Field to watch some of the best baseball ever played in Chicago. The fans understandably began to think of their Cubs as invincible. They looked forward to vanquishing the Philadelphia Athletics in the World Series.

On October 8, Wrigley Field was dressed up in its World Series best for the first time. The Cubs set up additional bleachers beyond the outfield walls, making it possible for 50,740 to cram the park for the opener. Manager Connie Mack of the Athletics surprised everyone by starting a little-used left-hander named Howard Ehmke against Charlie Root and the Mighty Cubs. All Ehmke did was to strike out thirteen Cubs, a new World Series record, and limit them to one run on eight hits. Jimmy Foxx homered for Philadelphia, one of three runs they scored to win the opener. In game two, Foxx hit a three-run homer and Al Simmons had four RBIs as the Athletics behind George Earnshaw and Lefty Grove pounded the Cubs, 9-3. Once again, thirteen Cubs whiffed.

When the Series moved to Philadelphia, the Cubs responded with a 3-1 win, thanks to a two-run single by Cuyler and superb pitching by Guy Bush. Then came the deluge. In the fourth game with the Cubs leading 8-0 in the seventh inning, the Athletics launched the most explosive inning in World Series history. Before the inning was over, they had scored ten runs, aided in part by Hack Wilson's losing the ball in the sun. The 10-8 loss shocked the Cubs and their faithful. But the surprises were not over yet. In the fifth game, the Cubs led 2-0 in the bottom of the ninth, only to lose the game, 3-2, and the Series, 4-1.

Cub fans today can only imagine what it would be like to be upset about losing a World Series. Such a luxury! But the fans of 1929 had been spoiled during the season by their Cubs, and they were in no mood to accept the Series outcome in docile fashion. That infamous seventh inning was the focus of attention, and the blame was put on Wilson for his fielding miscue and McCarthy for not making the proper pitching changes. All through the 1930 season the bitter taste lingered. The Cubs made a determined effort to repeat as league champions, but a strain existed between McCarthy and the Cub brass. For his part, Hack Wilson did everything humanely possible to erase the memory of the ball lost in the sun and to give McCarthy another pennant. He hit .356 with a league record of fifty-six homers and a major league record 190 RBIs. His slugging percentage was an incredible .723. But even that, along with great seasons for Cuyler, Stephenson, and Hartnett, was not enough. When it became apparent that the Cubs would not overtake the Cardinals, McCarthy resigned and was replaced for the last four games of the 1930 season by Rogers Hornsby. In later years, Cub management and fans would wish that McCarthy was still wearing Cub colors. Leading the Yankees to seven world championships, Marse Joe would be back in Wrigley Field to take two World Series from the Cubs.

Under Hornsby, the 1931 Cubs came in third behind the Cardinals and Giants. It was a frustrating season. The "Rajah" was outspoken in his approach to Veeck and to the players. He managed the team by standards players found difficult to meet. For while it may have been true that he never asked his players to do anything he wouldn't do himself, it was also true that he wasn't satisfied with anyone doing less than he did. Of course, the problem with this approach was that he was one of the greatest players in the history of the game. Hack Wilson's problems with Hornsby, along with his own fiery temper, took him into a prolonged slump. From his phenomenal pace of 1930, Wilson dropped to a .261 average, thirteen homers, and sixty-one RBIs. It was his last season as a Cub.

"New Faces of 1932" made for a smash hit. Billy Jurges was installed at shortstop. Woody English was moved to third, with Billy Herman taking over at second to hit .314 in this, his rookie year. Johnny Moore hit .305 as Hack Wilson's successor in center field. And Lon Warneke in his first full season won twenty-two and lost only six. In early August, with the Cubs locked in a three-way race with Pittsburgh and Brooklyn, Hornsby was fired. The genial Charlie Grimm replaced him as player-manager. Behind Grimm, the Cubs rallied to win the pennant by four games. Their opponent in the World Series was Joe McCarthy's New York Yankees. It was a mismatch. The Yankees swept the Series, outscoring Chicago 37-19. Yankee bench jockeys rubbed it in from start to finish. The Cubs even had to put up with the story that Babe Ruth had called his home run off Charlie Root in the third game. Whether he had pointed to center field or not, he may as well have. Cub fans were more tolerant of the Series result than they had been three years earlier. Perhaps they had the feeling that they would get another chance before too long. The Wrigley-Veeck combination that had brought a pennant-winning team to Chicago was ended in 1932 with Mr. Wrigley's death. Philip K. Wrigley inherited the team and kept Veeck as president until Veeck died in 1933. William Walker was then appointed president to succeed Veeck, but he was removed after one year when Mr. Wrigley himself assumed the presidency.

Even though the Cubs dropped to third in 1933 and stayed there through 1934, no one could deny that Grimm's charges played some pretty exciting baseball. In 1935 the Cubs put on the most thrilling stretch drive in the history of the game. They had won eighteen in a row when they went to St. Louis for the final head-on collision with the second-place Cardinals. With the Cubs' one-game lead on the line, Lon Warneke bested Paul Dean 1-0 to give the Cubs a two-game lead with two games to go. The lone score came on a home run by Grimm's successor at first base, a seventeen-year-old rookie named Phil Cavarretta. The Cubs won the double-header the next day, finishing the season with twenty-one straight victories and another flag for Wrigley Field. The infield of Cavarretta, Herman, Jurges, and Stan Hack combined with outfielders Chuck Klein, Frank Demaree, and Augie Galan, and catcher Gabby Hartnett to give Chicago the most potent attack in the league. Cub pitching, led by twenty-game-winners Lon Warneke and Bill Lee, was also the best in the league. This time the Series was against the Detroit Tigers, not the Yankees, and the Cubs figured to win it. Warneke won the opener in Detroit with a four-hit shutout, 3-0. The Tigers routed Root the next day for a 9-6 win. Then, in Chicago, the Tigers edged the Cubs 6-5 in eleven innings and followed that with a 2-1 victory, scoring the winning run on two Cub errors. Cub fans were disconsolate. Back to Detroit, the Cubs, behind Warneke again, won 3-1. But in a heartbreaking sixth game, the Tigers broke a tie in the bottom of the ninth to take the series four games to two.

With basically the same lineup, the Cubs were in contention in 1936 and 1937, but finished second both years. Time for surprises. On April 16, 1938, the Cubs made an incredible deal with the Cardinals. For $185,000 and three pretty fair players, the Cubs received what was

left of Dizzy Dean. With his fastball gone, what was left
was a reservoir of cunning and courage. But wait — there's
more. Slightly past the halfway mark of the season, Charlie
Grimm told Mr. Wrigley that for the good of the team he
would step down as manager. The Cubs were in third
place, more than six games out, and Grimm was convinced
that Gabby Hartnett was the man to take his place.
Hartnett, a superb catcher and hitter, was not as easygoing
as Grimm, but he did have a fine-tuned sense of humor.
And once when he was reprimanded by Judge Kenesaw —
Landis, Commissioner of Baseball, for allowing his picture
to be taken leaning over a box seat talking with the
notorious Al Capone, Hartnett responded, "If you don't
want anybody to talk to the Big Guy, Judge, *you* tell him."

Grimm joined Lew Fonseca as a radio broadcaster of
Cubs and White Sox home games. From the booth Charlie
watched as Hartnett's Cubs tried to catch the Pirates. On
September 17, the Cubs were three-and-a-half games back.
But the Pirates began to slide. On September 27 they came
to Chicago nursing a slim one-and-a-half-game lead. This
was a three-game shutdown series, and Wrigley Field
attendance would have its season peak. Game number
one: score yet another surprise move for the Cubs. Gabby
announced that Dizzy Dean would pitch the opener. Dean
hadn't started for five weeks, and his 6-1 record had been
attained with nothing but slow curves, pinpoint control,
and a lot of confidence. What could he do against the
Pirates? Hold them scoreless through eight innings. The
Cubs entered the ninth with a 2-0 lead. In the Pirate ninth
with two men on base and two out, Gabby called in his
tired ace, Bill Lee. Dean was given a standing ovation as he
left. Lee allowed a hit, and it was 2-1; but he fanned the
next batter, and the Cubs were now only a half game off the
pace.

The next afternoon saw Pittsburgh take a 5-3 lead into
the bottom of the eighth inning. To the delight of 34,465

fans, the Cubs scored twice and the game was tied. It was growing dark, and the umpires huddled to discuss whether to call the game in favor of a doubleheader the next day or to play one more inning. They decided to continue. Charlie Root retired the Pirates in the ninth, so the Pirates called in their ace reliever, Mace Brown, to protect the tie. When Phil Cavarretta flied out to right and Carl Reynolds grounded out, it seemed certain that the only winner would be the darkness. Then Manager Hartnett came to the plate. A swing and a miss. Strike one. A swing and a foul, strike two. Brown decided not to waste a pitch, and he threw his third consecutive curve ball. A mistake. Gabby was ready and drove it through the gloaming over the left-center-field wall. He was escorted around the bases by ecstatic fans and teammates. In later years he commented, "That was really the highlight of my career. When I got to second base, I couldn't see through the people, there were so many people on the field. And when I touched third base, believe me, my feet never touched the ground till I got to home." The Cubs were in first place! The Pirates were demoralized and lost the next day to Bill Lee, 10-1. At the finish, the Cubs were a full three games ahead of the Pirates, having won twenty-one of their last twenty-five games. Another miraculous finish in the glorious tradition.

The World Series against Joe McCarthy's Yankees opened in Chicago. Babe Ruth was gone, but the Yankees still boasted stars like Gehrig, Dickey, DiMaggio, Crossetti, and Red Ruffing. The Series lasted only four games with the Yankees scoring twenty-two times to nine for the Cubs. Only Dizzy Dean even came close to winning a game for the Cubs. He held the Bronx Bombers to two runs through seven innings, but they caught up with his "nothing" ball in the eighth and claimed a 6-3 win.

Cub fans were not happy. Neither was the management. It was decided that an overhaul was in order. Jurges,

Demaree, Collins, O'Dea, and Carleton were among those that were dealt away. But not much came in return. Dom Dallessandro and Bill Nicholson were brought up from the minor leagues. But the glory days were gone, at least for now. In 1939, the Cubs managed to finish fourth, and a year later they slipped to fifth. P. K. Wrigley decided that more drastic changes were needed for 1941. Hartnett was fired in favor of another ex-catcher, Jimmy Wilson. And James T. Gallagher, a sportswriter, was recruited to be general manager. The trick had worked twenty-three years earlier when William Wrigley had tapped Bill Veeck, Sr. But Gallagher wasn't the answer. His first trade of note sent Billy Herman to the Dodgers for an outfielder named Charlie Gilbert. Herman was one of seven ex-Cubs on the Dodgers' championship team. The Cubs fell to sixth place.

Then came the war. President Roosevelt said it would be good if baseball could continue, but it would get no special favors. Teams would have to make do with whatever talent they could find and for as long as they could hold on to it. Fans would simply have to be tolerant. For the most part, they were. But a sixth-place finish in 1942 followed by fifth a year later brought cries of "fire him" aimed at Jimmy Wilson, war or no war.

Finally, early in the 1944 season, Wilson gave way to Charlie Grimm. Charlie had done it before; maybe he could do it again. Some good players did grace Wrigley's friendly confines during these years: Bill Nicholson, Phil Cavarretta, Stan Hack, Clyde McCullough, Claude Passeau, and Hank Wyse among them. The Cubs had a second baseman named Eddie Stanky in 1943, but he was traded to Brooklyn a year later.

Grimm brought savvy as well as humor to his job, and he pulled the Cubs up to a fourth-place finish. In fact the Cubs were shaping up to be not a bad team even by peacetime standards. Second baseman Don Williams and rookie outfielder Andy Pafko looked especially promising. Still,

Cub fans were not so bold as to think that their favorites would challenge seriously for the flag in 1945.

When the season was half over, the Cubs were still dogging the Cardinals in the race for first. The Chicago infield of Cavarretta, Johnson, Merullo, and Hack, and the outfield of Peanuts Lowrey, Pafko, and Nicholson were doing pretty well. So was Mickey Livingston behind the plate. Hank Wyse, Claude Passeau, Paul Derringer, and Ray Prim were the starting four, and the only question was whether they could hold out for the whole season. That question never needed answering. Thanks to the carelessness of American League general managers, the Yankees managed to secure waivers on Hank Borowy, who was 10-5 at mid-season. The Yankees offered their star pitcher to the Cubs for $100,000 and a few players, and Gallagher was quick to accept. Borowy won 11 of 13 decisions as a Cub and compiled a classy 2.13 ERA. The Cubs won the flag by three games over the Cardinals. More than a million fans had come to Wrigley Field to celebrate the unexpected bonanza.

On to the Series against the Detroit Tigers. It was certainly not a classic in the sense of brilliant play. But it was exciting in its own way. Borowy opened with a 9-0 shutout, but Virgil Trucks came back the next day to even the Series with a 4-1 win. Game three went to the Cubs, 3-0, on a masterful one-hitter by Claude Passeau. Rudy York had the only Tiger safety, a single in the third. The Tigers won the next two games, 4-1 and 8-4. Chicago tied the Series at three apiece with a twelve-inning 8-7 decision. In the seventh game, Detroit scored five times in the first inning and coasted to a 9-3 victory. Sportswriter Warren Brown had predicted that this would be a Series that neither team could win — and he was nearly right.

In 1946, with the war over, some pretty good baseball players turned in their khakis for pinstriped uniforms. Unfortunately, too few of them belonged to Chicago. With pretty much the same cast as had won the pennant, the Cubs managed to finish third in 1946. The following year they slipped to sixth.

The story of what happened over the next thirty-two years is told in the chapters to come. It should be read against the backdrop of a proud tradition of sixteen pennants, ten of them since 1900, and four of them in the ten seasons from 1929-38. It is a story that continues the drama of unorthodox moves, calculated risks, mid-season surprises, and stunning peformances, despite the seasonal absence of World Series drapes from the walls of Wrigley Field. Baseball is a patient game — it is not run by a clock, but by rules, records, performances, and, yes, luck. The game does not end by a buzzer or a gun. It is never over till the last man is out. So, too, the story of the Cubs is far from over. The glorious tradition is only in the middle of the seventh. The top of the order due up. Jolly Cholly Grimm is in the dugout slapping players on the back. And WGN rookie broadcaster Jack Brickhouse is in the press box, singing the praises of Beautiful Wrigley Field. Take a stretch.

Chapter Four:
The Fifties: Fantasies and Failures

NINETEEN FORTY-EIGHT SEEMS LIKE A LIFETIME AGO. Sirloin steak sold for forty-nine cents a pound. Lettuce cost barely a dime a head. Fifty-one cents bought a pound of coffee (a *pound*, not a cup). And a gallon of gas rang up at fourteen cents — including tax! But forget prices; in many ways things weren't all that different. Nineteen forty-eight was an election year and incumbent Harry Truman was strongly criticized for the high inflation. When the Russians heated up the Cold War with their blockade of Berlin, Truman called for a reinstitution of the registration for the military draft. A new republic named Israel was proclaimed on May 14, and immediately was at war with its Arab neighbors. And Harold Stassen, then forty-one years old, was running for president. Sound familiar? What about these names? Ronald Reagan and Shirley Temple co-starred in *That Hagen Girl*. John Wooden coached the basketball team at Indiana State Teachers College. And Citation won the Kentucky Derby and went on to become the last triple crown winner until an incredibly beautiful horse named Secretariat captured the fancy of American sports fans in 1973.

But to American sports fans in 1948, baseball reigned as the country's "national pastime." On April 18, President Truman threw out the first ball to open the major league season at Washington's Griffith Stadium for a game between the Senators and the Philadelphia Athletics. It was a time of post-World War II energy, optimism, and change, and the sport of baseball itself reflected that national spirit of growth and rejuvenation. This was true especially in terms of personnel. Before the start of the 1944 season, over three hundred major league players had been pressed into military service. But by 1948, the teams were virtually back to full strength. Some new players entering these ranks were making history that reached beyond baseball. In 1945, Branch Rickey defied the "gentleman's agreement" to keep major league baseball segregated and signed the incomparable Jackie Robinson to play with the Dodgers. In 1947, Robinson made his major league debut and immediately distinguished himself by becoming the National League Rookie of the Year. (His salary for 1948 was tripled to $15,000.) Two years later, he received the league's Most Valuable Player award. Other black baseball players soon followed Robinson, bringing their impressive talents to the sport — players like Larry Doby, Satchel Paige, and Roy Campanella.

Baseball fans in 1948 could look, literally, to one other phenomenally promising source of growth for the sport — television. The first televised major league game had occurred in 1939 when NBC broadcast a game between the Brooklyn Dodgers and the Cincinnati Reds at Ebbets Field. Early baseball telecasting was, to say the least, technically wanting. Reception was generally poor, and the baseball field was rather broad for the limited range of the television cameras. However, the television audience itself was also rather limited. By 1945, only 5,000 television sets could be found in American homes. But by 1948, over 1 million sets were owned across the country, and the market for televised sports had grown dramatically. The first commercial rights for a season of baseball television broadcasts were sold in 1946 by Yankee president Larry MacPhail for $75,000. Indeed, by the late sixties, the big business, multi-billion dollar relationship between major league baseball and television would reach the point that ballclub owners would admit that baseball could not survive without the revenues from television. Television truly nurtured the sport. It is remarkable to realize that before 1955 no one living west of the Mississippi (except in St. Louis) would have been able to see a major league baseball game.

So spring of 1948 saw a country well primed for baseball. In Chicago that year, a young sportscaster named Jack Brickhouse was making his debut as an announcer for WGN-TV. Joe Wilson was already announcing Cub games for WGKB-TV (the station that first telecast a Cub game in 1946). The following year Rogers Hornsby, former Cub manager and player, would broadcast the games from the press box for WENR-TV. So in 1949, all Cub home games were being televised on three different networks. (Of course, radio broadcasts of Cub games reached a wide listening audience at that time. In 1947, the Midwest Baseball Network was formed with twelve member stations receiving WIND's Bert Wilson's play-by-play account of the games. Within a year, the number of stations in that network nearly doubled.)

Unlike many other baseball team owners who initially feared that television would hurt their attendance, Wrigley welcomed both increased radio and video coverage of Cub games. Accommodations were made to suit the media; holes were dug out for television cameras and crews in the first tier of boxes and on both sides of the dugout; and in

the press box, WGN set up its "advanced" cameras with
the protruding three-foot-long "zoomar" lens to bring the
action of the game "right into the lap" of the viewers.
Wrigley's largest accommodation was to give to the
networks the television rights to the game. Free. The
Chicago Cubs Newsletter reported that "The Cubs are giving
the televison rights to the stations at no charge . . . . The
Cubs realize that television is in its infancy, but believe
that some day video may play an important role in
baseball. Therefore, the Cubs feel it is only fair to give the
television stations in Chicago every opportunity to
develop, and improve on, techniques . . . without our
adding to the video industry's problems." The organization let it be known that "win or lose, the Cubs are
determined that their fans find out for themselves exactly
what happened during the Cub games."

Unhappily for Cub fans, more often than not, "lose" beat
"win" in those video verité days of broadcasting. The
Cubs, which had won the National League pennant in
1945, had, by 1947, dropped to a disappointing sixth place.
Only Philadelphia and Pittsburgh finished with worse
records. This dismal performance made it clear that the
Cubs could no longer compete by standing pat with
holdovers from the 1945 team. It was decided that what was
needed was youth; new faces, new talent. It was up to
general manager Jim Gallagher (who had taken the job in
1940 on the premise that he had to do better than his
predecessor because he couldn't do any worse) to find the
players. Once on the field, "Jolly Cholly" Grimm would
mold them into a team.

Nineteen forty-eight had barely started before the Cubs'
annual hyperenthusiasm began in earnest. The Associated
Press had sent word coast to coast that on February 5 the
Cubs had signed George Zoeterman, an eighteen-year-old
sensation who had pitched four no-hitters in high school.
"Cub plans call for a speedy indoctrination course which

could bring him to Wrigley Field late next season for his debut." With or without speedy indoctrination, Zoeterman never did make his debut, but many did — some earlier than they should have and others who never should have. Ever.

Spring training for this season opened at Catalina Island, also a property of Mr. Wrigley, twenty-four miles off the coast of southern California. Veterans like Phil Cavarretta, Andy Pafko, Eddie Waitkus, and Bill "Swish" Nicholson were joined by young hopefuls like Clarence Maddern, Roy Smalley, Cliff Chambers, Bob Rush, Russ Meyer, "Rube" Walker, and Hal Jeffcoat. Charlie Grimm allowed as how "We've got some good looking kids in camp. They show a lot of promise." But such restraint in the usually ebullient Grimm should have been a clear sign of what was to come. There was talent out there, but the Cubs couldn't seem to locate it. While the Cubs were working with Smalley, Maddern, and Jeffcoat, other teams in 1948 were developing players like Richie Ashburn, Whitey Lockman, Roy Campanella, and Duke Snider, to name a few.

The season opened on Friday, April 23, at Wrigley Field with a game against the Cardinals. The Cub loss was prophetic.

Seven weeks into the season the Cubs' destiny was clear.
Poor Chicago. Its two teams were on their way to finishing
dead last in their respective
leagues. Frustration ran
high. One Chicago newspa-
per did its best to bolster the
fans' spirits. It printed the
standings upside down,
boosting the Cubs and Sox
straight to the top. But the
Cub infield itself seemed as
though it was playing upside
down. Waitkus, Schenz,
Smalley, and Pafko were, to
say the least, erratic and
unpredictable. Cub hitting, on the other hand, was all too
predictable. So poor was the offense that Charlie Grimm
begged his scouts to comb the minor leagues for someone
who could knock in a run now and then. Within days he
received a wire from a scout which read, "Spotted a pitcher
who stopped a good team cold for nine innings. Only one
ball hit out of the infield and that was a foul fly." Grimm, so
the story goes, wired back, "Forget the pitcher. Send the
guy who hit the foul."

Opening-Day Lineup, 1948

Schenz, 2b
Waitkus, 1b
Jeffcoat, cf
Pafko, 3b
Cavarretta, 1f
Nicholson, rf
McCullough, c
Smalley, ss
Meyer, p

The 1948 Cubs finished in last place, winning sixty-four
games and losing ninety. This must have been a painfully
difficult season for those few players from the 1945
championship team who had survived the youth movement. Perhaps their only consolation was that the
crosstown White Sox, nicknamed "The Runless Hose" that
year, finished with the even worse record of fifty-one
wins, one hundred and one losses. Jim Gallagher, who had
earned his job by saying he couldn't do worse, had. Yet,
like so many Cub general managers, he found cause for
optimism, stating publicly that "The 1948 Cubs were the
best ball club ever to finish last in the National League."

No doubt many members of other last place teams were duly insulted. Still, in all fairness, it must be pointed out that this was only the second time the Cubs had ever ended up last, and the first time had been back in 1925.

Perhaps no one was more disappointed about the 1948 season than Wrigley himself. He seems to have felt a genuine obligation to give the fans a good brand of baseball. The fact that 1,237,792 people paid their way into Wrigley Field to see a last place team may have been financially reassuring, but it also seemed somehow unsporting. In fact the season had begun with an apology to the fans for the first increase in ticket prices since the early twenties; box seats went from $1.80 to $2.00. Now, at season's end, Wrigley placed a prominent ad in the Chicago newspapers:

> To Chicago Cub Fans
>
> The Cub management wants you to know we appreciate the wonderful support you are giving the ball club. We want you fans and Charlie Grimm to have a team that can be up at the top — the kind of team that both of you deserve.
>
> We also know that this year's rebuilding job has been a flop. But we are not content — and never have been — to just go along with an eye on attendance only. We want a winner, just as you do, and we will do everything possible to get one.
>
> If one system does not work, we will try another. Your loyal support when we are down is a real incentive for us to try even harder to do everything in our power to give us all a winner.
>
> Thanks,
> The Chicago Cubs

With the rebuilding effort having been declared a "flop," the Cubs decided to trade for veterans in preparation for 1949. "Experience" became the watchword as the Cubs bargained in the winter trading market. First baseman Eddie Waitkus and pitcher Hank Borowy were dealt to the Phillies for pitchers Emil "Dutch" Leonard, thirty-eight, and Walt "Monk" Dubiel, thirty. Catcher Clyde McCullough and young pitcher Cliff Chambers were sent off to Pittsburgh for veteran Frankie Gustine, a third baseman, and Cal McLish, the best ambidextrous pitcher ever to come out of Anaderko, Oklahoma. The Phillies took "Swish" Nicholson for Harry "the Hat" Walker. And young Russ Meyer, whose ten victories for the Cubs in 1948 included a one-hit shutout, a three-hit shutout, and a four-hit shutout, strangely was sold to the Phillies, a deal the Cubs would rue for years to come. To cap it off, the Cubs signed pitcher Mort Cooper, thirty-five, as a free agent. Mort had been 3-10 with the Braves and Giants in the previous season.

As the Cubs went to spring training in 1949, Grimm offered his own version of an apology for the 1948 season by announcing, "You won't be able to recognize the Cubs this season!" Of course, you could. The outfield of Peanuts Lowrey, Andy Pafko, and Harry Walker, and the infield of Phil Cavarretta, Emil Verban, Roy Smalley, and Frankie Gustine showed only one relative newcomer, Smalley, now in his second season. Still, there were rookie hopefuls in camp; Smokey Burgess, Carl Sawatski, Carmen Mauro, and Ransom Jackson among them. Indeed, spring reports from Catalina touted an outfielder named Cliff Aberson as the best young prospect in years. Charlie Grimm stated flatly, "Cliff Aberson is my left fielder until someone takes the job away from him." One wonders how Charlie kept a straight face. One week later, having watched Cliff called out on strikes three times in a row in an exhibition game, Grimm said, "Well, he doesn't charge after the ball in the outfield and he's slow besides. He'd have to hit a lot to compensate for all this, and I don't see how anybody can hit if he doesn't swing." (Aberson played four games with the Cubs that season.)

Asked why the Cub rookies were not of better calibre, Grimm explained that the Cubs do their scouting differently from other clubs. "When a prospect is presented, he must be reviewed by a committee which decides whether the kid should be scouted further and signed. By this time," said Charlie, "someone else has probably paid him a bonus and signed him." Apparently there was no shortage of young talent. At least on other clubs. During the exhibition season Grimm said in awe, "I've seen enough youngsters on the rosters of some clubs, the Indians in particular, to start a new league."

On opening day, April 19, 1949, Governor Adlai Stevenson, Mayor Martin Kennelly, and celebrity Bing Crosby were on hand to see forty-one-year-old Rip Sewell of the Pirates beat the Cubs 1-0. This was the third time he had shut them out on opening day at Wrigley Field and the first step toward matching his seven victories over the Cubs in 1948. Dutch Leonard pitched well for the Cubs, allowing only five singles. The run that lost the game was unearned — error Smalley.

Opening-Day Lineup, 1949

Walker, lf
Gustine, 3b
Cavarretta, 1b
Pafko, cf
Scheffing, c
Jeffcoat, rf
Smalley, ss
Verban, 2b
Leonard, p

By May 1, the Cubs were at home in the cellar, after the infamous "homer in the glove" game which they lost to the Cardinals on the previous day. (See Chapter 7, "Games to Remember.") Chicago sportswriters were not gentle to the Cubs. Ed Burns, commenting on the upcoming May 19 roster deadline (by which time six Cubs would have to be cut) said, "Since more than half of the Cubs have been playing like minor leaguers, it is difficult to speculate on the names of the inadequate half dozen who must depart." If nothing was working, why not trade? Hank Schenz went to the Dodgers for Bob Ramazzotti, pitcher Jess Dobernic was sold to the Reds, and outfielder Hank Edwards came from the Indians for cash. But it didn't make a bit of difference. What next? Rumors circulated to the effect that life was too easy for the Cubs under Grimm. Wrigley reaffirmed his faith in Charlie but said succinctly, "I am not happy with the number of Cub losses in ratio to victories."

And so it was that on June 14, Grimm was made a vice-president and Frankie Frisch, the Fordham Flash and fiery second baseman of the old Gashouse Gang, took over as manager. Frisch, a coach with the Giants, learned of the offer from Giants' manager Leo Durocher, who had taken the phone call in the Giants' dugout. Frisch could find no one, not friends, relatives, or especially his wife who thought he should accept the job. But he respected Grimm and Wrigley, and he simply loved to manage. He had managed the 1934 Cardinals to the world championship, and he knew he was Grimm's personal choice as his successor with the Cubs. Grimm's praise of Frisch revealed as much about Grimm's experiences as player and manager with the Cubs as it did about Frankie: "The Cubs have never had a fighting manager of the Frisch type for forty years. The last manager who'd compare with Frisch in my book is Frank Chance."

So the two of them set to work enthusiastically to bring major league baseball back to Chicago. Gallagher was being edged out of his function (if not his title) as general manager, but not before he engineered one of the best trades ever made by the Cubs. He sent Peanuts Lowrey and

Harry Walker to Cincinnati for outfielders Hank Sauer and Frankie Baumholtz.

Frisch's competitive fire may have made the Cubs less complacent on the field, but still they lost. And lost. Under Frisch, the Cubs won forty-two and lost sixty-two games, giving them a season total of sixty-one wins and ninety-three losses, the worse ever by a Cub team. They were back in the basement again. After the season, the Grimm-Frisch duo devised a three-year plan that sent them to the trading market in search of surplus talent from better teams. Their bargaining power was about as real as that of a panhandler in Las Vegas. Their chips had finished last in the league in fielding and runs scored and next to last in pitching.

Enter Mr. Branch Rickey of the champion Dodgers. Undoubtedly one of the shrewdest men in baseball history, Rickey had built a first-rate minor league system, developed a superior scouting force, and established a quasi monopoly on promising young talent. A good trader knows what to keep and what to sell. Buyer Beware! The Cubs sent Mr. Rickey a check for $100,000 in return for pitcher Paul Minner and first baseman Preston Ward. Remember Jackie Robinson's salary? While spending this kind of money, the Cubs were also busy reducing their support of their own farm teams. From twenty teams in 1947, to fifteen in 1949, they cut themselves to ten teams in 1950. This seemed to be in direct contradiction to one of the planks in "The Cubs Platform" announced with regularity in *The Chicago Cubs News*. It read in full:

The Cubs Platform
1. A world's championship.
2. Continued comfort for the fans.
3. To make Wrigley Field America's finest recreation center.

4. Baseball's no. 1 farm system.

The violation of number four would be notable except that they had already failed to deliver on number one.

Now that Grimm and Frisch were in charge of making deals for the Cubs, Gallagher felt free to speak his mind about the danger of any team (the Cubs weren't the only ones) giving their money to Rickey: "Rickey is the greatest salesman in baseball. He never sold a player who was worth a quarter, but he has received millions for them." Rickey replied that no one had a gun to the heads of the buyers. He also pointed out that by this time in the Cub organization Gallagher was little more than "a glorified office boy."

Despite their last place finish in 1949, the Cubs drew 1,157,200 fans, only a slight drop from the previous year. The newly formed Cub Junior Booster Club no doubt helped attendance that year — over 90,000 Chicago youngsters were issued membership cards which gave them a free visit to Beautiful Wrigley Field for a Cub game of their choice. But even with the boosters, the Cub efforts to improve had failed. Mr. Wrigley, reminded of his newspaper ad which had said, "If one system doesn't work, we will try another," said now, "The trouble is we are now on our third system." He noted that the Cubs had spent two million dollars in the past three years trying to find, develop, and buy talent. How poorly the money was spent can be seen from the following vignette: Grimm and Frisch met with Lou Perini of the Braves in an effort to buy Warren Spahn or Johnny Antonelli. Instead, they came away with Bill Voiselle in exchange for Gene Mauch and $35,000.

Thanks in part to a continuing feud with Gallagher, Charlie Grimm resigned as vice-president in January 1950 to accept the managerial post with the Dallas minor league team. "These hands were never intended to carry a brief case," said Charlie. So departed from the scene, at least for a while, one of the most colorful men in baseball. When

Frisch had taken over as manager of the Cubs, Charlie advised him to coach at third base himself, instead of sending out one of the junior coaches. Grimm reasoned that it helped the team's morale to know that the manager was out on the field taking the same abuse from the fans that they were. Charlie had a way of turning hostility into humor. Once when the Cubs were suffering a drubbing, Charlie used his spikes to dig a hole in the dirt by the coach's box and then proceeded to bury his scorecard, a gesture that showed how clearly he understood and shared the fans' disgust.

A poll of Cub fans, taken early in 1950 (the year the farm system had been reduced to ten teams), revealed that 87 percent of them felt that the Cubs should work on developing an outstanding farm system instead of relying on trades to acquire leftovers from other teams. The fans indicated that they were willing to stick with rookies and be patient until they developed into stars. They got their opportunity to be patient; very patient. On the spring roster in 1950, twenty-one of the thirty-nine players listed were products of Cub farm teams. Ah, youth! Frisch, in a moment of candor, wished for a few veterans, and the Cubs did buy thirty-five-year-old Johnny Vander Meer from the Reds. In addition, Andy Pafko, Phil Cavarretta, and Hank Sauer were still around. But the commitment to youth was to be tried again. Given that commitment, it was not surprising that they turned to the Dodgers' system to find someone who should know about such things. Wid Matthews was hired away from Branch Rickey and made director of player personnel for the Cubs. Frisch helped instigate the appointment as well as the transfer of Gallagher from player development and trades into the position of business manager. Matthews, with Frisch's help, worked out a five-year plan that would put the Cubs back in contention. Enter the Matthews era.

As the Cubs prepared for spring training in 1950, it seemed that things might take a turn for the better. Mr.

Wrigley spent $7,000 hosting all the players and brass for a week on Catalina Island prior to the opening of camp. The idea was for everyone to get to know each other better, to develop some genuine camaraderie. Wrigley said in an interview that the Cubs "have been failures the past two years because they lacked spirit. They just haven't had the will to win." Asked how this spirit could be instilled, Wrigley said he didn't know. He went on, "Recently I have been bombarded in that regard by an avalanche of letters, telegrams, and phone calls from a fellow in St. Paul who calls himself 'The Personality Kid.' He has never given me an explanation of what his plans are to inject that winning spirit into the boys. Maybe he just charms them with his personality." But Wrigley apparently felt that the Cubs already had what they needed. He told reporters, "Grimm was a leader; Frisch is a driver. He'll drive these fellows and tongue-lash them into hustling. Perhaps that will turn them into a fighting ball club."

At Catalina Island, Frisch was determined to live up to expectations. He did put up a sign in the training camp locker room that read, "If you like your job it should be fun." But the camp was tightly organized, and Frankie told the press, "The players are going to run until their tongues hang out." Problem: Of twenty pitchers on the spring roster, a grand total of two had struck out more batters than they walked in the previous season. Solution: Frisch ordered two catcher's mitts made of white leather. He explained: "Maybe these fellows can't see the dark colored gloves." It was going to be that kind of year. Matthews and Frisch had a massive task in front of them. Wid's self-proclaimed slogan was, "If what you did yesterday still looks big to you, you haven't done much today." A lot of doing seemed in store for the Cubs.

As spring training ended, Mr. Wrigley hosted a final party. Captain Phil Cavarretta, on behalf of the team, gave Wrigley a watch engraved, "In appreciation of the splendid vacation you gave the 1950 Chicago Cubs." That turned out to be prophetic. Cavarretta told Wrigley, "We hope we can give you a better present by winning a few ball games for you this season." That also turned out to be the case.

The 1950 season opened with Frisch's promise that "Nobody will outhustle us." Three hustling rookies were in the Cubs starting lineup: Preston Ward, Wayne Terwilliger, and Bill Serena. It was Serena who was regarded as the prize of the lot. In 1947, with Lubbock of the West Texas-New Mexico League, Bill had hit fifty-seven home runs and driven in 190 runs in 137 games. (He also committed sixty-four errors at third base that year.) The Cubs had purchased him from Dallas for $35,000. It seemed a bargain, especially since Branch Rickey was not involved in the transaction.

> *Opening-Day Lineup, 1950*
>
> *Terwilliger, 2b*
> *Jeffcoat, rf*
> *Ward, 1b*
> *Sauer, lf*
> *Pafko, cf*
> *Serena, 3b*
> *Smalley, ss*
> *Owen, c*
> *Schmitz, p*

The Cubs surprised everyone by playing almost even with the league for the first half of the season. As might be expected with a young team, their play ranged from brilliant to miserable. Wid Matthews summed it up: "They break your heart one day and have you wondering whether they'll ever win another game and then the next day they look so wonderful they have you floating in the clouds."

There were bright spots; Hank Sauer, whose forty-ounce bat was the heaviest in the majors, Roy Smalley and Bill Serena were hitting with power and young Bob Rush was pitching well. But the defense was terrible, and the pitching staff spotlighted the team's inconsistency. On July 26, Walt Dubiel was pitching a strong game and had a 4-0 lead in the sixth inning. He proceeded to lose control and walked six batters, five of them in a row, gave up six runs, and lost the game 6-4. Asked why he didn't take Dubiel out, Frisch replied, "I would have kept Dubiel in there for ninety-nine runs. I'm determined to find out what's going on. I'm sick of watching some of my pitchers getting into jams, then peeping out to the bullpen to see if a reliever is ready to take over their work for them. I want to find out if Cub pitchers have to have a lantern on the plate to find out where it's located."

By August, the frustrated Frisch had found out. The .500 season was a bust and the Cubs, Reds, and Pirates were fighting for the cellar. The young Philadelphia Phillies, nicknamed "The Whiz Kids," were headed for a dramatic pennant. Four members of this championship squad were ex-Cubs: Waitkus, Nicholson, Meyer, and Borowy.The Cubs, meanwhile, were setting a new national league record for strikeouts by a team (757). Sportswriters started calling them "The Whiff Kids."

Unlike the previous two teams, these 1950 Cubs did not lose the fight for the cellar. Their seventh-place finish put them only two games behind the sixth-place Reds. Home attendance climbed slightly to 1,165,944, not because the Cubs were lowest in the league in hitting and fielding (their 201 errors were high in both leagues), but because there actually were some causes for joy and, even, real optimism. Pafko hit 35 home runs; Sauer, 31; Smalley, 21; and Serena, 17. Among the pitchers, Frank Hiller was 12-5; Bob Rush, 13-20; and Johnny Schmitz, 10-16.

In this season of ups and downs, nothing seemed to play to form for this young team. Hank Sauer, voted by the fans as the starting left fielder on the All-Star team, became the focus of ridicule when manager Burt Shotton of the Dodgers tried to keep him out of the game on the grounds that he was too poor defensively. Shotton wanted to use his Dodger, Duke Snider, in place of Sauer. "We want to win this one," he explained. To Chicago fans, it looked like an

Eastern conspiracy. Frisch led the uproar: "Shotton says he wants to win, huh, well, Snider sure looked great in the world series last year (1949). He couldn't hit a ball past the pitcher and he looked lousy in centerfield. I wouldn't trade one Sauer for three Sniders." Sauer was restored to the lineup, played four innings, and drove in a run with a sacrifice fly in the National League's 4-3, fourteen-inning win. Nor did the Cubs take Shotton's remarks lightly; they beat the Dodgers twelve out of twenty-two games in 1950, and that reversal of form was one of the reasons the Dodgers finished in second place by two games.

Post-season trading in 1950 was slow. North Korean Communist troops had invaded South Korea and in December President Truman reinstituted the draft to meet the crisis. Bad news from the front meant that young players and even veterans of military service were liable to be called. The Cubs began to think more fondly of forty-one-year-old Dutch Leonard and thirty-six-year-old Johnny Vander Meer. They also ventured to buy a few more players from Branch Rickey before he left the Dodgers to become general manager of the Pirates. They obtained Kevin "Chuck" Connors, Dee Fondy, and Omar "Turk" Lown. But by and large, the Cubs were ready to stand pat. After all, no less an authority than Leo Durocher, manager of the New York Giants, was quoted as saying that the Cubs should be regarded as the dark horse team of 1951. Citing the Cubs' young infield as evidence, Durocher said, "Just remember what I'm telling you: look out for the Cubs in 1951."

During these years a south-side movement had also been taking place. While the Cubs were pinning their hopes on Smalley, Terwilliger, Serena, Ward, and Mauro, the White Sox under Paul Richards and Frank Lane had come up with Chico Carrasquel, Nellie Fox, and Billy Pierce. Guess who they bought Carrasquel from? Of course. Branch Rickey and the Dodgers. Gallagher notwithstanding, it was clear some people could deal with Rickey and win. Chico was a steal.

The 1951 season started out well. Instead of a celebrity, a loyal Cub fan was selected to throw out the first ball and this seemed to help for a while. In the first month of play the Cubs looked as sharp as any team. Could Durocher have been right? On May 20, with 42,088 cheering fans at Wrigley Field, the Cubs staged two ninth-inning rallies to sweep a doubleheader from the Braves and move to within a game of the league-leading Dodgers. Dutch Leonard was the winning pitcher in both games. By June 1, they were still as high as third place, only three-and-a-half games from the top. Then came one of those patented June Swoons and a fall from third to sixth place. In mid-June, in part as an effort to shake the team out of its June slump, the Cubs made an eight-player deal with Wid Matthews' old employers, the Dodgers. Going to Brooklyn were two established stars, Andy Pafko and Johnny Schmitz, and two good prospects, Rube Walker and Wayne Terwilliger. Coming to Chicago were lefty Joe Hatten, infielder Eddie Miksis, outfielder Gene Hermanski, and catcher Bruce Edwards.

Opening-Day Lineup, 1951
Terwilliger, 2b
Baumholtz, rf
Sauer, lf
Jeffcoat, lf
Serena, 3b
Pafko, cf
Smalley, ss
Walker, c
Minner, p

Other pennant contenders were flabbergasted at the deal and claimed that they had offered more than the Dodgers did to get Pafko. Sportswriters used phrases like "the great daylight robbery" and "the deal that defies the laws of sanity" to describe the trade. Only the $3.5 million Brinks robbery in Boston the year before seemed more larcenous. The baseball world reckoned it was such a steal for the

Dodgers that a rumor circulated claiming the Dodgers had promised to sell Duke Snider to the Cubs for $200,000 at the end of the season, thereby completing the deal. Wid Matthews said that he "deeply resented the stories of what suckers the Cubs were." He surely must have felt confident that his days in the Dodger organization gave him a better knowledge than his critics' of the players he had acquired. In addition, the deal was effective for drawing attention away from the rags-to-riches White Sox, who were beginning to sparkle.

But while the trade may have gotten notoriety, it did not stop the headlong slide of the Cubs. Stories of dissension on the team began to appear, culminating in an article quoting Cub players to the effect that Frisch was a "lousy" manager, berating players in public, and ranting and raving to excess. Frisch held a clubhouse meeting at which he demanded to know who had said these things. No one owned up. Frisch said later, "You don't find real ballplayers talking like that. There weren't any .320 hitters or twenty-game winners among those gripers." Frisch knew what he was talking about. Not one Cub was hitting .320 or winning twenty games that season.

June was a trade. July was a manager. On July 21, Frisch was fired. Hired for his fiery temperament, he was apparently fired for the same reason. Cub Captain Phil Cavarretta, thirty-four, was named player-manager. In making the announcement, Wrigley said that Phil would manage only for the rest of the season, unless, of course, the Cubs by some miracle won the pennant. He then would be sent to manage in the minors before returning later as manager of the Cubs. Wrigley's reasoning went like this: "Suppose we hired him outright and things didn't go well. We'd have to fire him and no one else would hire him and he'd be through." "In the meantime," said Wrigley, "we thought that he could transmit some of his indomitable spirit into the ball club."

Cavarretta, although not exactly "The Personality Kid," was a great competitor. When the Cubs won sixteen of the first thirty-four games played under his direction, Wrigley relented and gave Phil a contract extending through the 1952 season. Thereupon the Cubs lost fifteen of the next nineteen games and settled into the cellar. The foursome recently acquired from the Dodgers didn't do much. Bruce Edwards, a sore-armed catcher, was tried at first base, and his play there was said to make Zeke Bonura look like a ballet dancer by comparison. Hermanski hit .281 and Miksis .266; Hatten won 4 and lost 4. For the Dodgers, Pafko hit .248 with 18 homers and 58 RBIs in half a season.

But 1951 was the season of Bobby Thomson's home run in the playoff that won the pennant for the Giants over the Dodgers. It was the season that the White Sox rose to fourth place. And it was the season that the Cubs' attendance, at 894,415, dropped below the million mark for the first time in seven years. Bert Wilson's "Beautiful Wrigley Field" wasn't enough to draw crowds anymore. The fans wanted to see good baseball. The Cubs finished last in the standings, last in fielding, and seventh in hitting and pitching. And so ended the second year of Matthews' Five-Year Plan.

At season's end, Wid had a moment of candor and admitted, "We have to do something to get by the next two years. We'll try to make some deals." He was elated that two National League clubs called to talk possible trades with him: "For nearly two years I've been wearing out shoe leather chasing after other people. But nobody seemed interested in what we had. Now they are finally coming around. It's the best evidence we've had so far that we have some topflight players." Wid was grateful for signs of approval no matter how slight. Meantime, the Cubs traded Carmen Mauro to the Dodgers' Montreal farm team for catcher Toby Atwell, and sent Frank Hiller to the Reds for Willie "The Knuck" Ramsdell. Smoky Burgess and Bob

Borkowski also went to Cincinnati for catcher John Pramesa and outfielder Bob Usher.

In January, 1952, at a luncheon with press, radio, and TV sportspeople, Matthews began his annual speech about how good the Cubs would be next season. He said that if Bruce Edwards' sore arm responded to treatment, the Cubs could build a winner around him. Mr. Wrigley, often wrongly accused of not caring about the Cubs, stunned the audience by interrupting Matthews. He said that it was time for some realism. He gave his own assessment of the situation: "At the moment I will regard Edwards as no more than a patched-up ballplayer out of whom we hope to get as much service as possible until we can get somebody better. If and when his arm heals there will be enough time to celebrate." Wrigley went on to say that the Cubs had spent more than $2.5 million since 1947 on player development. He said that he didn't have much hope for improvement in 1952 and cited the team's needs as a first baseman, two outfielders, and three catchers.

In 1952, the Cubs moved to a new location for spring training. Instead of Catalina Island, they met at Rendezvous Park in Mesa, Arizona, where they were welcomed by a local civic group named the Ho-Ho-Kams (named, disturbingly, after an Indian tribe that had mysteriously disappeared). The rendezvous, however, was a promising one. Cavarretta was impressed by the rookie prospects, especially pitchers Bob Kelly and Fred Baczewski and catcher Harry Chiti. But with nearly a third of all Cub farmhands, 101 out of 335, now in the armed forces, there was not a surplus of material to choose from. Still there were indications that young Cub regulars like Dee Fondy, Ransom Jackson, Eddie Miksis, and newcomer Toby Atwell might combine with the experience of Hank Sauer, Frankie Baumholtz, Warren Hacker, and Bob Rush to pull the Cubs out of the cellar and maybe even more.

The Cubs got off to a fine start in the regular season, winning ten of their first fourteen games. As late as June 18, they were in second place only four games behind the Dodgers. Well, why not? Now in the third year of the Five-Year Plan, Matthews had had enough time to assemble a twenty-five man roster consisting of fourteen ex-Dodgers. Sportswriters began to call the Cubs the Dodgers' B team. Wid defended his plan for development: "I know the potentialities of these kids. I nursed some of them along in Brooklyn. Why take a chance on someone I know nothing about?" On the other hand . . .

Opening-Day Lineup, 1952

Miksis, 2b
Fondy, 1b
Baumholtz, rf
Sauer, lf
Jackson, 3b
Atwell, c
Jeffcoat, cf
Smalley, ss
Minner, p

But alas, not even our version of the Dodgers could avoid a June Swoon; nine straight losses. Still, they were in the first division at the All-Star break and several Cubs were having great seasons. Hank Sauer, Bob Rush, and Toby Atwell (none of them ex-Dodgers) had been selected for the All-Star team. In the rain-shortened game, Cub fans could easily have found themselves "Singing in the Rain." Sauer's two-run blast over the roof at Shibe Park in Philadelphia won the game, and Rush was the winning pitcher. Sauer was reported to have said, after circling the bases, "Maybe that'll convince Shotton." He might have been as anxious to convince Leo Durocher, who had commented, "Hank Sauer? Well, he's Hank Sauer. He certainly won't get any better. He's inconsistent. He runs hot and cold." Maybe so, but Hank ran hot this season!

On July 27, the Cubs gave up their hold on fourth place and slipped into fifth, where they finished the season ahead of the Reds, Braves, and Pirates. It was their best finish since 1946, and their .500 season was a cause for joy. No one was shouting "Break up the Cubs," but Sauer's 37 home runs and 127 RBIs had brought thrills to Cub fans all through the season. His recognition as the Most Valuable Player in the National League may have been a decision as controversial as his election to the All-Star team two years earlier, but to Cub fans it was icing on the cake. The team seemed to have real potential. Frankie Baumholtz had done a creditable job in center field and hit .325, second only to Stan Musial's .336. Dee Fondy hit .296, and Bob Addis, obtained from the Braves, finished at .295. Pitcher Warren Hacker was 15-9 with a classy 2.59 ERA, and Rush was 17-13 and 2.70. The Cubs were fourth in the league in fielding, third in pitching, and second in batting. All in all, something to cheer about. Cubs' attendance climbed to 1,024,826, and the third-place White Sox drew 1,231,675 fans. Chicago baseball was major league again. Maybe Matthews did know what he was doing.

Well, maybe. Over the winter, Wid called the Dodgers and offered them Bob Rush for Gil Hodges, Carl Furillo, and Bobby Morgan. Presumably he did not ask for the Brooklyn Bridge too. The Dodger brass smiled and shook their heads. Instead, Wid traded Walt Dubiel to the Braves for Sheldon Jones.

Nineteen fifty-three brought some changes to the country. We were still in Korea, but with the new leadership of Dwight Eisenhower and Richard Nixon. In baseball, the Boston Braves announced that they were moving to Milwaukee for the new season and that Charlie Grimm, who had been hired early in the previous season, was to continue as their manager. In effect, this put some pressure on the Cubs. Cub fans in Wisconsin might be lured away by the Braves as had other fans by the Go-Go White Sox. Of course, the Braves had finished behind the Cubs in 1952, so there seemed no cause for immediate alarm, the colorful Grimm notwithstanding.

After a reasonably good spring, the Cubs opened the 1953 season on a downbeat. Hank Sauer, their MVP, was hampered by a broken finger, so was infielder Bob Ramazzotti. Bob Rush, their first potential twenty-game winner since Hank Wyse in 1945, had a sore arm, as did Bill Serena. The fans, now with raised expectation, no longer were in the mood to be tolerant. Roy Smalley became the focus of their frustration, but the team received its share as well. One sportswriter even suggested that the Cubs move to Gary, Indiana, and the reader was left to decide whether that was an insult to the Cubs or to Gary. By the end of May, the Cubs were in seventh place. This time Wid didn't go to the Dodgers for help. Instead, he went to his old boss Branch Rickey and, on June 4, made a deal with the Pirates. Preston Ward, Gene Hermanski, Bob Addis, Toby Atwell, and pitcher Bob Schultz, plus an estimated $100,000 went to Pittsburgh. Chicago received Ralph Kiner, George Metkovich, Howie Pollet, and Joe Garagiola.

> *Opening-Day Lineup, 1953*
>
> Miksis, ss
> Baumholtz, rf
> Fondy, 1b
> Serena, 2b
> Ward, cf
> Jackson, 3b
> McCullough, c
> Hermanski, lf
> Rush, p

With Ralph Kiner in left and Hank Sauer moved to right, center field doubled in size. Poor Frankie Baumholtz. One can only speculate how many playing years he lost from chasing down balls hit into that outfield. The Cardinal relievers used to taunt Kiner in the outfield: one bellowed over the bullpen fence, "Get some circulation in those legs of yours. You're killing the grass out there!" To make matters worse, Kiner had a leg injury. So, after seven consecutive years as National League home run king, a title he shared with Hank Sauer in 1952, he spent the early part of the season struggling. In fact, the Cubs as a team seemed to forget how they had played the previous year. The 105 errors they made in the first seventy-four games, for example, hardly filled the pitchers with confidence. Even Matthews' annual mid-season trade didn't help. He sent pitchers Bob Kelly and Fred Baczewski to Cincinnati for righthander Bubba Church. Baczewski went on to an 11-4 season with the Reds while Church was 4-5 as a Cub.

By mid-June, it was apparent that the Cubs would be lucky to finish seventh. To the north, the Braves' five-year plan, begun in Boston, was paying off. Talent makes a difference. And the Braves had lots of it with youngsters like Del Crandall, Johnny Logan, Eddie Matthews, Joe Adcock, and Billy Bruton. The Cubs took a look at their own youngsters in September, calling up their best farmhands for some experience. Fortunately, some of them deserved a good long look. From their Los Angeles club came infielder Gene Baker, the first black player in the Cubs' system, outfielder Bob Talbot, and pitcher Bill Moisan. From Springfield the Cubs brought up pitchers Jim Willis and Don Elston. And they announced the purchase of a twenty-two-year-old shortstop named Ernie Banks from the Kansas City Monarchs for $35,000. All were to report to the Cubs on September 14.

Banks played his first game as a Cub on September 17, 1953. The Cubs lost 16-4 to the Phillies, and Ernie was hitless in three tries. He finished the season with eleven hits in thirty-five trips, 2 home runs, 6 RBIs, and a .314 average. The Cubs finished in seventh place: in the standings, in hitting, and in pitching. In fielding they were last thanks to a sad total of 192 errors. Only Fondy at .309 and Baumholtz at .306 were consistent hitters. Kiner did hit 35 homers and drive in 116 RBIs, but Sauer slipped to 19 home runs and 59 RBIs. The battered pitching staff was led by Warren Hacker, 12-19, and Bob Rush, 9-14. Home attendance plunged to 763,658: Wrigley estimated that the Cubs lost $500,000 for the year. Meanwhile, the third-place

Milwaukee Braves drew 1,826,397, and the third-place White Sox attracted 1,191,358. Happily, the biggest news of the year was that the Korean War was finally over.

The fact that the Cubs' farmhands helped them to ten straight victories in September, their longest winning streak since 1946, enabled Wid to make some claims for the progress of his Five-Year Plan. It also got Cavarretta another contract. After the season Matthews acknowledged that the Cubs needed a deeper bench, but he also went on to lament the Cubs' peculiar fate. Mistakes cost most teams a run or so, Wid pointed out, but they always managed to cost the Cubs a game. He wondered aloud what many Cub fans have secretly feared: were the Cubs under some kind of whammy, curse, or jinx?

During the winter, Matthews wrote to Cavarretta: "The thought just occurred to me that with all the trials and tribulations we had in 1953, our won and loss record in Chicago wasn't so bad after all." Wid was right as far as he went. The Cubs were 43-34 at Wrigley Field. But he'd apparently forgotten that they were 22-55 on the road. By January, if one listened to Wid at the annual sports luncheon in Chicago, one would have thought it time to start preparing for an all-Chicago World Series in 1954. The White Sox would have to go only from third place to first and the Cubs only from seventh to first. It would be as easy as that.

Seventeen of the forty players reporting to spring training in 1954 were rookies, the prize products of Wid's rebuilding plans. When other clubs were bringing up rookies like Harvey Kuenn, Junior Gilliam, Hank Aaron, Harvey Haddix, and Bob Buhl, the Cubs' camp included pitchers John Pyecha, Bob Hartig, and Jim Brosnan, catchers Chris Kitsos, Harold Meek, and Bob Murray, outfielder Jim McDaniel, and infielder Burdette Thurlby. Of course, it also included Ernie Banks. With Banks installed at shortstop, Roy Smalley, the symbol of Cub frustration, became expendable. He was sent to the Braves for pitcher Dave Cole and cash. "I'll have to admit," Roy said, "that I'm relieved at getting away from the fans at Wrigley Field."

Manager Cavarretta had only four serious problems as the Cubs assembled for training at Mesa, Arizona. They were: (1) pitching, (2) catching, (3) fielding, and (4) hitting. By March 29, the Cubs had lost fifteen of their twenty exhibition games. Cubs' pitching (and fielding) had allowed 135 runs in those twenty contests. Cavarretta went directly to Mr. Wrigley and told him his honest opinion of what 1954 would be like, and 1955, and 1956, and so on. Cavarretta said bluntly, "The Cubs have to win now. They are losing fans by the thousands. But the material isn't there. The future looks even worse. There just isn't any good talent coming up. The Cubs have to get some big league talent or they're sunk." Phil became the first major league manager ever fired during spring training. Mr. Wrigley commented sadly about his former "indomitable" manager, "Phil seems to have developed a defeatist attitude. We don't believe he should continue in a job where he doesn't believe success is possible." Phil replied, "Evidently I made a mistake when I told Mr. Wrigley the truth about the ball club. I was never a defeatist in my life. I have never quit!"

Stan Hack, great Cub third baseman and a former teammate of Cavarretta, became the new manager of the Cubs. Cavarretta refused Mr. Wrigley's invitation to replace Hack as manager of the Los Angeles Angels, an offer which in its way foreshadowed the revolving coaches scheme that would bedevil the Cubs a few years down the road. Hack was a mild and friendly man, apparently capable of manufacturing enough optimism to please Mr. Wrigley. Said Stan: "I'm not conceding anything to anyone. We'll all start even on April 13 and we'll be out to win."

It was true that they all started even on April 13, but within eight weeks the Cubs were home in seventh place for good. But at least it wasn't eighth. The infield of Fondy, Baker, Banks, and Jackson was not a bad one, and the outfield of Sauer, Kiner, and Baumholtz, with help from Talbot, was still interesting, particularly on fly balls. But the pitching was atrocious. In fact, Hal Jeffcoat, after years of showing great promise as a speedy outfielder, was given a chance to pitch in an exhibition game and threw five shutout innings at the Orioles. That was enough to win him a job on the Cubs' pitching corps. It turned out that "Hotfoot Hal" could throw a curve much better than he could hit one. Of the Cubs' pitchers, only Bob Rush, 13-15, Paul Minner, 11-11, and rookie Jim Davis, 8-10, had reasonably good seasons. Johnny Klippstein, 4-11, Dave Cole, 3-8, and Warren Hacker, 6-13, were generally hit often and hard. The staff ERA was 4.51. The Cubs were able to score 700 runs for the season, but their opponents scored 766. Only the eighth-place Pirates were worse. Phil Cavarretta had known whereof he spoke in the spring. In fact, he had managed to join the White Sox as a player and hit .316 in seventy-one games for them.

Highlights for the 64-90 season were Hank Sauer's comeback to 41 home runs and 103 RBIs and Ernie Banks' fine play in his first full season in the majors. However, Cubs' attendance slipped to 748,183. The Braves again finished third, but their attendance shot up to 2,131,388. The White Sox, also third for the second year in a row, drew 1,230,629. There was one notable event at Wrigley Field

> *Opening-Day Lineup, 1954*
>
> Talbot, cf
> Fondy, 1b
> Kiner, lf
> Sauer, rf
> Jackson, 3b
> Banks, ss
> Baker, 2b
> McCullough, c
> Minner, p

that season — a "first" in fact. Would you believe a night game? Try again. Would you believe a basketball night game? In August, the Harlem Globetrotters moved into the park with their portable court and lighting system to perform a "doubleheader" with their traveling opponents. The Cub organization billed the event as "one of the great sports evenings of all Chicago history." Given the way things were going for the Cubs that season, that statement seemed dangerously close to the truth.

Incidentally, this season was also the culmination of Wid Matthews' Five-Year-Plan. The record showed a fifth-place finish in 1952, bracketed by one eighth-place and three seventh-place finishes. In these five years the Cubs won 332 games and lost 437, a winning percentage of .432 with .500 as their best season.

Undaunted, Wid spent the off-season telling anyone who would listen of the talent fairly overflowing in the farm system. He predicted that prize youngsters such as Bob Thorpe, Solly Drake, Ed Winceniak, Joe Stanka, and Joe Hannah were ready to come to the rescue. And then, of course, there were more of his trades. Johnny Klippstein and Jim Willis went to the Reds for Harry Perkowski, Jim Bolger, and Ted Tappe. Bill Serena was sold to the White Sox for $30,000. Wid also announced the sale of Frankie Baumholtz to the White Sox and then had to call off the deal when it was discovered that he had forgotten to secure waivers on him. Oh, brother! In an uncharacteristic trade, however, Wid managed to recover most of the $100,000 the Cubs had sent Branch Rickey for Ralph Kiner. This time Kiner was sold to the Cleveland Indians for $60,000, pitcher Sam "Toothpick" Jones, and outfielder Gale Wade. It might also be noted that Rickey was still pulling off some good ones. His Pirates may have finished eighth, but they wouldn't stay there for long; not while he was picking up ballplayers in the winter draft like Roberto Clemente. The Cubs, in the same draft, secured Vincente Amor and Jim

King. Finally, to make room on the roster, Matthews sold
Dave Cole, the pitcher acquired from the Braves for Roy
Smalley, to the Phillies. Told of the sale, Dave said, "That's
too bad; they're the only team I can beat." He was right.
Two of his three wins in 1954 had been against the Phillies.

Euphoria! Spring training for the 1955 season had barely
opened when Stan Hack, noting that the Cubs had called
up the cream of their minor-league crop, let it be known
that "we have improved more than any other team in the
League. We'll be in the first division this year." In
addition, Wid announced the signing of a bonus baby
pitcher named Don Kaiser for $50,000. Even more, Wid
gave his solemn opinion that Harry Chiti was "the best kid
catcher since Gabby Hartnett." As for pitching, Wid did
seem to have logic on his side. He pointed out that there
were eight rookie pitchers on the spring roster and "it is
not conceivable that all of those kids will flop on us." Even
Clarence "Pants" Rowland, who was hired to monitor
Wid's optimism, could not contain himself. "Pants"
avowed as how "I have never been impressed so much
with any bunch of kids in a training camp." First-division
fever was beginning to spread.

But not without a centerfielder. In the exhibition and
early regular season, Gale Wade, Jim Bolger, Lloyd
Merriman, Frankie Baumholtz (whose legs must have aged
a decade since the acquisition of Kiner) were each given a
shot at the job. Those who were barely adequate fielders
couldn't hit, and those who could hit fairly well had trouble
fielding the position. Someone pointed out that the best
centerfielder on the team was enjoying a seat in the
bullpen, meaning, of course, Hal Jeffcoat.

In early April, Chicagoans went to their polling booths and elected Richard J. Daley their mayor. Celebrations followed. Too bad he was a White Sox fan. He could have taught the Cubs how to build a machine that could win and win and win. In early May, the newly acquired Sam Jones pitched a dramatic no-hitter against the Pirates at Wrigley Field. (See Chapter 7, "Games to Remember.") More celebrations. With good reason. Jones had supplied the fans with a gutsy, professional piece of pitching; the kind the Cubs hadn't seen in a while. By the end of May, the team was in second place with a record of 23-16. They were winning, often in exciting fashion, and the fans were beginning to come back. Heroics were the order of the day. In addition to Jones' no-hitter, Warren Hacker tossed a one-hitter at the Braves, and Hal Jeffcoat won his first five decisions in relief. But the biggest hero of them all, the man Cub fans hailed as their new superstar, was a rookie first baseman/ outfielder named Bob Speake. Playing left field in place of Hank Sauer whenever the opposing pitcher was right-handed, Speake had hit eight home runs, and five of them had won games outright. Now a celebrity, Speake said that it was easier to hit in the majors than it was in the minors because major league pitchers had better control and the batter could stand in there and take his cuts. It was a wonderful May and even Hank Sauer's deep slump did not cripple the team. After all, along with Speake there was Ernie Banks to take up the slack.

The Cubs continued to win and by the All-Star break in July they were still second only to the Dodgers. But it was

Opening-Day Lineup, 1955

Wade, cf
Baker, 2b
Baumholtz, rf
Sauer, lf
Jackson, 3b
Banks, ss
Fondy, 1b
Chiti, c
Rush, p

not to last. When the second half of the season opened, it seemed almost as though a group of imposters were wearing Cub uniforms. Speake was no longer hitting effectively, apparently having discovered that a major league curve ball is elusive even if controlled. The pitching and fielding began to deteriorate and the July Swoon was on. In May, the Cubs had won dramatic, come-from-behind victories; in July they lost them. Once, leading the Phillies 11-4 in the sixth inning, they lost 12-11. By the end of July, after a 1-12 road trip, the Cubs were six games under .500. Dashed expectations led to unhappiness, and not even Stan Hack's genial manner could prevent dissension on the team. Mild-tempered Hank Sauer complained that he was being benched too often and that he was not being given a fair chance to get in the groove. Team veterans agreed, although not always in the most flattering terms; one said, "Hank is being made to look like a bum." By August 26, the Cubs were 59-71 and headed down. The descent stopped at sixth place, and it was there that they finished the season, ahead of the Cardinals and the Pirates. The Cubs were seventh in hitting, fifth in fielding, and sixth in pitching. The early season success enabled Cubs' attendance to increase to 875,800, but this was still considerably less than the 2,005,836 drawn by the second-place Braves or the 1,175,788 attracted by the third-place White Sox.

Thank goodness for Ernie Banks. During this terribly disappointing season for the Cubs, Banks had managed to hit 44 home runs (the most ever hit by a shortstop) while leading the league in fielding for shortstops (a league that included star shortstops like Pee Wee Reese, Roy McMillan, Al Dark, and Johnny Logan). In addition, he set another major league record by hitting five grand-slam home runs. An amazing season. But as all Cub fans know, one man, even an Ernie Banks, does not a team make. For the rest, it was time to reevaluate and to clean house.

Matthews lost no time. He released Howie Pollet and sent Perkowski, Bolger, Merriman, Cohen, and Hillman down to the Los Angeles Angels. Hal Jeffcoat went to the Reds for catcher Hobie Landrith; Ransom Jackson became a Dodger in return for Don Hoak and Walt Moryn, and Frankie Baumholtz was sold to the Phillies, a deal that, fortunately for Wid, did not require waivers. In the winter draft, the Cubs picked up Vito Valentinetti and thirty-seven-year-old Monte Irvin, who had earlier enjoyed three fair years with the Giants before developing a chronic ankle problem that forced him back to the minors in 1955. Such was the Cubs' need for outfielders that Monte, bad ankle and all, was immediately touted as the key to the Cubs' rise in 1956. Then, in a moment of shrewdness, Wid ended Russ Meyer's personal jinx against the Cubs by trading rookie pitcher Don Elston to the Dodgers for him. Russ came back to the Cubs after having beaten them twenty-four times in twenty-seven decisions. Even if he didn't win any games for the Cubs, at least he wouldn't be beating them anymore.

Spring training for the 1956 season (Wid's seventh) opened with some confidence that the Cubs actually had a deeper bench and a chance to make it into the promised land of the first division. But the spectre of an outfield composed of Sauer, Irvin, and Walt "Moose" Moryn was too much to contemplate. So before the season opened, Sauer was traded to the Cardinals for Pete Whisenant and $10,000. Cub fans were sorry to see Hank go. In seven years as a Cub he had hit 198 home runs. During some of the leanest years in Cub history he had been, in his own lumbering way, a hero one could genuinely cheer for.

After the usual spring rites of ballyhoo and buildup, the Cubs this year gave up their quest for the first division early and almost without a fight. They lost fourteen of their first nineteen games in the regular season and were back in the cellar again. Don Hoak, counted on to be the holler guy and team leader, may have hollered, but he didn't hit. Harry Chiti, "the new Gabby Hartnett," hit less than he weighed. And despite Wid's logic, all of those young pitchers touted in the previous spring were proving to be flops.

Opening-Day Lineup, 1956

Hoak, 3b
Baker, 2b
Wade, cf
Banks, ss
Moryn, rf
Irvin, lf
Fondy, 1b
Landrith, c
Rush, p

Predictably, this team lacked spirit even more than it did talent. Wrigley thought that it might help to have an oxygen tank installed in the dugout. But it didn't. The only person who used it was Pat Pieper, the field announcer. There was no May outburst, no "Speake explosion" this year. Occasionally, a few glimmers of hope would shine through the gloom; a well-pitched game here or there, especially from the reliable Bob Rush, good infield work by Baker and Banks, and the added talent of two more bonus babies, infielder Jerry Kindall and pitcher Moe Drabowsky. Reputed to be a flame thrower, Drabowsky pitched batting practice the day he joined the club. Outfielder Jim King stood at the plate and took a pitch: "I didn't see it but it sounded low," he quipped. Moe threw a couple of good games and Pee Wee Reese said after facing him, "In two years he'll be the best pitcher in baseball."

Early in July the Cubs did manage to climb into sixth place, but almost immediately they settled back near the bottom. Almost typical of the season was a game with the

Pirates in late July at Pittsburgh. In the top of the eighth inning, pitcher Bob Friend of the Bucs was coasting along with a 4-0 four-hitter. The Cubs erupted to score seven runs off Friend and reliever Roy Face. Chicago returned one run in the bottom of the eighth, but got it back in the top of the ninth. Leading 8-5 with their best reliever, Turk Lown (back this season after a year in Los Angeles), on the mound, it looked safe. Lown gave up a single and two walks prompting Stan Hack to call to the bullpen for Jim Brosnan. Roberto Clemente blasted Brosnan's first pitch off the left field light tower, but the ball was still in play. By the time the Cubs had retrieved it and set up a relay, Clemente had sped around the bases, ignoring his coach's signal to stop at third, to score the winning run.

As the season wore on, there were stories of dissension and clubhouse fights. Hack was accused of being too lenient. By August 25, the Cubs were in the cellar to stay, on their way to a 60-94 record. A real bottom. This was the worst record in the team's history. Attendance went down to 720,118, while the White Sox drew over a million and the Braves topped the two million mark again. As a team, the Cubs were last in hitting with a .244 team average, sixth in fielding, and seventh in pitching. Banks, plagued by injuries, had slipped to 28 home runs and 85 RBIs. Wid Matthews shook his head and said that he had been the victim of seven years of bad luck. Seven years. Bad luck.

The worst of times led to the biggest of shakeups. On October 11, 1956, Mr. Wrigley announced that Gallagher, Matthews, and Hack had all "resigned." Charlie Grimm, who had been fired as manager of the Braves early in the '56 season, was to return to the Cubs as a vice-president. John Holland, President of the Los Angeles Angels, was also made a vice-president and was to take over Matthews' duties. And Bob Scheffing, former Cub catcher, was named as manager. Scheffing had managed the Los

Angeles Angels to the Pacific Coast League flag. Like Hack before him, Scheffing had first-hand knowledge of the young prospects on whom the Cubs would have to build. Again. This time, however, there was no Five-Year Plan. Holland simply promised to make things interesting again.

From the looks of the trading market, things definitely got interesting. Warren Hacker, Don Hoak, and Pete Whisenant went to the Reds for infielder Ray Jablonski and thirty-six-year-old pitcher Elmer Singleton, who had been 18-8 with Seattle in 1956. Asked about Elmer's age, Scheffing replied that it didn't matter if he was ninety as long as he could win. Catchers Charlie Silvera and Cal Neeman were acquired from the Yankees and Denver respectively. Silvera had been Yogi Berrra's backup for nine years and had appeared in only two hundred and one games during that span. No one, including Casey Stengel, knew what Charlie could do as a regular. A ten-man trade with Frankie Lane of the Cardinals brought pitchers Tom Poholsky and Jackie Collum, catcher Ray Katt, and three minor leaguers for Sam Jones, Jim Davis, Eddie Miksis, and Hobie Landrith. It couldn't exactly be called a sting, but time showed that the Cardinals got more out of the deal than the Cubs. Scheffing also asked Holland to bring up some of his Los Angeles stalwarts including infielder Casey Wise, outfielder Bob Will, and pitchers Dick Drott and Bob Anderson.

With so many new faces in camp, spring training was a wide open affair. Only Ernie Banks was assured of a starting job, though after tryouts in the outfield and at first base, even he didn't know where he would be playing. Unimpressive in spring games, the recently acquired Jablonski and Katt were shipped to the Giants for pitcher Dick Littlefield and outfielder Bob Lennon. The latter's claim to fame was that in 1954 he had hit 64 home runs for Nashville. He was to hit a total of one as a Cub.

On opening day of 1957, Cub fans got a surprise. The team entered the field sporting new home uniforms, with blue pin stripes and a slightly changed insignia. Wearing those uniforms were sixteen new Cubs on the roster. One week later, outfielder Jim King was traded to the Cardinals for centerfielder Bobby Del Greco who, in his first game as a Cub, dropped a fly ball against the Braves allowing the three unearned runs that beat Bob Rush, 4 to 1. Welcome to the '57 Cubs.

Opening-Day Lineup, 1957
Fondy, 1b
Wise, 2b
Will, cf
Banks, ss
Baker, 3b
Bolger, lf
Moryn, rf
Neeman, c
Rush, p

In the third week of the season, Holland sent Gene Baker and Dee Fondy to Pittsburgh for first baseman Dale Long and outfielder Lee Walls. That proved to be one of those rare trades that really benefits both teams. Long would hit .305 for the Cubs that year and Walls .304 the following season. But with the exception of Dick Drott, the youngsters from Los Angeles proved a disappointment. Wise, replacing Baker, made six errors in four games. Bob Speake and Bob Will were only so-so, and Bob Anderson was returned to the Angels. The seemingly endless shuffle continued. Bobby Morgan was purchased from the Dodgers and installed at second base, Ed Winceniak was farmed out, infielder Jack Littrell and outfielder Frank Ernaga were brought up, Del Greco was optioned out, Collum and Valentinetti went to the Dodgers for Don Elston. Ernaga homered in his first at-bat in the major leagues, but a month later he was back at Fort Worth. What a year. When Bobby Adams and Johnny Goryl were purchased they became the tenth and eleventh Cubs to play third base that season. Outfielder Chuck Tanner, bought from the Braves, was unspectacular but at least managed to win and then to keep the center-field job, something six other Cubs had tried and failed to do. It was a "Hello-Goodbye" season in more ways than one.

Nothing worked. By July 5, the Cubs were 24-44, in seventh place by a game over their perennial companions in the dungeons of the league, the Pirates. The script for the year seemed to call for the Cubs to blow leads in late innings. It was a script they followed faithfully. On their way to a last-place tie (could we call it seventh?) with the Pirates, the Cubs lost twenty-nine games by one run! Their only real achievement in this 62-92 season was to take six games in a row from the Cardinals during a nine-day stretch in late August, thereby knocking them out of first place and giving the Braves their first pennant in Milwaukee.

Cub fans were quick to note that Holland's house cleaning had created some pretty good ex-Cubs. Fondy had hit .313 as a Pirate, and Hoak had been the starting third baseman on the All-Star team and gone on to hit .293 as a Red. Still, it could be argued that with so many trades some ex-Cubs were bound to have had good years. And the Cubs did have some bright spots of their own. Knowledgeable observers agreed that Drabowsky (13-15, 3.53 ERA) and Drott (15-11, 3.58 ERA) were the most talented pair of young pitchers on any team in the major leagues. It had been a glorious Sunday afternoon in late May when Drott set a new Cub strikeout record by fanning fifteen first-place Braves. (See Chapter 7, "Games to Remember.") Moreover, Ernie Banks, healthy again, had hit 43 home runs with 103 RBIs. And Walt Moryn proved himself to be a hustling fielder with a good arm, as well as a good hitter (.289, 19 homers, 88 RBIs). But weakness up the middle (catching, second base, and center field) still plagued the Cubs. As did attendance problems. The 1958 Cubs drew only 670,627 fans. The second-place White Sox enjoyed attendance of 1,135,757, and the pennant-winning Braves drew 2.25 million fans to County Stadium.

Nineteen fifty-eight was the season that the Dodgers moved from Brooklyn to Los Angeles. To do so, they had to buy the Los Angeles franchise from Mr. Wrigley who, to his credit, had for several years been laying the groundwork so that major league baseball could go to the West Coast. The top Cubs' farm teams would now be Portland and Fort Worth. The New York Giants also moved west to their new home in San Francisco. In preparing for 1958, Holland and Scheffing were not anxious to repeat 1957s enormous upheaval of personnel. For once there seemed to be a good mix of young talent and experience on the roster. Despite their .403 winning percentage, it could be argued that the team had real potential. Better to let things settle and to work on improving individual spots.

Spring training in 1958 brought some happy surprises at some of those spots. Tony Taylor, a second baseman picked by Holland in the winter draft, was impressing everyone with his speed and hustle. Outfielders Moryn and Walls were improving as was catcher Sammy Taylor. Center field was still a problem but Holland was able to persuade the Braves to part with Bobby Thomson for Bob Speake and cash. Speake, trying to come back after a good year with Los Angeles, never recovered anything like the form he showed that glorious May of 1956. Thomson moved into center field and, although not speedy, did better there than any Cub had for years. And with Dale Long at first, Taylor at second, Banks at short, and Johnny Goryl at third, the Cubs appeared to have a pretty good infield.

The happiest surprise of all was a sweep of the first four games against the Redbirds; .500 ball for the next ten games was good enough for first place on May 1. Lee Walls, who had come to the Cubs with Dale Long for Fondy and Baker in May of 1957, was doing act one of a Bob Speake. By May 2, he had nine home runs. On the mound, the starting rotation of Drott, Drabowsky, Brosnan, and rookie Glenn Hobbie, with relief help from Don Elston, looked really solid. So solid that Holland felt he could send Turk Lown to the Reds for Hershel Freeman.

Opening-Day Lineup, 1958

T. Taylor, 2b
Walls, rf
Banks, ss
Moryn, lf
Thomson, cf
Long, 1b
Goryl, 3b
Neeman, c
Brosnan, p

But then came May and with it a seven-game losing streak. Time for changes? The newly arrived Freeman was farmed out to make room for left-handed reliever Bill Henry from Portland. Jim Brosnan was traded to the Cardinals for thirty-five-year-old infielder Al Dark, who immediately became the Cub third baseman. There, his take-charge attitude seemed to generate a Cubs team that wouldn't give up. On May 30, for example, they beat the Dodgers twice at Wrigley Field before nearly 38,000 fans. In the first game, the Dodgers behind Johnny Podres were leading 2-0 with one out in the ninth. Then Walls hit his thirteenth homer. Dark struck out, but Banks walked, and Moryn doubled, scoring Banks. Tie game, two out. The Dodgers brought in Ed Roebuck to face pinch-hitter Sammy Taylor. But a single by Taylor scored Moryn and the Cubs had the game, 3-2. In the second game, the Dodgers were leading 6-1 in the fourth before Banks and Moryn hit successive home runs. In the seventh, Moryn and Tanner homered to knot the score at 8-8. In the ninth with Sandy Koufax pitching in relief, Banks singled and Moryn homered again, giving the Cubs a 10-8 win.

By June 18, the Cubs were in sixth place with a 27-29 record, but they were only five games out of first. For the next month, no team was able to pull away from the rest; as late as July 14 the Cubs found themselves in fifth place but only two-and-one-half games behind the first-place Braves. And the heroics continued. Trailing the Phillies 9-5 in the ninth, the Cubs scored four times to send the game into extra innings. Then, in the eleventh, the Cubs made three errors to give the Phillies a 10-9 lead. Undaunted, the Cubs went to work again. In their half of the eleventh, Walls fanned but Banks singled, followed by a single from Sammy Taylor. With Walt Moryn at bat, everyone knew that those "boos" were only the fans cheering for their "Moooooose." His response? A double to win the game. Two days later, July 16, the Cubs scored three times in the ninth to beat the Reds 5-4 in the first game of a doubleheader, then tallied three in the eighth inning of the second game to win 7-5. Oh, you Cubs!

Until the end of July the Cubs were talking seriously about the pennant. They could certainly hit — consistently and with power, more than any previous team in Cubs' history. But hitting alone could not overcome the problems caused by their fielding and especially by a hurting pitching staff. Drabowsky was out for nearly two months with a strained elbow; Drott's control had left him, and he was giving up an average of five runs a game. Hobbie, Briggs, and Hillman were doing what they could and Elston and Henry were often brilliant in relief, but there just wasn't enough talent to carry the team all the way. The Swoon came in August. With a double loss on August 22, the Cubs had dropped twenty-three of their last thirty-three games. On August 24, they were in the cellar. Oh, you Cubs.

But this team had been coming from behind all year.

Now, led by first baseman Jim Marshall, just acquired from the Orioles, the Cubs managed a brief rally. Marshall had five hits, three of them homers in his first two games as a Cub. By season's end, the Cubs had climbed ahead of the Dodgers and Phillies into a fifth-place tie with the Cardinals. Where was Pittsburgh? For nearly a decade, they had been the only team worse than the Cubs, but now they had moved all the way to second place. But why quibble; the Cubs also appeared to be on the move. They were definitely an exciting team, and if their pitching had lived up to expectations, they would have been genuine contenders. As it was, the Cubs led the major leagues in home runs with 182 (Banks had 47; Moryn, 26; Walls, 24; Thomson, 21, and Long, 20). In addition, Sammy Taylor and Tony Taylor were both named to the *The Sporting News* rookie team. And most important, Ernie Banks was named the Most Valuable Player in the National League. For the season Banks had hit .313 with 47 home runs and 129 RBIs. Jimmy Dykes, interim manager of the Reds, approved the choice of Banks by saying, "If the Cubs didn't have Banks they would have finished in Albuquerque." And the fans were coming back to Wrigley Field; 979,994 to be exact, their best since their other fifth-place finish back in 1952. Interestingly, the second-place White Sox drew only 787,936, and the pennant-winning Braves, 1,971,101, down a quarter of a million from 1957.

Early in 1959, John Holland moved to strengthen the Cubs. Pitcher John Briggs, who had been 5-5 in 1958, and outfielder Jim Bolger, who had hit .225, went to Cleveland for Earl Averill, Jr., and Pitcher Morrie Martin. Averill had played eight positions for San Diego and been named the Most Valuable Player in the Pacific Coast League. Before making any other trades, however, the Cubs wanted to see what new surprises this year's spring training might bring. The idea seemed to be to hope for Drabowsky and Drott to return to form while watching a few other spots carefully. After all, they had the power and their other young pitchers, Hobbie, Buzhardt, and Anderson, appeared to have bright futures. They even had a promising trio of catchers in Taylor, Neeman, and Thacker. In addition to all this promise there were two pleasant surprises that spring. One was a nineteen-year-old catcher-infielder named Ron Santo who had signed with the Cubs for $18,000. The other, a tall, swift, powerful, young outfielder: twenty-three-year-old George Altman. Santo was eventually sent to Fort Worth for seasoning, but Altman survived the final cut. A final trade of the spring sent Chuck Tanner to the Red Sox for erstwhile pitcher Bob "Riverboat" Smith. With the Cubs ready for the season Scheffing quietly understated the team's confidence when he said, "We will win more games than we did last year."

The Cubs began the season by spoiling the Giants' home opener 5-2. Ernie Banks hit a pair of two-run homers off Jack Sanford, something Sanford didn't forget, hitting Banks with pitches three different times during the course of the season. But in the first month of the season, homers were not so abundant. In early May the team batting average was only .229. It was pitching, in fact, that kept the Cubs alive. Drabowsky was erratic and Drott's sore arm had become chronic (six of the most painful words written in this book — oh, the splendid promise of that young man). Hobbie and Anderson, relieved by Elston and Henry, were giving the Cubs superb pitching. But with no hitting, it seemed that for every game the Cubs won they lost the next. By June 12, the Cubs were 29-28 in fourth place, but only five

---

Opening-Day Lineup, 1959

T. Taylor, 2b
Altman, cf
Banks, ss
Moryn, lf
Averill, 3b
Long, 1b
Thomson, rf
S. Taylor, c
Anderson, p.

games out of first. Tony Taylor was playing well, hitting .313 with only 2 errors in his first 248 chances. But of the fearsome fivesome of Banks, Moryn, Thomson, Walls, and Long, only Banks was producing.

Then even the pitching began to falter. Hobbie and Anderson were simply not stoppers. Sixteen straight games without a complete performance by a starter meant that Elston, Henry, or Elmer Singleton was working or at least warming up every day. Scheffing summed it up: "They say that pitching is seventy-five percent of a ball club. Well, then the way we're going, I'd say that fifty percent of our effectiveness is in the bullpen." By June 21, Cub starters had achieved the grand total of eight complete games!

Time out! June 30 of this year produced one of those really strange occurrences at Wrigley Field that Cub fans remember. Not surprisingly, the Cardinals were involved. On a three-and-one pitch to Stan Musial, the ball skipped to the backstop. The umpire called it ball four, but catcher Sammy Taylor claimed that it had hit Musial's bat and was a foul strike. While Taylor and pitcher Bob Anderson were arguing with the umpire, Musial went to first and his teammates yelled at him to keep running. Meanwhile, Al Dark had run in from third all the way to the screen to retrieve the ball, but it had already been picked up by the Cardinal bat boy and tossed to the field announcer. Dark pursued it, picked it up, and threw to Banks at second. While Dark had been on his errand, the umpire had absent-mindedly handed a new ball to Taylor while they argued. Anderson, seeing Musial break for second, grabbed this ball from Taylor and threw to Banks. It arrived at the same moment as the one thrown by Dark. Dark's throw was low and Banks fielded it on one hop. Anderson's throw was high and sailed into center field. Musial slid in safe at second, but, seeing the ball over Banks' head, got up and started for third. Banks, using the ball thrown by Dark, tagged him. Safe or out? The umpires huddled and finally affirmed that the befuddled Musial was out. The Cardinals won the game anyway, 4-1.

At the half-way point in the season, the Cubs were 36-37 and only four-and-a-half games out of first. Scheffing noted that the hoped-for Cub power had not materialized, "so we'll try to win with pitching, defense and speed." Speed? At this point in the season Luis Aparicio of the White Sox had stolen 25 bases; the entire Cubs team had managed 15. Well into July the Cubs stayed in the race simply by playing .500 baseball. The pitching got a boost from Art Ceccarelli, called up after the All-Star break. Ceccarelli won his first three assignments in eleven days, including two complete games and a shutout. Then in late July and early August, the Cubs won seven of nine games from the three teams above them. It began to look like a miracle was possible. Scheffing said, "We've tangled with the Giants, Dodgers and Braves the past few weeks and, frankly, I don't see much difference between them and us. We've got as good a chance as any of them to go all the way."

But the miracle couldn't happen. The Cubs won twelve and lost seventeen in August and yielded fourth place to the Pirates. Scheffing had platooned his players, and now, as the pennant disappeared, some of them started to grumble. Two Cubs publicly accused John Holland of filling in Scheffing's lineup card every day and added that Holland knew more about race tracks and poker than he did about baseball. One veteran Cub surmised that Holland would be active when interleague trading opened. "What's it like in the American League?" he asked.

About the only thing the Cubs were able to do in September was to knock the Giants out of contention by beating them twice on homers by the rookie George Altman. When the final out of the season had been recorded, the Cubs were fifth with a record of 74-80, thirteen games behind the Dodgers. Their hitting from the previous season had practically disappeared. A .249 team batting average put them seventh in the league, although their fielding and pitching had improved to fourth and fifth respectively. Oh, but what a year for Ernie Banks. He had the greatest season of any shortstop in baseball history. Not only did he hit .304 with 45 home runs and 143 RBIs, he also set two major league fielding marks for shortstops: the highest percentage, .985, and the fewest errors ever by a regular, 12. Moreover, he played in every game, running his consecutive streak to 498 games. Small wonder that for the second straight year he was named the Most Valuable Player in the National League.

The Cubs second consecutive fifth-place tie was not as promising as their first had been. There were good young players on the team, but there had been some real disappointments as well. These disappointments were reflected in the attendance drop to 852,255. Across town, the White Sox had a super season, winning the pennant with dramatic, exciting baseball. Their attendance had swelled to 1,422,864. And the second-place Braves had drawn 1,749,112. Something had to be done. As usual, the manager was to be offered as victim.

On September 28, P. K. Wrigley announced that Scheffing's contract would not be renewed. The new manager was to be none other than Charlie Grimm. After all, Charlie had led the Cubs to their past four pennants. Besides, his style would be at least something of a Cub counter to the south side's colorful Bill Veeck. At sixty-one, Charlie could give it all he had for a year, just to see what might happen. Mr. Wrigley, voicing a philosophy that would later make the Cubs unique in baseball, commented, "I believe that managers are expendable. In fact, I believe there should be relief managers just like relief pitchers, so you can keep rotating them." Wrigley said that the Cubs had good player personnel and that what they really needed was luck. "Grimm has always brought us luck before," he said. Charlie agreed: "Somehow the ball has always bounced lucky for me when I've managed the Cubs. I hope it happens once more." Thus the Cubs, who left the forties with Charlie Grimm bowing out in favor of Frankie Frisch, now left the frustrations of the fifties with Charlie back, and with their fingers crossed.

Chapter Five:
The Sixties: From Chaos to Contention

IF THE FIFTIES SEEM A LIFETIME AGO, THE SIXTIES MAY SEEM TO
some too painfully close in memory. Perhaps no two
decades in America were so opposite in character. The
optimistic, post-war fifties agreeably sought change by
consensus. The sixties defiantly challenged change to
occur. With consensus replaced by complaint the temper of
the national spirit was at once idealistic and cynical. Strong
feelings and attitudes were wrenched into actions, and the
toll of that approach to change remains etched in our sense
of life's possibilities. The contrasts which marked the
movements of the sixties are revealing: from the formation
of the Peace Corps to the escalation of the Vietnam War,
from the establishment of civil rights legislation to the
destruction and violence of the race riots, from the broad
social reforms promised by the New Frontier and the War
on Poverty to the harsh realism of political and racial
assassinations. But life in the sixties was not all tension and
turmoil.

America was letting its hair down, literally. In 1960,
Chubby Checker's record, "The Twist," set a whole

generation of swaying, bending teenagers to rock the rafters at New York's Peppermint Lounge, beginning the "discotheque" fever that would spread across the country. Add miniskirts, marijuana, and the pill, mix well, and eventually you have the Woodstock Generation of 1969. Throw in some technology — the first nuclear generating power plants, computers, calculators, laser beams, and satellites. Bring the Star-Trek fantasy of space travel that Americans watched on television to the historic reality of Neil Armstrong's walk direct from the moon in July 1969. And wonder at the Amazin' Mets winning the World Series against 100 to 1 odds. There you have the unpredictable, daring, and free-wheeling decade of the sixties.

For baseball, the decade held many surprises. A team that didn't even exist in the fifties would become World Champions in the sixties. The unbreakable records of baseball were broken. Babe Ruth's sixty home runs and Ty Cobb's ninety-six stolen bases received national attention while being pursued, in the first case by Roger Maris and Mickey Mantle and in the second by Maury Wills. Baseball made headlines throughout the decade. It was to be seen and followed by more fans than ever before; new fans. Growing from sixteen teams to twenty-four, baseball had increased its potential for fan attendance by an additional 50 percent.

The Cubs would also be full of surprises in the sixties, some of them actually quite shocking to the baseball world. But let's look at those surprises in order, starting with the 1960 season. Having concluded the fifties with consecutive fifth-place finishes and the rehiring of Charlie Grimm, the Cubs turned to the trading market to search for the players that could move them into the first division. After two seasons as a Cub, Al Dark, now thirty-eight years old, went along with pitcher John Buzhardt and minor leaguer Jim Woods, to the Phillies for Richie Ashburn, now thirty-three. Ashburn had been with the Phillies for twelve

seasons and was a lifetime .300 hitter, but had fallen off to
.266 in 1959. To get slugger Frank Thomas from the Reds,
the Cubs gave up Bill Henry, who had appeared in
sixty-five games the previous year, and Lee Walls, who
had fallen from .304 in 1958 to .257 in 1959. And
thirty-six-year-old Bobby Thomson, who had slipped to
.259, was sent to the Red Sox for a pitcher named Al Schroll.
With the hitting of Banks and Altman, now complemented
by Ashburn and Thomas, the Cubs could, it was hoped,
finish better than seventh in hitting. Add to these bats
comebacks by Drott and Drabowsky, and things seemed to
look interesting for 1960. Mr. Wrigley proudly pointed out
the good feeling on the club. He was especially pleased
with the harmony between the front office and the players.
"Just take a look at our organization," he said. "We have a
group of level-headed fellows who keep on an even keel."
Maybe he hadn't heard Charlie Grimm's prediction in
January: "We can win the pennant if the ball bounces
right."

The spring roster showed the usual number of new faces.
But this time the names were worth remembering: Ken
Hubbs, Dick Ellsworth, Billy Williams, Lou Johnson, and
Ron Santo were among them. Hubbs had been offered a
scholarship to the University of Southern California in any
one of five areas: baseball, football, basketball, track, and
academics. But he had chosen a professional career in
baseball, and the Cubs had managed to sign him. Ron
Santo's signing had been somewhat different from
Hubbs'. After high school, Santo was courted by several
teams. But before signing with any of them, he wanted to
play in an amateur all-star game he had been selected for.
Though a third baseman by trade, he was pressed into
catching the game when the intended catcher got sick.
Santo recalls, "I had two passed balls, threw wild into
center field, muffed a pop foul, and dropped the ball at
the plate after having the guy out by ten feet." Skeptics

might say, "No wonder the Cubs signed him." Grimm felt that these youngsters, except for Johnson, still needed more seasoning in the minors. So more deals were made for experienced players to tide the team over until the new crop of kids were properly ready. Third baseman John Goryl, outfielder Lee Handley, pitcher Ron Perranowski, and $25,000 went to the Dodgers for Don Zimmer. And Dick Gernert came from the Red Sox to alternate with Altman at first.

For the Cubs' entry into the sixties, then, only three of their nine regulars had played on the teams that had climbed to fifth place during the last two seasons. These new Cubs started miserably, losing eleven of their first sixteen. The opposition quickly learned the secret to stopping the Cubs cold: walk Banks. No one else was hitting, and the pitching was poor. Bonehead plays were not even restricted to those actually in the lineup. On April 14, Drabowsky was warming up in the Cubs' bullpen when Frank Thomas smashed a shot down the third-base line. The ball bounced into the bullpen and to everyone's amazement Drabowsky fielded it cleanly. Thomas was made to return from second to first thanks to Moe's interference. Said Moe, "I saw the ball coming toward me, and my first reaction was to field it." Would that Cub infielders felt the same way.

> *Opening-Day Lineup, 1960*
>
> Ashburn, cf
> T. Taylor, 2b
> Banks, ss
> Thomas, lf
> Gernert, 1b
> L. Johnson, rf
> Zimmer, 3b
> Rice, c
> Hobbie, p

By May 4, the Cubs were 5-11, in last place. What to do? Would you believe a trade with WGN? Charlie Grimm went to the broadcast booth in return for announcer Lou Boudreau, the new Cub manager. Charlie's health was not up to the strain this team was placing on him. He was given a title of vice-president of the Cubs and permitted to do color commentary for WGN. In Boudreau's first game as manager, the Cubs were leading the Pirates 7-2 at the end of six, only to lose the game 9-7. More changes. Tony Taylor and catcher Cal Neeman went to the Phillies for first baseman Ed Bouchee and pitcher Don Cardwell. Lou Johnson was farmed out and Walt Moryn reinstalled in right field. Young Jerry Kindall was recalled from the minors to play second base. On May 13, the Cubs were 6-13 and in last place.

Then, on May 15, Don Cardwell made his debut as a Cub. He was on that day a great pitcher. In the first inning, the second Cardinal batter, Alex Grammas, reached base —on a walk— and then Cardwell retired the next twenty-six batters. A no-hitter near perfection. (See Chapter 7, "Games to Remember.") But such glimmers of brilliance could not disperse the impending gloom. Losses continued to mount, and on July 1, the Cubs were 27-39 in seventh place, barely ahead of the Phillies. Best to give the remainder of the season to those promising spring youngsters. Ron Santo, Danny Murphy, a seventeen-year-old bonus baby, Dick Ellsworth, and Jim Brewer, a southpaw prospect, were all given a taste of the majors. Drabowsky was sent to the minors. Drott, troubled by a sore arm, found himself watching games from the bullpen. Of the regular starters, only Glen Hobbie was pitching well.

Boudreau tried every imaginable combination to put together a winning lineup, but nothing worked. The most notable event in the second half of the season occurred on August 4 when Cincinnati infielder Billy Martin charged the mound and punched Jim Brewer in the face, breaking the orbit bone under the right eye. In the ensuing fight, both benches emptied and Frank Thomas was roundly decked by Martin. The next time the Reds were in Chicago,

Martin was served with a subpoena and notified that Brewer and the Cubs were suing him for $1 million. Cub fans pelted him with eggs and tomatoes, and he needed a police escort to leave the park safely. It took years for a court decision to come down in favor of Brewer, awarding him $100,000. Martin's comment: "How will they ever collect it? I haven't got that kind of money."

The final 60-94 record equaled the Cubs' worst, set in the 1956 season. To make matters worse, the Pirates, the Cubs' cellar companions just three seasons ago, won the pennant. The Cubs were thirty-five games away from such lofty heights. As usual, there were some individual bright spots. And as usual, Ernie Banks was one of them. Forty-one homers to lead the league, a .271 batting average, and 117 RBIs were impressive figures. Ashburn had regained some of his form to lead Cub hitters with a .291 average, and Santo had looked good hitting .251. Only Hobbie and Don Elston pitched well for the season, although neither could achieve .500 records with this team. Hobbie went 16-20 and Elston in sixty relief appearances finished 8-9. Attendance dropped another 40,000 to 809,770. The second-place Braves drew 1,497,799 and the third-place Sox, 1,644,460.

Something had to be done. Lou Boudreau suggested that he be given a two-year contract but was returned to the radio booth. Some fifty applications came in for the position of manager, with Billy Jurges and Casey Stengel rumored as the top candidates. It was not until late November that Mr. Wrigley met with the other Cub brass to discuss the situation. Into December and still there was no appointment. "We're studying this from all angles," said Mr. Wrigley. Jack Quinlan, voice of the Cubs on WGN, speaking at the Notre Dame Football banquet that year, denied that both Grimm and Boudreau would be in the radio booth to free him to be the next manager. And he consoled the Irish who had lost eight straight in their season. "As broadcaster of the Cubs I can tell you that at least you lost eight in a row only once in the season."

Finally, shortly before Christmas, it was announced that the Cubs would not have a manager for the 1961 season. Instead, an eight-man coaching staff would run the team. The coaches would circulate throughout the Cubs' system and take turns working with the parent club. This rotation system changed the traditional position of the manager to a head coach of the month. Predictably, the baseball world was shocked by the move. Even Cubs' General Manager John Holland admitted that when he had first heard the idea he thought Wrigley was nuts. But there was some logic in the system. In the first place, the system was not set up simply for the major league Cubs. The idea was to hire first-rate coaches for infielders, outfielders, and pitchers and to send them from top to bottom in the system to give uniform instructions. Every player in the organization received a manual explaining how the Cubs play baseball, how the Cub system works. "This is the day of specialists," Wrigley pointed out. "It makes sense to get the best man for each job. It works in football; I don't see why it can't work in baseball." He added, "We certainly cannot do much worse trying a new system than we have done for many years under the old."

Secondly, the system was devised to speed up the development of the young players in the farm system. The college of coaches would have personal knowledge of the strengths and weaknesses of each player and could consult with one another on their individual progress. Initially, there were to be eight coaches: Rip Collins, Vedie Himsl, Harry Craft, El Tappe, Gordie Holt, Charlie Grimm, Verlon Walker, and Bobby Adams. Speaking of the selection of these pioneers, John Holland had said, "We had to be careful. We couldn't hire a Durocher or Stanky, although they're good baseball men. We didn't want the type of guy who wants it done his way or else. We needed harmony, men who can be overruled and not take it personally. We needed men of varying capabilities and personalities. And that's what we got." The plan was that there would always be four coaches with the Cubs and four circulating throughout the minors. The rotation of the head coaches would be maintained. Holland guaranteed that "no one man will run the Cubs this season, no matter how well he's doing. In fact, Mr. Wrigley said he'd love to see a head coach win nine straight and then step down. I'm sure that won't happen, at least not this year." Leo Durocher, then a coach with the Dodgers, said the plan really wasn't a bad idea. Thanks, Leo. But Bill Veeck, asked if he would follow suit and hire eight coaches to run the White Sox, said, "No, I'll go along with tradition. I guess I'm just an old stick-in-the-mud."

Everyone had his laugh, and soon it was time for spring training. The Cub players went on record as liking the new system. One said that he felt more relaxed and another that he worked harder than ever. The coaches certainly sang its praises. El Tappe thought it "the best thing that's happened to baseball since the spitball." And Gordie Holt reasoned that since there would always be four coaches with the Cubs at any given time "we'll have the advantage — we'll have four minds working and the other teams only one." Harry Craft reported, "I see no flaws. The plan has created harmony." Catcher Sammy Taylor summed it up, tongue-in-cheek, "My Lord, I can't even belch without one of the coaches hearing it."

In March, Mr. Wrigley added a further wrinkle. Since everyone from Ernie Banks to the newest kid on a class C team would be getting the same instruction from the revolving coaches, the word *minor* would be erased from the Cub vocabulary. "A player in the organization is a Cub no matter where he plays." A wag suggested that the Cubs should keep the word *minor* and banish the term *major* instead.

As spring training continued, everyone was anxious to prove himself. Reports glowed with pitchers so ready and

Opening-Day Lineup, 1961
Ashburn, 1f
Zimmer, 2b
Williams, rf
Banks, ss
Santo, 3b
Heist, cf
Rodgers, 1b
Thacker, c
Anderson, p

willing to start the season they almost had to be restrained. Billy Williams was slated to start in the outfield, Santo was ready for his first full season at third, young speedster Al Heist would be in center. Moe Drabowsky, who had pitched only fifty innings in 1960, was sent to Milwaukee for infielder Andre Rodgers. Just prior to the opening game, in a plane flight over Texas, Vedie Himsl was appointed head coach and given two weeks' notice at the same time. All four coaches would have a vote on the starting lineup, but once the game began, the head coach would be in charge. The Cubs lost the opener to the Reds, 7-2, and made it two in a row the next day, falling 5-2. Then, on April 14, with two outs in the ninth, catcher Sammy Taylor hit a two-run homer to beat the Braves, and the next day with the score knotted at 5-5, Al Heist grandslammed in the ninth for a victory. A week later, Don Zimmer homered with two out in the eleventh for a 6-4 win over the Phillies. Himsl finished his two weeks with a 5-6 record and headed for San Antonio; Harry Craft was the new head coach. After winning four of twelve games, Craft and Himsl traded places. By May 15 the Cubs were 10-17, in seventh place.

During the month of May, Mr. Wrigley issued a twenty-one-page, 5000-word defense of the no-manager plan. It began, "We have started out under an extreme handicap because of all the ridicule and criticism from the press at daring to try something different in baseball." (The press had dubbed the college the "enigmatic eight.")

Wrigley went on to point out that in the last fourteen years, there had been 103 managers in the big leagues. Clearly managers and their coaches are expendable. But the constant changeover creates a loss of continuity. According to Wrigley, the Cubs' new system was designed to get first-rate coaching and instructional ability in the organization from top to bottom, thus insuring continuity. Obviously, the plan could only be judged from the perspective of several years. Would continuity be achieved? Would it help develop stars more rapidly? Only time would tell.

In the meantime the Cub defense was mediocre, the pitching was ineffective, and the hitting weak. It was not just the coaches who were shuffled. In the first twenty-eight games, nine different outfield combinations were tried and found wanting. In May the Cubs sent Frank Thomas to the Braves for utility player Mel Roach. Thomas went on to have an excellent year for the Braves. Roach slipped back to the minors. Banks, tried in left field and first base, was having an off-season due to a depth perception problem in his left eye and loose knee cartilage. On June 23 he removed himself from the lineup after 717 straight games, placing him tenth among baseball's all-time "iron men."

In June, George Altman did what hitting there was for the Cubs. Knuckleballer Barney Schultz took over as relief star for the no-longer-effective Don Elston. Once again, young Cub pitchers were coming down with arm miseries. Drott still was suffering, and now Glen Hobbie and Dick Ellsworth were also ailing. No doubt their problems were aggravated by the fact that the Cubs made 134 errors in the first 111 games of the season. By mid-August the Cubs were 48-66, and neither El Tappe nor Lou Klein could rally them. But in the midst of all this, there were some rays of sunshine. Ron Santo was developing into a good hitter and fine fielder, and Billy Williams was on his way to Rookie of the Year honors. Early in September two more youngsters were called up from the minors: Lou Brock, with rave notices from the St. Cloud, class C team; and Ken Hubbs, thanks to the recommendation of Coach Bobby Adams, came up from San Antonio. On September 10, they made their debut. Brock singled but made two errors. Hubbs was two for three. The college of coaches notwithstanding, baseball had much to be excited about in 1961. The American League had expanded to ten teams and had broken with tradition to extend the schedule to 162 games. Yankees Roger Maris and Mickey Mantle created headlines with every home run as they pursued Babe Ruth's sixty-home-run mark. It was Maris who reached the magical sixty-one with a shot into the right-field stands on the closing day of the season.

The Cubs finished this eventful season with a 64-90 record. They were not in last place, having finished well ahead of a terrible Phillie team, but they were still far behind the rest of the league. Cub pitching was seventh with a 4.50 ERA, the hitting was seventh despite 176 home runs, and their 182 errors ranked the Cubs last in fielding. Attendance dropped alarmingly to 673,057, compared to 1,151,999 for the fourth-place White Sox and 1,101,441 for the fourth-place Braves.

In 1962, the National League would expand to ten teams and a 162-game schedule, and the Cubs would continue with their own innovation. Don Zimmer asked to be traded. "I've been unhappy under this system," he said, "and I think the same thing goes for most of the men on our roster." That particular trade was unnecessary, as the New York Mets claimed Zimmer, Sammy Drake, and Ed Bouchee in the expansion draft. The Houston Colts took Drott and Al Heist. Zimmer left a parting shot: "Next year when I'm with the Mets I'll look over at all my friends on the Chicago bench and feel sorry for them. They don't have a chance to do their best." He said that the coaches were competing with one another. "I've seen one coach wagging Santo to play deeper at third while another was motioning to him to come in further. They are driving him crazy." Indeed, one of the head coaches had complained that his predecessors had been unable to hide their glee when the Cubs lost while they weren't calling the shots. Nor did the newspapers help by printing the won-lost records of each head coach.

But Mr. Wrigley was committed to the experiment. At the annual January press meeting, he personally predicted a first-division finish in '62, and coach Tappe was talking about a pennant. Twenty-three men on the roster of forty for spring training in 1962 were rookies. Unlike the youth movement in the fifties, this one had a coaching system to support it. The Cub clubhouse at Mesa was covered with signs reading, "WINNING IS A HABIT — GET THE HABIT!" and "NOW IS THE FUTURE — LET'S GO!" Everyone hoped that this would be the year when rookies like Brock, Hubbs, and catcher Cuno Barragan were going to parade the merits of the Cubs' coaching system. An incident from spring training illustrates how serious the Cubs were. Pitcher Bob Locke, acquired from the Indians for Jerry Kindall, was traded to the Cardinals for cash and a minor leaguer because he walked off the mound when his shoulder stiffened in an exhibition game. "With this all-coach system," he said later, "I just didn't know who to talk to."

But the season didn't start well. After losing the opener 6-2 to Houston, playing its first major league ball game, the

Opening-Day Lineup, 1962
Brock, cf
Hubbs, 2b
Williams, 1f
Banks, 1b
Altman, rf
Santo, 3b
White, ss
Barragan, c
Cardwell, p

Cubs managed only one win in their next eight games. Seven of the losses were to left-handers, prompting sportswriter Edgar Munzel to quip, "It wouldn't be surprising if some of the old lefties long gone to their reward are stirring in their graves yearning to get one more fling at these pushovers from Chicago." On April 24, Sandy Koufax whiffed eighteen Cubs, tying a record. A few days later catcher Sammy Taylor quit the team and went home.

Mr. Wrigley demanded that something be done to improve on the 5-17 record of the club. El Tappe was replaced as head coach by Lou Klein, and pitcher Jack Curtis was sent to the Braves for Bob Buhl. Writers began blaming the Cubs' plight on lack of hustle and determination. Klein said that the real problem was bad pitching and fielding. He had a point. In the first twenty-six games, the Cubs made thirty-two errors. As for pitching, Cub starters failed twenty-three straight times to complete a game. The staff earned run average was 5.50. Klein was unable to prevent the Cubs from falling into the cellar in May, behind the two expansion teams. Ignominy. In early June Charlie Metro became head coach, and the Cubs climbed to ninth place, ahead of the Mets.

By August, it was plain that the Cubs would not make it higher than eighth at best. Even so, not everything was bleak. Andre Rogers improved dramatically at short and, with Ken Hubbs at second, formed a solid double-play combination. Hubbs set two major league records for second basemen by playing seventy-eight straight games without an error and handling 418 chances. On June 24 Brock reached base nine times in eleven tries in a double header with the Pirates. Three days later he became only the second player ever to hit a ball into the center-field bleachers at the Polo Grounds, a blast of more than five hundred feet. And he showed his speed by scoring from second on an infield out. His fielding was not unimpeachable, but it was hoped that experience would cure that. Through it all Charlie Metro stayed on as head coach and was winning the respect of players, fans, and writers in Chicago.

On September 26, 903 loyal fans gathered at Wrigley Field to see the Cubs suffer their 101st loss of the season. A week later the final record stood at 59-103, the most losses ever by a Cub team. Only the Mets, with the worst record in the history of baseball, saved the Cubs from the cellar. The Houston Colts in their first year had finished ahead of the Cubs by six games. Needless to say, attendance at Wrigley Field dropped still more to 609,802, the lowest in the majors. The fifth-place White Sox drew 1,131,562 and the Braves, also fifth, attracted 767,221. Ken Hubbs was named Rookie of the Year (receiving nineteen of a possible twenty votes), the second straight time this award went to a Cub. Last season's winner of the award, Billy Williams, had not suffered a sophomore slump, hitting .298 with twenty-two home runs and ninety-one RBIs. The irrepressible Banks, having settled in at first base, drove in 104 runs with thirty-seven homers. And George Altman's twenty-two home runs and .318 average were noteworthy.

After the season, however, John Holland gave up Altman along with Cardwell and catcher Moe Thacker to the Cardinals, getting pitchers Larry Jackson and Lindy McDaniel and catcher Jim Schaeffer in return. Critics attacked Holland for giving up Altman, but the trade would prove to be an excellent one. In November, Coach

Charlie Metro was fired. There was speculation that other coaches and some players had complained directly to Mr. Wrigley that Metro was too strict. Metro would later be offered $2,500 by a national magazine to tell the inside story of the Cubs, but he refused, saying that he would rather say nothing than to say anything negative. But some Cub officials, recognizing that he had been popular, kept dropping subtle criticisms of him. Metro, now hired as chief scout for the White Sox, warned that if the Cub brass kept sniping at him, he would "really blow the lid off one of these days." Fortunately, Bob Kennedy was selected to be Metro's replacement in the college. Kennedy was a former Indian and White Sox player, who had managed the Cubs' team in Salt Lake City in 1962. Another Kennedy, President John F., jokingly praised the Cubs for hiring ten coaches instead of one manager. It was a small step toward easing the country's unemployment problem.

The new year of 1963 was still young when Mr. Wrigley proved that he was not yet finished with his revolutionary experiment. If you have a college of coaches and you want things to be systematized, what comes next? An athletic director, of course. And so a retiring Air Force colonel named Robert Whitlow, who had served as the first athletic director at the Air Force Academy, was named athletic director of the Cubs. He was to have complete charge of the Cub organization. Whitlow said that what the Cubs' coaching complex needed was "centralized direction and a centralized objective." (What they really needed was an outfielder, a catcher, and a few pitchers.) Thankfully, John Holland remained as vice-president in charge of player personnel, but even he was under the colonel. Moreover, Whitlow threatened to suit up and sit on the bench. Perhaps his size, 6'4", 240 pounds, would be a deterrent to squabbling among the coaches. At any rate, his first official announcement in this regard was a good one: he announced the elevation of Bob Kennedy from coach to head coach. Aside from baseball, Kennedy's experience included service as a Marine pilot in World War II and Korea. Kennedy showed himself to be a baseball realist by predicting that the Cubs might possibly finish as high as fifth. He wrote down on a slip of paper that his goal was a record of 82-80. Whitlow, now sitting in Wid Matthews' chair, sounded like Wid himself when he offered that "by just analyzing our team on paper — and I admit games aren't won on paper — I say it's possible for us to take all the marbles." To which Charlie Metro quipped. "Oh, is that what we're playing, marbles?" Baseball or marbles, the Cubs still needed a catcher.

After a good spring training, the season opened with the Cubs splitting their first fourteen games. Cubs' pitching was sensational, but their defense was anemic. Bob Buhl, the Cubs' best pitcher in 1962, was doing even better. In thirty-one innings, he had an 0.87 ERA. His 1-2 record testified to the Cubs' offense. Dick Ellsworth had recovered from his arm trouble and, along with new Cubs Jackson and McDaniel, was reminding Cub fans what major-league pitching looks like.

Opening-Day Lineup, 1963

Landrum, cf
Rodgers, ss
Williams, 1f
Santo, 3b
Banks, 1b
Brock, rf
Hubbs, 2b
Bertell, c
Jackson, p

Although Banks was in a deep slump, Brock, Santo, and Williams kept the Cub offense going. After spending May hovering around .500 and fourth place, the Cubs won ten of their next thirteen games and on June 6th climbed into a first-place tie with the Giants and Cardinals. McDaniel was one of the heroes. Coming in against the Giants with the bases loaded and one out in the tenth, he picked Willie Mays off second and fanned Ed Bailey. Then in the bottom of the tenth, he homered to win the game.

Lindy had nine saves to go with three wins. Ellsworth was 8-3 with a 1.50 ERA and was voted the National League Player of the Month in May. The same honor went to Santo in June.

Even though they slipped somewhat by the half-way point, the Cubs were still in third place and only three games out. A good share of the credit belonged to pitching coach Fred Martin and to Bob Kennedy, who was calm and fair with his players. Wrigley had not given Kennedy the title of manager, but as head coach the team was his for the season. Then in mid-August the Cubs seemed to run out of gas. Col. Whitlow offered advice until Kennedy confronted him directly: "Keep your nose out of my business with the players, now and forever." The Cubs slid to seventh place but finished with an 82-80 record, exactly as Kennedy had hoped before the season. It was the first time the Cubs had finished above .500 since 1946. And there were any number of signs for a bright future. Lou Brock's twenty-four stolen bases were the most by a Cub since Kiki Cuyler swiped thirty-seven in 1930. Dick Ellsworth's 2.11 ERA placed him second in the league to Cy Young winner Sandy Koufax (15-5; 1.88!). And Ellsworth's won-lost record of 22-10 gave him more wins than any Cub lefty since Hippo Vaughn's twenty-one victories in 1919. Lindy McDaniel won thirteen and saved another twenty-two; Larry Jackson was 14-18 with thirteen complete games. In fact, the Cubs' pitching staff was second in the league to the Dodgers, recording forty-five complete games and a team earned run average of 3.04. One wonders where the Cubs would have been without the trade that brought them Jackson and McDaniel. On the other hand, what if (isn't this fun?) the Cubs had not sent Ron Perranowski to Los Angeles back in 1961. This season he had gone 16-3 with a 1.67 ERA and led the Dodgers to the pennant. Another Cub bright spot was fielding. Yes, fielding. The Cubs finished fourth in fielding and Ron Santo's 374 assists set a major league record for third basemen. It was in the hitting department that the Cubs failed. Only Santo at .297 (25 HRs and 99 RBIs), Williams at .286 (25 HRs and 95 RBIs) and Brock at .258 had reasonably good seasons. The five other regulars averaged less than .240 at the plate.

The Cubs' attendance escalated by 370,000 to 979,551. This was still below the third-place White Sox total of 1,158,848, but it outdistanced the sixth-place Braves' 773,018. Never far away, the fans were clearly happy to be coming back. They sensed that with Banks, Hubbs, Rodgers, and Santo in the infield and Williams and Brock in the outfield, the basis was there for building a real challenger. After the season, Colonel Whitlow came out from hiding and took some bows. He announced that the farm system would be providing more young stars for the 1964 season in the persons of outfielder Billy Cowan and infielders John Boccabella and Jim Stewart.

But the off-season this year was a time of tragedy. In the nation, President Kennedy was shot down on November 22, 1963. And for the Cubs, their young second baseman was killed when on February 13, 1964, the plane he was piloting crashed through a foot and a half of ice near Provo, Utah. Although not flamboyant, Ken Hubbs had emerged as a steady, talented professional baseball player and a genuine leader on the field. The Cubs were stunned by his death, and spring drills took on an air of sadness and grim determination. The Cubs wanted to have a good season in memory of Ken Hubbs, but, unfortunately, it was not to be so.

The 1964 season was in some ways the reverse of the previous year. Bob Kennedy was still at the helm, but the pitching (except for Larry Jackson) seemed to disappear. The Cubs hovered around the .500 mark until late May, but on May 26 they were walloped by the Mets 19-1 at Wrigley Field. By the end of May, it was ninth place and a 15-21 record. What games the Cubs did win were won with hitting, particularly by Santo and Williams. As the pitching faltered, the pressure increased to trade one of the good young players for an established starter. The Cubs remembered what a shot in the arm it had been to acquire Larry Jackson not only for his steadiness but for the experience and cunning he imparted to the younger members of the staff. Moreover, rookie Billy Cowan was proving to be a happy surprise in center field. So the Cubs traded Glen Hobbie for ex-Brave star Lew Burdette, now thirty-seven. Since his two good seasons of 1959 and 1960, Hobbie had compiled a 19-37 record. The Cubs also bought outfielder Len Gabrielson from the Braves for $40,000 and catcher Merrit Ranew. Unfortunately, that was not enough. On June 15, the Cubs sent Lou Brock and pitchers Paul Toth and Jack Spring to the Cardinals for Ernie Broglio, Bobby Shantz, and outfielder Doug Clemens. In theory the Cubs now had another young (twenty-nine years old) winning pitcher (18-8 in 1963, 21-9 in 1960), and even if it was not the steal that the Jackson-McDaniel acquisition was, at least it would help both teams equally.

Opening-Day Lineup, 1964

Stewart, 2b
Brock, rf
Williams, 1f
Santo, 3b
Banks, 1b
Rodgers, ss
Cowan, cf
Bertell, c
Norman, p

As a Cub, Brock had hit .263, .258, and was hitting .251 at the time of the trade. But the trade seemed to turn things around for him. As a Cardinal that season, he hit .348 and led the Cardinals to the pennant and the World Series Championship. Also helping the Cardinals that season was former Cub Barney Schultz, who had been traded to the Redbirds back in 1963 for infielder Leo Burke. Schultz saved eleven games in the last two months of the season, and in the stretch drive he appeared in seven consecutive games without yielding a run. Burke disappeared into the minors in 1965. Meanwhile back at the Cubs, Broglio's elbow problems caused Cub fans to think back on the infamous Andy Pafko trade. It must have pained Broglio as much as it did the Cubs to see Brock's name in the headlines almost daily. The fact that Lou had twenty-three hits in fifty-five trips to the plate against the Cubs didn't help either.

Injuries and inconsistency were too much for the Cubs this season. Andre Rodgers was hampered with a bad back and was in and out of the lineup at shortstop. Jim Stewart was not able to fill Hubbs' shoes at second. Gabrielson and Clemens, the two outfielders acquired to replace Brock, were simply inadequate. Centerfielder Billy Cowan was indeed fast and had some power (19 homers for the season), but he struck out with more regularity than he hit. In New York while Billy was fanning six times in a doubleheader, the fans gave him the Bronx cheer every time he swung and missed. When he managed to hit a ground ball to third they gave him a standing ovation. The next night in his first time up he belted a home run. Going around third, he tipped his cap to the fans, who then gave him another standing ovation.

Of the pitchers, only Larry Jackson had a good season. His twenty-four wins were the most by any big-league pitcher in 1964 and the most by a Cub since Charlie Root's twenty-six in 1927. Dick Ellsworth fell off to 14-18; Bob Buhl was 15-14, and Lindy McDaniel lost seven of his eight decisions. When the last out of the season was recorded, the Cubs stood in eighth place with a 76-86 record. Attendance fell off to 751,647. Except for Williams and Santo, things were looking bleak again. Williams and Santo finished third and fourth in the league in total bases with Santo's .564 slugging percentage second only to Willie Mays' .604 and Williams' thirty-three home runs second, again to Mays, who had forty-seven. In addition, Santo's 114 RBIs put him second to — no, not Mays — Ken Boyer and for the third straight year he led the league's third basemen in assists and in putouts.

After the 1964 season the Cubs announced that Al Dark, who had been fired as manager of the Giants, was returning to the Cubs as a coach. Ernie Broglio underwent surgery for bone chips in his pitching arm. And shortstop Andre Rodgers was traded to the Pirates for infielder Roberto Pena. George Altman was reacquired, coming from the Mets in return for Billy Cowan, already a Met hero. Then, on January 8, Colonel Whitlow resigned as athletic director. Mr. Wrigley commented that "baseball simply refused to accept him and his ideas. He was too far ahead of his time." One of his ideas had been to install a fence on top of the bricks in the vacant area of center field. Said one Cub official, "The fence will be down by opening day. The one thing we don't need around here is any reminders of Whitlow."

Bob Kennedy was still head coach when the squad gathered for spring training for the 1965 season, which would be the last year they would train at Mesa, Arizona. Kennedy gave a strong and dramatic speech to the players. In the course of telling them that it was time to play to win, he stopped and asked two rookies to stand up. "I want everybody in this room to take a long look at these two boys and then remember something very important," he said.

"They were both born in 1946. That is the last time this club finished in the first division. Now does everybody understand me when I say that things are going to be different on this club this year?"

This spring brought another tragic death to the Cubs. Jack Quinlan, their radio broadcaster on WGN, was killed in an automobile accident. Quinlan was a fine announcer, respected and appreciated by fans, players, and colleagues. Fortunately, Vince Lloyd was available to take his place at the microphone, along with Lou Boudreau.

During the exhibition games, the Cubs tried a new keystone combination with the recently acquired Roberto Pena and their own farm-system graduate, Glenn Beckert. In addition, a young shortstop, signed in 1964 from the University of Mississippi, was in camp for a look; but he was sent down for more seasoning. You guessed it — Don Kessinger. Relief pitcher Don Elston, now thirty-six, was given his unconditional release. Elston had been a workhorse, appearing in 447 games in his eight years as a Cub. Whatever can be said of the Cubs in the fifties and sixties, they had some superb relievers, and the names of Dutch Leonard, Turk Lown, Don Elston, Bill Henry, Lindy McDaniel, and Ted Abernathy still stir many proud memories. Elston had been obtained from Brooklyn during John Holland's first season as general manager, 1957, and had pitched as a spot starter and reliever. But from 1958 on, he had worked from the bullpen, averaging close to sixty appearances a year over those seven seasons. Lefthander Bill Henry shared the relief duties with Elston in 1958 and '59. His 109 games and 216 innings for those two years, coupled with Elston's 134 games and 195 innings, demonstrates how crucial these players were to those Cub teams that tied for fifth place in consecutive years. Lindy McDaniel's outstanding 1963 season had helped the Cubs break the .500 barrier that year. Pitching only eighty-eight innings in fifty-seven appearances, McDaniel's every pitch had a game riding on it; twenty-two saves and thirteen wins to be exact. Now, in 1965, McDaniel would recover from an off-season and contribute to the brilliant year that the newly acquired Ted Abernathy would have.

But let's begin with the season opener, an unusual one to say the least. After eleven innings the game was called on account of darkness with the Cubs and the Cardinals tied 11-11. Would the elevens be lucky for the Cubs or Cardinals? Roberto Pena was the highlight and lowlight of the game. He made three errors in seven chances, including two dropped pop-ups. But he also had three hits in six at-bats, one a homer, another a two-run double, and the third a single in the eleventh which led to his scoring the tying run. Said Kennedy, "It looks like we're going to have some excitement with this fellow." Unfortunately his hitting fell off quickly, so the only excitement left was when a ball was hit in his direction. By June 6, Pena had seventeen errors to complement his .218 average. Some compliment.

Opening-Day Lineup, 1965
Beckert, 2b
Pena, ss
Williams, cf
Santo, 3b
Altman, 1f
Banks, 1b
Clemens, rf
Bertell,c
Ellsworth, p

After thirty-two games, the Cubs were even with the league. Included in this tally were a sixteen-inning 3-2 win over the Dodgers (See Chapter 7, "Games to Remember") and a 3-2 loss to the Reds ending when hardluck Ernie Broglio balked with the bases loaded in the ninth. Run production was limited pretty much to Banks, Williams, and Santo. Outfielders Doug Clemens and Don Landrum were both under .230, as were rookie catchers Vic Roznovsky and Chris Krug. The starters were ineffective, but the bullpen of McDaniel and Abernathy, recently acquired from Cleveland, was excellent. Pena had become

Four Cub stars of the late forties: outfielder Frankie Baumholtz *(top, left)*, pitcher Bob Rush *(top, right)*, outfielder Hank Sauer *(bottom, left)*, and shortstop Roy Smalley *(bottom, right)*.

Phil Cavarretta *(right)* visits the Cub dugout on March 30, 1954, the day after becoming the first major league manager to be fired during spring training. With him is Coach Bob Scheffing.

The Cubs' College of Coaches meets the press (January, 1961). Standing (from left): James (Rip) Collins, Goldie Holt, Verlon Walker, and three-time Cub manager Charlie Grimm. Seated (from left): Elvin Tappe, Harry Craft, owner P. K. Wrigley, and Vedie Himsl.

The incomparable Billy Williams tips his hat to 41,000 fans as teammates surround him on "Billy Williams Day" at Wrigley Field (July 1, 1969).

Cub fans celebrate their seemingly invincible lead in the National League East, 1969.

For the 500th time in his career, Mr. Cub, Ernie Banks, knocks one out of the park (May 12, 1970).

so unreliable that the inexperienced Kessinger was called up in June to replace him. But Don committed nine errors in his first eleven games.

By June 10, the Cubs were 22-29, in ninth place. Four days later Bob Kennedy was moved upstairs as an administrative assistant and Lou Klein was made head coach. Lou held the fort but there just weren't enough troops to rally. At the end of July, the Cubs were in eighth place, where they remained at the end of August, and September, and the season. It was the kind of season in which Dick Ellsworth could pitch a one-hitter against the Dodgers and lose 3-1. With one out in the eighth, an error and a fielder's choice put two men on base. Someone named Al Ferrara then homered. It was the kind of season that the Cubs could be no-hit for ten innings by Jim Maloney of the Reds and victims of a perfect game by Sandy Koufax. It was the kind of season that could see these same Cubs sweep a three-game series from the Braves in the following fashion: in the first game Williams grandslams and the Cubs win 5-3; in the second game Williams homers, singles twice, and drives in three runs as Cubs win 3-2; in the third game Williams homers and then is walked three times in a row but scores each time as Santo and Banks each homer twice in a 10-2 win. Notice the names.

There is no doubt that the Cubs had stars; Banks, Santo, and Williams between them hit ninety-five homers and drove in 315 runs. Williams had an especially good year, finishing among the top five National leaguers in seven different hitting categories. But while Williams was batting .315 with 203 hits, and Santo and Banks were at .285 and .265, no other Cub regular could break the .240 barrier. Ted Abernathy appeared in a major-league record eighty-four games, saving thirty-one with a 2.57 ERA, and Lindy McDaniel pitched in seventy-one games with a 2.59 ERA. Buhl had a winning season at 13-11, but Jackson went from twenty-four wins the year before to twenty-one losses in 1965. Dick Ellsworth was 14-15.

With a final record of 72-90, the Cubs' attendance fell off another 100,000 to 641,361, but even this was more than the Braves attracted (555,584) in their last year in Milwaukee. The White Sox had attendance over 1,100,000. When asked whether the Cubs would install lights to draw better crowds, Wrigley said, "It's not night baseball we need; it's winning baseball." After the season, Bob Kennedy resigned from the Cubs' organization.

With the end of the 1965 season, the verdict was clear on the college of coaches. It had probably contributed to the rapid development of players like Santo, Williams, Hubbs, and even ultimately Beckert and Kessinger. But in terms of providing strong leadership at the major-league level, it was a flop. One flop too many? No doubt reacting to the major flaw of their experiment, the Cubs reached for a manager unlike any they ever had before. After ten years away from managing, Leo Durocher was named to head the Cubs. Moreover, he was the first Cub manager to get a three-year contract. Leo wasted no time in making three things perfectly clear: (1) "If they haven't given me a title, I'll give myself one. I'm the manager and the only manager. Don't ever call me a coach." (2) "This is definitely not an eighth place ball club. The Cubs are better than that." and (3) Leo maintained that the Cubs seemed to bring up players with outstanding ability, keep them for several tantalizing years and then trade them only to watch them excel for their new teams. Therefore, he reasoned, the Cubs were just not handling them right. Was Leo starting his years with the Cubs with a well-placed needle in the sensitive Lou Brock area?

Needles or no, John Holland was busy making one of his better trades for the Cubs. He sent Lindy McDaniel and Don Landrum to the Giants for pitcher Bill Hands and catcher Randy Hundley, both untested rookies. The Cubs had been without a standout catcher for a long time. Sammy Taylor held the position from 1958 to 1962. He shared some of that time with Dick Bertell who worked at the job for four undistinguished seasons before he was traded to the Giants during the 1965 season. The door was open for Hundley.

As the weeks went by, Leo began to hype the Cubs. He apparently saw no need to "back up the truck," a phrase he had used in 1948 when he told Horace Stoneham of the Giants that he wanted to get rid of slow-footed power hitters like Johnny Mize, Sid Gordon, Walker Cooper, and Willard Marshall. He told reporters, "I wouldn't trade Billy Williams for three Frank Robinsons," and "Dick Ellsworth is the best left-hander in baseball after Sandy Koufax." He was consciously trying to develop in the players and fans the belief that the Cubs were good, that they could win. Still, he was enough of a realist to laugh when Glenn Beckert reminded him of his own playing limitations. Beckert, honored at the Chicago Baseball Dinner as Chicago's Rookie of the Year, quipped, "It's not very often that a .240 hitter gets invited to sit at the head table. But I see that Mr. Durocher is up here too, so I know I'm not alone." Leo's diagnosis was that the Cubs had plenty of hitting but not enough alertness. He was going to do something about mental errors, throwing to the wrong base, missing the cut-off man, failing to charge the ball, and so forth.

As spring training began, this time in a new location at Long Beach, California, Leo went to work to prepare the players to rid themselves of mental lapses. He did not run the tightly organized camp that the college of coaches had. He wanted to see the players in game conditions. He did all he could to restrain his criticisms, continuing his efforts to get the Cubs, after decades of second-division baseball, to think of themselves as winners. He was particularly pleased with three of the young players. Hundley won the catching job, speedy Byron Browne would be installed in center field, and twenty-year-old Ken Holtzman impressed Leo as another Koufax. (Along with Ellsworth, this now gave Durocher two virtual Koufaxes on the same staff!)

There was speculation as to how Leo would get along with eccentric pitcher Bill Faul, a self-proclaimed hypnotist, preacher, and karate expert who was 6-6 with a 3.53 ERA for the Cubs in 1965. Said Leo, "All I know is that he can fire the ball. If he can win, I'll let him hypnotize me. You know, every ball club should have some sort of kook on it, someone who is different, somebody the other guys can kid about and laugh about and get relaxed." Fans could hardly wait for the season to begin.

It had been an eventful off-season. The Cubs' hiring of Leo had brought a lot of press attention. And with Eddie Stanky having signed as manager of the White Sox, Chicago fans could be sure of excitement in both of their ball parks. In the nation, the Vietnam War was escalating rapidly. Many baseball players joined the National Guard and did the largest share of their military training during the off-season.

When the season finally opened, it didn't start well for the Cubs. On April 20, they were 1-7, in last place. The next day, Holland announced another of his trades that would benefit the Cubs in the years ahead. Larry Jackson and Bob Buhl went to Philadelphia for pitcher Ferguson Jenkins, outfielder Adolfo Phillips, and first baseman John Herrnstein. On April 23, Jenkins pitched five-and-one-third innings of relief and knocked in both runs with a homer and a single to lead the Cubs over the Dodgers 2-0. The next day Holtzman pitched six innings of shutout ball to help topple the Dodgers by the same score. But that was it. April 27 showed the Cubs in ninth place with a 3-9 record.

> **Opening-Day Lineup, 1966**
>
> Cline, cf
> Beckert, 2b
> Williams, rf
> Santo, 3b
> Altman, lf
> Banks, 1b
> Hundley, c
> Kessinger, ss
> Jackson, p

Santo, Williams, and Banks were off to slow starts. With Jackson and Buhl gone, the pitching staff was headed by Ellsworth and the three rookies, Jenkins, Hands, and Holtzman. Not even Bill Faul's magic helped. Faul would turn his back on the hitters to let them see the number thirteen on his back and then turn back and wave his hand in front of his face a few times before delivering the ball. But he was no mystery to the opposing batters, so Leo didn't have to worry about being hypnotized.

By May 25 the Cubs were 10-24, in last place. In a strange deal, they sent Ted Abernathy, their ace reliever of the previous season, to the Braves for outfielder Lee Thomas. The tailspin continued. On June 8, the Cubs were 15-35, and two weeks later they were 18-41, with a team batting average of .236 and an ERA of 4.58. Only Santo with a twenty-eight-game hitting streak, a Cub record, had begun to hit with regularity. Leo was being as patient as he could be, but it was clear that more experienced players were needed. Thirty-seven-year-old Curt Simmons was purchased from the Cardinals and in his Cub debut pitched a 7-0 shutout. On July 13, thirty-nine-year-old Robin Roberts was signed as a free agent. Now a Cub, Roberts recounted how sixteen years earlier the Phillies had brought him to Chicago from his hometown of Springfield, Illinois, and let him work out with them for three days at Wrigley Field before signing him right under the Cubs' nose. To make room for Roberts on the roster, Bill Faul was shipped to Tacoma. The day before he had been hit for a homer by Bob Skinner of the Pirates after shaking off a pitch which was then called again by catcher Boccabella. Faul said his release was "spiteful and unfair." He wanted to know who, really, called for the curve he hung to Skinner, Boccabella or Leo?

The Cubs maintained a .333 winning percentage through the middle of August. When Robin Roberts failed as a starter, Ferguson Jenkins was finally put into the rotation. About the only tension left to be resolved was which Cub hitter would lead the league in strikeouts. It was a battle to the wire and ended in a tie. Both Phillips and Browne fanned 133 times for the season.

The 1966 season ended, mercifully, with the Cubs owning a 59-103 record. Unlike 1962, when the Cubs had an identical record, the Mets weren't losing 120 games. So the Cubs were dead last in the league, a full thirty-six games behind the pennant winning Dodgers. Attendance was 635,891, down 6,530 from 1965. Of course, Cub fans were not without cause for optimism. After all, how could things really get worse? Adolfo Phillips may have struck out a lot, but he also stole thirty-two bases, fourth best in the league. Hundley caught 149 games, the most ever by a rookie catcher in the major leagues, and was impressive in fielding and hitting. The Cub infield was the best hitting infield in the league, led by Santo at .312; Beckert hit .287, Kessinger, .274, and Banks, .272. Cub power was again evident: in the home run column, Santo had 30, Williams 29, Hundley 19, Phillips 16, and Banks 15. Understandably, none of the starting pitchers had a winning record. The veteran of the group, Dick Ellsworth, finished with a dismal 8-22 record. After the season he was dealt to the Phillies for pitcher Ray Culp. Rookie Ken Holtzman was 11-16, and in the final home game he had gone to the ninth with a no-hitter, then gave up two hits and one run. The Cubs scored twice with four hits. The losing pitcher? The *real* Sandy Koufax!

Reminded incessantly of his now-famous prediction that the Cubs weren't an eighth-place team (proven true by their tenth-place finish), Durocher was more cautious in looking ahead. All he would predict was "We are not going to win the pennant in 1967."

Nineteen sixty-six may have been tenth place, but spring training for 1967 — this year at Scottsdale, Arizona — revealed a new confidence on the part of Cub players, much of it attributable to the presence of Durocher. The fact that Leo was respected as a shrewd baseball man cast a mantle of respectability on the whole team. Ron Santo pointed out that Leo must have seen the real possibility of developing a good team or he would never have accepted the job as manager. For his part, Leo kept heralding individual Cub players and in so doing he created more than a little self-belief on their part. Except in the case of Mr. Cub, now thirty-six years old. Leo began referring to Banks as "old grey beard," named him a player-coach, and announced that John Boccabella would get a full shot at the first-base job. Banks, always a team man, was determined to keep his place in the starting lineup, but he intended to do so with his hitting and fielding, and not simply on his past record.

As the exhibition season ended, the Cubs were the talk of the league. The pitching of Jenkins, Holtzman, Hands, rookie hopeful Rich Nye, and new acquisition Ray Culp were very impressive; the Cub infield was solid; and in Hundley they had one of the best young catchers in baseball. Leo might have said with good reason that this was no tenth-place team. He didn't. But he did say, "There's no reason why we shouldn't have a terrific start," Well, they did win three of their first four games, with complete performances by Jenkins, Simmons, and Culp. And they did so without Hundley, who missed the first few games with an injury. But it was clear that the Cubs needed another outfielder. George Altman's comeback effort over the past two seasons had failed, and Browne could not cure his strikeout problem. Both were farmed out. Right field was turned over to Lee Thomas and rookie Norm Gigon. At the same time, the Bleacher Bums were beginning to adopt a new favorite — the unpredictable Adolfo Phillips. Unpredictable? How about a game against the Phillies in which he dropped a fly ball allowing three unearned runs to score but also hit a triple and a home run to lead the Cubs to an 8-4 win.

Opening-Day Lineup, 1967

Kessinger, ss
Beckert, 2b
Williams, lf
Santo, 3b
Banks, 1b
Thomas, rf
Bertell, c
Phillips, cf
Jenkins, p

After the first month of the season, the Cubs were 16-11, in third place. Something was different about this team. Billy Williams pinpointed it: "We used to play a lot of lay-back baseball. We'd be waiting for something to happen. Now we're making things happen. It's a whole different kind of thing." For example, on May 10, Adolfo

Phillips stole home with the winning run in a 5-4 defeat of the Giants. Yes, a Cub stole home!

Ken Holtzman was called to a six-month tour of duty with the Illinois National Guard. On May 20, two days before he reported, the Cubs gave him a going-away present, twenty runs against the Dodgers enabling Ken to win 20-3 and to take with him a 5-0 record. Phillips had six RBIs on a homer and double, Hundley five on a grand slam and sacrifice fly, Beckert three on a homer and double.

But the outfield situation was still a major problem. The Cubs acquired Ted Savage from the Cardinals and were happily surprised with the play of Adolfo Phillips. Spurred on by standing ovations and "oles" from the fans, Adolfo made June 11 his day with six hits, including four homers, eight RBIs, and two diving catches in the Cubs' sweep of a doubleheader from the Mets.

In the third week of June the Cubs caught fire. They won seven straight, lost one, and then won six more. CUB POWER lapel pins were seen all over Chicago, and fans were so enamored of these Cubs that the upper deck had to be opened for a weekday game for the first time in five years. On July 2, a crowd of 40,000 gathered at Wrigley Field to help the Cubs beat the Reds 4-1 for their seventeenth win in nineteen games. With the game finished, the fans stayed in their places, chanting "We're number 1" and watching the scoreboard report the progress of the first-place Cardinals. More than an hour later, the score finally went up, reporting the Cardinals' defeat. The fans' chant was true. It was July, and the Cubs were in first place!

Even a seven-game losing streak early in July didn't turn into a full-scale Swoon. On July 18, the Cubs were 50-38 and only two games behind the Cardinals. They then won six out of eight and on July 25 moved into a first-place tie. There were plenty of heroes to go around: Santo, Williams,

Hundley, Phillips, Jenkins, and Nye. But perhaps the greatest was Ernie Banks. His fielding at first was impeccable, and his hitting was timely. More than that, Banks had been able to overcome Durocher's desire to ease him out of his job. Durocher had said to newsmen, "Why don't you knock off that 'Mr. Cub' stuff? The guy's wearing out, He can't go on forever." Now he was wondering what Ernie's formula for staying young was.

If the Cubs had not lost Holtzman to military service, there is no telling how far they might have gone. Holtzman was able to pitch on weekend passes and won four without a loss as a part-timer. But it wasn't enough. The staff was being overworked. Jenkins, Culp, and rookies Rich Nye and Joe Niekro, aided by Hands and Chuck "Twiggy" Hartenstein in the bullpen, were simply worn out by August. By the middle of the month, an 8-16 stretch dropped the Cubs to 64-56 and third place, ten full games behind the Cardinals. The second half of August brought only four victories with twelve more losses. But there was no giving up. Winning seventeen of their last thirty contests, including two out of three from the Reds in a head-to-head battle for third place, the Cubs finished behind only the Cardinals and Giants. Their 87-74 record was the best winning percentage for a Cub team since 1945.

The fans were back as surely as the Cubs were; 977,226 came to Wrigley Field, about 11,000 more than the fourth-place White Sox drew. The Cubs showed a profit of $342,346. Ferguson Jenkins, who set an all-time Cub record with 236 strikeouts, won twenty and lost thirteen, with a 2.80 ERA; Holtzman was 9-0 and 2.52; Nye, 13-10; and Hands, working primarily from the bullpen, had pitched in forty-nine games with a 2.46 ERA. The Cub offense produced more runs than any other team in the league. Of the regulars all but Kessinger and Savage hit over .265. Banks had had a fine year with twenty-three homers and ninety-five RBIs, while Santo had been excellent with a .300

average to go with his thirty-one homers and ninety-eight RBIs.

It seemed clear that with one more outfielder and one more good pitcher . . . Lou Brock this season had again led the Cardinals to the world championship, hitting .414 in the Series against the Red Sox. And Ted Abernathy, traded the previous year, was 6-3 with the Reds and led the league in saves with twenty-eight. The Cubs' total was also twenty-eight. Abernathy's ERA was a cool 1.27. But trades are always a risk. Where would the Cubs have been without Hundley, Jenkins, or Hands? The problem now was to fill the gaps and go for it all. The season was barely ended when John Holland announced that he had obtained veteran outfielder Lou Johnson from the Dodgers for Paul Popovich. Lou's .270 average compared to Savage's .211 was enough to give Cub fans pleasant dreams over the winter.

Cub players themselves began to sense the possibility of a pennant. Citing the fact that the Cubs had led the league in 1967 not only in runs scored but in fielding average as well, Ron Santo sloganed that "the pennant date is '68." Ernie Banks told fans, "Don't fear, this is the year." And Ken Holtzman observed, "There is a fine spirit on our ball club and that will be a factor this year when we're up there fighting for a pennant. I think we'll make it. . . . And do you know who I believe could be the key to the pennant for us? Adolfo Phillips, that's who." And even the Chicago sportswriters, generally a hard group to convince, stated publicly that if Cub pitching held up they would win the flag. And the only real problem with the pitching appeared to be that Ken Holtzman still had to report for monthly duties and a two-week session during the summer with the Illinois National Guard.

Everybody worked hard in Scottsdale in 1968. Practice field number 2 with coach Pete Reiser in charge was nicknamed "Iwo Jima" by the players. In his playing days, Reiser had been famous for denting outfield walls with his bat and his body; he believed in 100 percent effort. One day after a long practice session, one of the players picked up a rock and handed it to Reiser. "Pete," he said, "your heart just fell out."

The opening-day lineup, even without the injured Glenn Beckert, was formidable. Still the Cubs lost the curtain-raiser 9-4 to the Reds. In fact, they won only three of their first ten games. It was clear that the Cubs needed a strong bullpen. John Holland got on the phone and got even with the Dodgers for the Pafko trade of years ago. He talked them out of relief pitcher Phil "the Vulture" Regan and outfielder Jim Hickman, while giving up Ted Savage and pitcher Jim

Opening-Day Lineup, 1968
Johnson, rf
Kessinger, ss
Williams, 1f
Santo, 3b
Banks, 1b
Hundley, c
Arcia, 2b
Phillips, cf
Jenkins, p

Ellis. No one seemed particularly concerned when the Cubs went through April and May barely able to stay even with the league. The inconsistency of Cub pitching and the silence of Cub bats were bound to change. On May 28, the Cubs were 22-21, in fifth place. But they were only two games out of first, and one of these days it would all come together. Adolfo Phillips led the slump parade with a batting average of .180 and three hits in his last forty-three trips to the plate.

But the hoped-for revival didn't take place in June. It was frustrating because the pitching and defense were splendid; the problem was, of all things, hitting. In mid-June the Cubs suffered the ignominy of tying a sixty-two-year-old major league record set in 1906 by the Philadelphia Athletics in the era of the dead ball. They went forty-eight consecutive innings without scoring a run. Beginning with their failure to score in the final eight innings of a loss to

Atlanta on June 15, they followed with a 1-0 loss to Phil Niekro in eleven innings, a 1-0 loss to Nelson Briles of the Cardinals, a 4-0 one-hit whitewashing by Steve Carlton, and a 1-0 shutout by Bob Gibson. On June 21, the Cubs finally got a run in the third inning off the Reds' George Culver. He helped by walking the bases full with one out, setting up a sacrifice fly by Billy Williams. During this offensive silence, Fergie Jenkins allowed one run in eighteen innings and got a loss and a no-decision for his efforts. In a classic understatement, Durocher noted, "We wasted some good pitching."

By June 25, the Cubs were 31-38, in ninth place, twelve-and-a-half games behind the Cardinals. Time for a shake-up. Durocher focused his frustration on Phillips and fined him $200 for loafing on the bases. John Holland sent Lou Johnson to the Indians for Willie Smith. Johnson was hitting only .244 as a Cub and had become as disillusioned with the Cubs as they with him. He took a parting swipe at Durocher: "The man never talked to me. He relayed his orders through messengers." The surest sign that something was wrong was the fact that by mid-season the Cubs had been able to come from behind after trailing in the fifth inning in only five games. Even worse, on July 11, Jenkins lost 1-0 for the fourth time that season. It was the sixteenth time the Cubs had been shut out.

But after the All-Star break the Cubs came to life, winning twenty and losing nine in the rest of July. Jenkins continued to be brilliant, performing pitching extravaganzas like fanning thirteen Dodgers for a 2-1 win on July 27. Holtzman, who lost two two-week periods with the National Guard (part of it to the crisis in Chicago during the Democratic National Convention), now was in the groove and pitched three straight shutouts. But there were signs that Ken wasn't overly fond of Durocher after being openly criticized by the Lip for being lackadaisical and not competitive enough.

Phil Regan was doing so well that everyone started accusing him of throwing illegal pitches. On August 8, umpire Chris Pelakoudas went to the mound and inspected Regan's glove and cap and claimed later that he could feel Vaseline on the inside of the cap. When the game continued, Pelakoudas charged Regan with throwing three illegal pitches. He nullified a fly ball and a strikeout and changed a strike call to a ball. The result was one of the biggest rhubarbs in Wrigley Field history: 30,942 of the faithful booed loudly and threw debris on the field. Durocher, Hundley, and Al Spangler were all thrown out of the game. Nonetheless, the Cubs held on to win. After a special hearing, National League President Warren Giles said that from now on umpires should have better evidence before calling pitches illegal. Durocher had gotten in a few comments of his own during a talk show with Bernice Gera, a woman who wanted to be an umpire. Said Leo, "She probably wouldn't do any worse than some of the guys who are umpiring right now." Way to go, Leo. That must have helped the Cubs on close calls!

The Cubs' 17-12 mark in August moved them up to fourth place but still far behind the Cardinals, who were running away with the race. The month of September was typical of the season. The Cubs displayed all of the elements of championship baseball but lacked the overall consistency and good fortune that would allow it all to gel. For example, on September 9th and 10th, Billy Williams hit five home runs in two consecutive games. But on September 11th, Fergie Jenkins suffered a 1-0 loss to the Mets. This loss marked the fifth time this season that Fergie had been bested 1-0, equaling a major league record. Not exactly the kind of record one wants to equal. Despite these five frustrating losses, Fergie would not be denied his second consecutive twenty-victory season. His forty starts tied a Cub record set by Grover Cleveland Alexander in

1920, and his 260 strikeouts surpassed his own Cub record of the year before.

The Cubs rallied at the end of the season to win their last five games and claim third place again from the Reds. Their record of 84-78 put them thirteen games behind the Cardinals, who went on to lose the Series to the Tigers, led by Denny McLain who had won thirty games during the regular season. Leo said, "It was a nice finish. I'm pleased and grateful." Cub fans felt the same way. The 1,043,409 gate was the best at Wrigley Field since 1950.

All the signs were there that this team could go all the way. The Cubs led the league in fielding and in home runs. The infield of Banks, Beckert, Kessinger, and Santo was probably the best in the major leagues. Beckert had a particularly good year, leading the league in runs scored and hitting safely in twenty-seven consecutive games, one short of Santo's club record set in 1966. Moreover, for the third consecutive year he was the most difficult National Leaguer to strike out. Ernie Banks, now having passed Cap Anson's record of 2,253 games played as a Cub, was still supplying outstanding fielding and his thirty-two home runs and eighty-three RBIs were good by any standard. Santo's average slipped to .248, but he still hit twenty-six homers, had ninety-eight RBIs, and led the league in walks for the third straight year. In addition, he won a Gold Glove for his work at third. Kessinger hit only .240, but it was clear that with his excellent range at shortstop even that would suffice. Hundley also had an off year at the plate, but was certainly one of the premiere receivers in baseball. In the outfield, Billy Williams again played in every game, hitting thirty homers, driving in ninety-eight runs, and leading the league in total bases with 321. In fact, he and Santo tied for second place in RBIs that year.

The pitching staff, led by Jenkins, Hands, Holtzman, and Joe Niekro, was solid. Hands was 16-10 in his first season as a starter, and Niekro went 14-10. Regan won the Fireman of the Year award with a 10-5 mark and a major league high twenty-five saves. Holland had done well by the Cubs in getting Regan, but one can only wonder what might have been if the Cubs had still had Ray Culp (sold to the Red Sox for cash and a minor leaguer), who had a 16-6 season for his new club, or even Dick Ellsworth, who had gone for Culp in 1967 and had just finished a 16-7 season, also for the Red Sox.

Nineteen sixty-eight brought an end to the first wave of expansion. The second wave would begin in 1969, with each league expanding to twelve teams. These twelve teams would be divided into an east and west division in each league with six teams in each division. At the end of the season, the divisional champions would participate in a best-of-five play-off for the league championship and the right to play in the World Series. The Cubs were placed in the National League East along with the Pirates, Phillies, Cardinals, Mets, and Expos. It seemed certain that the Cubs would be in serious contention in 1969 even in the same division with the National League Champion Cardinals. There were a lot of echoes to Ferguson Jenkins' statement that "the Cubs are two players away from being a pennant winner. All we need is another good outfielder and a starting pitcher who can win about fifteen games."

In January, Cub pennant hopes got a boost with the reacquisition of reliever Ted Abernathy. Durocher admitted that it had been a mistake to let him get away two years before. In those two years with the Reds, Abernathy appeared in 148 games, won 16 and lost 10, while chalking up 41 saves. The Cubs gave up catcher Bill Plummer, infielder Clarence Jones, and a minor-league pitcher to get him back.

Durocher, no longer reluctant to make predictions, came out of hiding: "The Cubs are now ready to go for all the marbles," he said. "We have sound hitting, the best defense in the league, and pitching that is constantly improving." Leo went on to discount the need for another trade: "People sometimes wonder about our outfield situation, but I'm not one of them. We have three of the hardest hitting prospects you could ever hope to see . . . Oscar Gamble, Jim McMath, and Jim Dunegan." Sportswriter Jerome Holtzman, unconvinced, wrote a column saying that the Cubs could indeed win it all, but to do so they still needed another starting pitcher and another outfielder. Rumors that had the Cubs dealing with the Reds for Vada Pinson stopped abruptly when the Reds traded him to the Cardinals.

The outfield hole got deeper when Adolfo Phillips fractured a bone in his right hand during spring training. Thanks to a dispute between owners and the Players' Association over the pension package, spring training was shortened and, as it drew to a close, Leo was still groping for a starting outfield. Gamble showed promise, but at age nineteen, he was still too green. Thus Don Young, who was not even on the spring roster, was invited to camp. At twenty-three, he had more experience than Gamble, including a two-week stay with the Cubs in 1965.

Observers compared Young to Jim Landis and said that he could be a Gold Glove center-fielder. According to Leo, "He could have a great future, but it's up to him. I don't care what he hits. I want to see more enthusiasm from him. He's got to be more aggressive." How many players over the years had been judged too unaggressive for Leo's tastes? How many Cubs? Holtzman? Kessinger? Beckert? As it was, Durocher kept Young and sent his "three hard-hitting prospects," Gamble, McMath, and Dunegan, down to the minors. Before opening day, Leo made a rather foreboding statement: "The only thing I'm concerned about is our lack of depth."

As the season opened the Cubs' efforts to secure that elusive pennant got off to a good start. Banks hit two homers and drove in five runs, and in the eleventh, pinch-hitter Willie Smith hit a two-run homer to give the Cubs a 7-6 win over the Phillies before 40,796 cheering fans. (See Chapter 7, "Games to Remember.") The next day Billy Williams hit four doubles to lead the Cubs to victory, and the day after that Santo homered twice for a sweep of the series. On to

Opening-Day Lineup, 1969

Kessinger, ss
Beckert, 2b
Williams, 1f
Santo, 3b
Banks, 1b
Hundley, c
Hickman, rf
Young, cf
Jenkins, p

Montreal, where a two-out, twelfth-inning single by Williams beat the Expos 1-0. They then lost 7-3, but won the next two. And so it went through the month of April, which ended with the Cubs in first place with a 15-6 mark. In late April the Cubs went after that needed starter by obtaining Dick Selma from San Diego for Joe Niekro, Gary Ross, and a minor-league infielder. Even Jimmy the Greek began to believe. Or so it would seem. The Cubs were now 7-5, co-favorites with the Cardinals, to win the National League East.

Two of the Cubs were off to poor starts, however. Glenn Beckert was injured in a collision with Mike Shannon of the Cardinals on April 16 and was slow to come back. Adolfo Phillips, still nursing his hand from spring training, was not playing well. Durocher, in early May, blasted Adolfo in a dinner speech: "Adolfo is ready to play, but he doesn't want to play," Leo said. Asked why he publicly berated one of his players, Durocher responded, "In three years I've tried everything else. I'll do everything I can to wake him up." Phillips was deeply disturbed by the attack but seemed genuinely unable to play to form. A month later he was traded to Montreal for Paul Popovich. Many of the Cubs were angered by the deal. Adolfo was popular with his teammates and more than one felt he would be important in the stretch ahead. When leaving the clubhouse for the last time, Phillips refused to shake hands with Leo. He said that Durocher hadn't talked to him for a month. Shades of Lou Johnson.

But back to the story. In mid-May, Jenkins, Holtzman, and Selma pitched consecutive shutouts as the Cubs continued on their way. When Beckert was hit in the face by a pitch, Nate Oliver took over at second base and in his first game hit a homer, a double, and a single, driving in four runs. The next day he doubled in the ninth and scored the winning run in a 3-2 win over the Padres. Meanwhile, Don Kessinger, who after two years of prodding from Durocher to be aggressive, was finally allowed to be himself and not Leo's "holler guy." He responded by fielding and hitting in spectacular fashion. On May 27, the Cubs were 29-15 and their pitching staff had posted thirteen shutouts and a 2.65 ERA. Dodger manager Walt Alston said, "If they left it up to me, I'd pick the entire Cub infield and their catcher for the All-Star team."

On to June. Swoon time? Not this year. On June 15, Kessinger set a major-league record for shortstops by playing fifty-four consecutive games in a single season without an error. Banks had ten homers and fifty RBIs in his first fifty-three games. Randy Hundley, the Iron Man, caught 416 of a possible 425 innings in the first forty-seven games. The hero list goes on. Holtzman had a mark of 10-1 on June 17, including a string of thirty-three scoreless innings. Holtzman credited Hundley as "the key to my improvement." He went on to say, "Everybody's sitting back waiting for the Cubs to blow it. It seems like people think our big lead is going to be reduced to nothing and pretty soon the Cubs will be back where they used to be. Well, I don't think it will happen." On June 29, Billy

Williams broke Stan Musial's National League record for consecutive games played by extending his string to 846.

Even a five-game losing streak in June didn't signal a swoon. On July 1, the Cubs were 49-27, still comfortably in first, seven full games ahead of the surprising New York Mets. With Phillips gone, Don Young was now the regular centerfielder and Willie Smith and Jim Hickman were platooned in right field. But on July 8, in New York, the pressure began to show. The Cubs were leading the upstart Mets 3-1 in the ninth. For some reason, Don Young missed two routine fly balls, aiding and abetting a Met rally to win the game, 4-3. Banks said of the game that in all his years as a Cub it was the toughest defeat the club had taken. Durocher and Santo both fixed the blame squarely on Young. Santo told reporters, "He was just thinking of himself. He had a bad day at the plate so he's got his head down. He's worrying about his batting average and not the team. . . . All right, he can keep his head down and he can keep going, out of sight for all I care."

What apparently angered Santo was that after the game Young had dressed quickly and left without waiting for the team bus. The next day, Santo called a press conference and apologized. He had apologized personally to Young and would do so again in front of the whole team. He said, "I've been guilty of the same thing myself. I've fought myself so hard at the plate that I forget you can win games with your glove."

Cub fans back in Chicago were shocked. They bombarded radio and newspaper offices with calls blasting Santo for publicly criticizing a teammate, especially a rookie. In his first game back at Wrigley Field, Santo was loudly booed.

This series in New York set the stage for further dramatics. In mid-July the Cubs had two more three-game series scheduled with the Mets, one in New York and one in Chicago. When the Mets took two of the three games in

A souvenir of Cub optimism: tickets for the 1970 playoffs that the Cubs almost made.

Who is that man smiling? Pete Rose seems to be the only one enjoying the discussion as Leo Durocher challenges a call by Umpire Frank Pulli (July 20, 1972). Five days later Durocher resigned as manager.

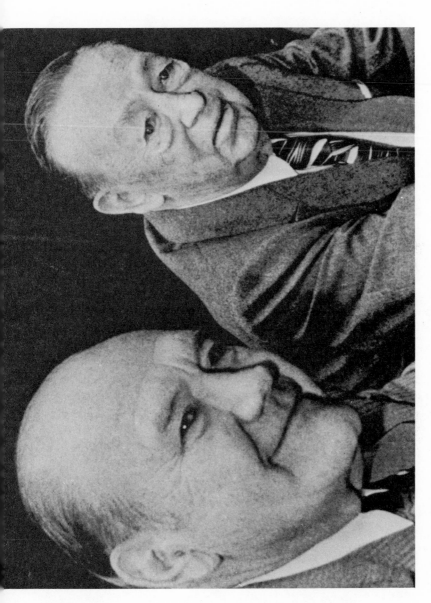

Starting over (October 1973). Cub executive vice-president John Holland (*left*), the architect of the Cubs' near-pennant-winning teams, meets with owner P. K. Wrigley. It was time for drastic changes in the Cub roster.

Cub glee (July 29, 1977). Rick Reuschel scores the winning run in a dramatic 16-15 victory over the Cincinnati Reds.

His finest day as a Cub (May 14, 1978). Dave Kingman crosses the plate, after the first of three home runs scored in a fifteen inning victory over the Dodgers.

Jack Brickhouse responds to a standing ovation from a capacity crowd of Cub fans on hand to honor him at his 5,000th WGN Cub broadcast. At left is Cub president William J. Hagenah, Jr., Illinois Governor James R. Thompson, and Chicago Mayor Jane Byrne.

New York, Santo said, "Wait till we get them next week in Wrigley Field." Earlier in the season, Santo had started a routine of jumping up and clicking his heels after every home victory for the Cubs. The fans loved it. When the Mets arrived and Tom Seaver lost the opener 1-0, Santo clicked several times. The Mets let it be known that this was bush-league stuff. Met Coach Joe Pignatano sent a message directly to Santo telling him so. The next day, when Santo and Met Manager Gil Hodges met at home plate to exchange lineups, Ron asked Hodges to tell Pignatano that the heel-clicking was for the fans. Hodges answered, "You remind me of someone, of Tug McGraw. When he was young, immature, and nervous, he used to jump up and down. He doesn't do it anymore."

When the Mets won the second game of the series, 9-5, Seaver raced out of the dugout, jumped up, and clicked his heels. Other Mets were heckling Santo with his own words from the week before, "Wait till we get them in Wrigley Field." The Mets won again the next day, and this time they gave the business to Durocher, who had just finished making a series of commercials for Schlitz beer. After disputing a call, Leo was on his way back to the dugout when Seaver intercepted him. Leo got a pat on his seat from Seaver who suggested, "Have a Schlitz, Leo." Durocher was speechless. The Mets clearly had the Cubs thinking too much.

When the All-Star break came in July, the Cubs welcomed it. "We need a couple of days of rest," said Kessinger. Hundley seconded: "We're really exhausted, all of us, but we'll get our second wind." But Cub pitching from mid-July was hampered. Holtzman was off to Camp McCoy for two weeks, and Bill Hands was out with a strep infection. Phil Regan pitched in seven straight games; in fact, he appeared in 49 of the first 106 games with an 11-5 record and 10 saves to his credit. The point is that although they were tired, the Cubs seemed safely in the lead. On

July 22, they were 60-37, four-and-a-half ahead of the Mets. They had played at a break-even pace for nearly a month, but the Mets had been able to gain only four games in all that time. Given their chance, the Mets had not really taken advantage of it. Now the Cubs were ready to take off and leave the league behind. They won eight of the first twelve games after the All-Star break and increased their lead of seven games. In mid-August the Cubs were eight-and-a-half games ahead. Who would have guessed that starting August 15, the amazing Mets would win twenty of their next twenty-five games? Even so, the Cubs were also playing well. From July 29 to September 2, the Cubs won nineteen and lost thirteen. And there were some splendid events in August, such as Ken Holtzman's no-hitter against the Braves at Wrigley Field on August 19, and Jim Hickman's .301 average for the month, and the play of Oscar Gamble, who was recalled from San Antonio in time to make two dazzling catches in the ninth to preserve a 2-1 victory over the Braves on August 29. In fact, the Cubs ended August by winning four in a row.

So on September 2, the Cubs still had a five-game lead. What happened next reads like a chronicle of disaster. On September 3, Jim Maloney and the Reds beat the Cubs 2-0. Pittsburgh came to Chicago, September 5-7, and swept three, cutting the Cubs' lead to two-and-one-half games. Well, a split of the two games at Shea Stadium would protect that lead. The only problem was that the Mets took both games by identical 3-2 scores. The Cubs now led by only one-half game. On to Philadelphia for a September 10 date with the Phillies. The Cubs lost 6-2. The Mets took two from the expansion Expos. September 10: a day that should be remembered with flags at half-mast and black armbands. September 10. After 155 consecutive days in first place the Cubs lost their seventh straight, lost their first-place perch, and lost their composure. Durocher was to recall later, "I never saw anything like it in my life. Our offense went down the toilet, the defense went down the drain, and I'm still looking for the pitching staff. I could have dressed nine broads up as ballplayers, and they would have beaten the Cubs."

That's not what he said at the time, however. Then his words were, "These guys are playing their hearts out. Billy Williams has been playing a month with a bad back. Randy Hundley has been catching with a bruised hand, and Ron Santo has been playing even though he's banged up. Not one of them is complaining. We'll come out of it." But why were they playing hurt? Leo's bench had Willie Smith (.246, nine HRs), Paul Popovich (.312), Al Spangler (.211), Ken Rudolph (thirty-four at-bats), and others could be had from the minors. Not great to be sure, but the Mets were getting by handsomely with the likes of Al Weis, J. C. Martin, Ed Charles, Rod Gaspar, and Bobby Pfeil, none of whom hit over .232 even though together they had 1,019 official trips to the plate.

Hundley tried to rally the Cubs by pointing out that "all we have to do is stay within two games of them, because we play them twice at the end of the season." But on September 11, the Cubs lost again while the Mets won again. On the 12th, finally, the Cubs scored a victory to end the eight-game losing streak. But the Mets won another two, increasing their lead to two-and-one-half games. By the time the last two games were played, the Cubs were eight full games behind and the colossal collapse was now history. As Ron Santo said, "Those last three weeks were a nightmare." The last two games? The Mets won the first, but the Cubs came back to win the last one on a three-run homer by Ernie Banks. Empty consolation for bitter disappointment.

But genuine congratulations to Gil Hodges. The Mets finished with a record of 100-62; the Cubs, 92-70. The Cubs scored 720 runs; the Mets, 632. But New York was second in pitching with a team ERA of 2.99, while Chicago was fifth with a 3.34 mark. The Mets were second in fielding at .980, and the Cubs fourth at .979. The Mets stole sixty-six bases to the Cubs' thirty. The Mets had moved from a ninth-place finish to first in one season. And the miracle wasn't over. They took the league play-off from Atlanta and beat the Orioles in five games for the World Championship. Amazing!

A great variety of theories have been advanced to explain the Cubs' swoon. A psychiatrist opined that the Cubs may have had an unconscious drive to lose the pennant. He said they were like school kids who do well for a good part of the year, only to take a good look at their grades, panic, and fail. Another theory was that the Cubs were so distracted by the outside interests generated by their success that they lost their concentration. They did have a team agent named Jack Childers who was in charge of building up a huge pot from endorsements, a pot the players split at the end of the season.

But most of the theories focused on Durocher himself. His constant feud with sportswriters created a tense atmosphere in the clubhouse. So did his willingness to publicly berate his players after a mistake. Many of the players disliked him for this, resenting the way he seemed to have absolutely no regard for people's feelings. For Leo, winning was everything. He didn't care whether he was liked or not. He criticized and ridiculed writers, coaches, and players alike. It was even said that he had informants among the second stringers so that no clubhouse conversation was really safe from his hearing. Twice during the season he had taken off without even telling his coaches that he would miss a game or two. Such behavior seemed a measure of his respect for the players. When the pennant race got tight, the players had to tread too lightly around Leo. Little wonder if they treaded lightly on the field as well.

It may seem unfair to focus so much blame onto Durocher. But he surely would have been the first to take the credit if the Cubs had won. And in terms of managing, it only needs to be mentioned that Gil Hodges led a less-talented team from ninth place to the pennant.

P. K. Wrigley spoke like a true Cub fan in summing up the season. Even though the Cubs set a team attendance record of 1,664,857, Wrigley said, "Naturally, I'm disappointed that the Cubs didn't win. By this time, though, I'm used to disappointments." The Cubs' financial sheet showed a profit of $909,099 for the season. It was a profit Wrigley would have willingly traded for a pennant.

From the college of coaches to the great collapse, the Cubs had come a long way in the sixties. And they still had a great team to begin the seventies. In fact, shortly after the end of the season, John Holland announced that he had acquired the outfielder the Cubs needed. The Lou Brock experience notwithstanding, Holland sent Oscar Gamble and Dick Selma to the Phillies for thirty-year-old Johnny Callison. But the Cubs would be a year older in 1970; it was a calculated risk to give up a bright prospect in the hope of getting a great year from an experienced player. The Cubs were going to put it all on the line in 1970.

Chapter Six:

The Seventies: Déjà Vu, The Instant Replay

SOME THINGS CHANGE. SOME DON'T. MANY PERSONALITIES making headlines in 1970 — in fact, many headlines themselves — were remarkably reflective of those in 1948. By 1970, Shirley Temple had graduated from The Good Ship Lollipop to become the United States delegate to the United Nations. John Wooden, a long way from back home in Indiana, won his sixth NCAA championship with the incomparable UCLA Bruins and was named, for the fourth time, the college basketball coach of the year. Ronald Reagan, whose first job was broadcasting Cub games for station WHO in Des Moines, Iowa, in the thirties, retired from the movies (if not from acting) for a career in politics and was reigning over the great state of California as its governor. And Harold Stassen, ever-optimistic, was polishing up his presidential campaign speeches for his efforts in the next election. Of course they weren't getting older, just better.

But some of the headlines were getting a little old. President Nixon was denouncing inflation and unemployment as America's most serious economic crises, as Truman had done twenty-two years earlier. With good reason. By 1970, the 1948 food prices had doubled, and within a decade, the 1970 prices would triple. The Arab/Israeli conflict of 1948 was still capturing international attention in 1970, as violent and tenacious border disputes raged. They too would continue through 1980. And in 1970, as in 1950, we found ourselves bogged down in a land war in Asia. Inflation, unemployment, war. The patterns surface again and again.

Some things change. Some don't. The Cubs have always managed to do both. They change — players, managers, coaches, pennant plans, and hopes. And they don't change — sunlight, grass, ivy, the Wrigleys, Ernie Banks, and Jack Brickhouse. Through it all, the fans remain. As the team gets older, the fans get better. Patience is their virtue. In 1979, while broadcasting his 5,000th game, Brickhouse jokingly, but perhaps all too accurately, said it best: "So the Cubs have not won a pennant in thirty-four years. Why not look at it this way. Take it in terms of eternity. That's not even a fly speck. Just tell yourself that some time in the next one thousand years the Cubs will get their share of the pie." Atta boy, Jack. Meet you at Wrigley Field in 2945.

For the twentieth-century Cubs, however, the decade of the seventies began with a no-change policy. Cold Chicago winds and a record snowstorm ushered in the January 1970 meeting between John Holland, Leo Durocher, and the coaches. They discussed the late-season collapse of 1969 in an attempt to learn from it. The Bleacher Bums, who held their winter meetings at Ray's Bleachers, could have told them that Cub pennant chances were riding on getting a fourth and fifth starter and a solid centerfielder to play with the new Cub rightfielder, Johnny Callison. But Cub management seemed satisfied with the roster they already had. Young pitchers Jim Colborn, Archie Reynolds, and Joe Decker had all enjoyed good seasons at Tacoma, and the coaches felt that two of them could be starters for the Cubs. Randy Bobb and Ken Rudolph were on hand to back up Hundley behind the plate. And Boots Day, acquired from the Cardinals, was a possible answer for the center-field problem. If not, Jim Hickman was another possible answer; although slow, he was also steady.

So the January meeting focused on spring training, and the Cub brain trust decided on three new tactics for implementation at Scottsdale. First, R & R. All veterans would be requested to take mineral baths at Buckhorn Spa for a week. The directive had the ring of "Out, out, damned spot" no matter how physically rejuvenating the mineral waters might prove to be. Was this a subtle way for management to acknowledge that the regulars really were tired last September? Could they really soak away their memories of the great collapse? Some fans might have preferred "Out, out, damned Leo." Second, the order came down that there would be no intrasquad games this spring. All exhibition games would be in direct competition with other teams. Third, regulars would not play as much as they had in the previous spring. The message was clear. Let us conserve the energy of our stars for the time we need them to glow their brightest.

With spring came healed wounds and the annual outpouring of Cub optimism. Ernie Banks allowed as how "with this kind of lineup I'd like to be pitching for this club." Durocher, after watching the young pitchers, said, "If I can't find myself two starters from among that bunch of kids, I'm not trying." Johnny Callison said that being with the Cubs was like having a new lease on life. His words were tinder for Cub fever: "It's a good feeling to be with a winner." All of this helped erase the memory of '69, despite continued references by the media. When a national magazine ran a story pinning the blame on Durocher, his only comment was, "I'm too busy to bother reading that stuff." But Leo was generally cooperating with newspeople this spring, and it was a more pleasant atmosphere for all concerned.

Prior to opening day, catching loomed as a problem. The Cubs sent rookie catcher Randy Bobb to the Mets for J. C. Martin. Hundley was expected to miss the first week of the regular season with a broken thumb. The season did not exactly start with a bang. They lost on opening day. They lost the following game. But you know the Cubs. In the third game of the season, with two out in the ninth, and trailing 1-0 against Montreal, Santo singled and Callison homered for a typical 2-1 Cub win. After a loss to Montreal the next day, the Cubs hit their stride, won their next eleven in a row, and claimed first place on April 28. Cub fans had waited seven months for this. The streak was marred, however. Randy Hundley suffered a partial tear of the ligament on his left knee when Carl Taylor of the Cardinals rammed him at the plate. It appeared that Hundley would be in a cast for a month.

During the first home series, Wrigley Field witnessed a new phenomenon: gangs of rowdies were roaming through the stands, starting fights, throwing debris on the field, and jumping over outfield walls, interrupting play. Said one veteran Bleacher Bum, "These kids are animals. They dress like us and try to look like us. But they're bums, not Bums." The Cubs took quick action to stop the shenanigans. Park security was beefed up, and a wire netting was fastened to the outfield wall, thirty inches from the top, angling out like a basket. The debris filtered through from time to time, but it stopped the fence-

---

Opening-Day Lineup, 1970

Kessinger, ss
Beckert, 2b
Williams, lf
Santo, 3b
Banks, 1b
Callison, rf
Hickman, cf
Martin, c
Jenkins, p

jumpers. But nothing could stop Durocher from making obscene gestures at the umpire during a three-game losing streak. The National League office warned Leo with a one-day suspension and a $200 fine.

Leo's frustration would increase, however, as the Cubs lost nine of their first twelve games in May. They managed to cling to first place, but the absence of Hundley was taking its toll. Fergie Jenkins summed it up succinctly: "Having Hundley catch for you was like sitting down to a steak dinner with a steak knife. Without Hundley all you had was a fork." Trying to solve this problem, the Cubs traded for catcher Jack Hiatt from Montreal. With Hickman hitting well, they felt that centerfielder Boots Day was expendable.

On May 12, Mr. Cub hit his 500th home run for his 1600th RBI. When Ernie crossed home plate with a tip of his cap to the standing, cheering fans, everyone knew that here was something special. He thanked everyone who helped him to these milestones, especially the Cub fans. "They have been an inspiration to me," he said. Cub fans could certainly say the same. (See Chapter 7, "Games to Remember.")

Nine days after Banks' milestone, the Cubs received depressing news from the team physicians. A rediagnosis of Hundley's knee indicated cartilage damage. Immediate surgery was required, and Hundley would spend two more months on the disabled list. Nonetheless, the rest of the team put on a rally and beat the Mets in the following road trip, *at* Shea Stadium, three games out of four. As the season was developing, the Mets, Pirates, and Cardinals were all experiencing troubles, and the Cubs were able to enter June in first place. The heroes? Jim Hickman and Billy Williams. Through May, Hickman was hitting .329 with eleven home runs and Billy was .283 with fifteen homers. In late May, for some reason, the Cubs traded Ted Abernathy to the Cardinals for infielder Phil Gagliano. It was the second time Abernathy had been traded from Durocher's Cubs. Later in the season, the Cardinals sent Abernathy to Kansas City where he appeared in thirty-six games and won nine of twelve decisions. Fortunately, however, the Cubs would manage to pick up Milt Pappas from Atlanta for $50,000. Pappas later credited the Cubs' traveling secretary Blake Cullen for his arrival to the Chicago team. "Blake kept bugging John Holland until he finally got me." Pappas would dramatically prove his worth to the Cubs.

June started well with victories bustin' out all over; seven wins in ten games and a four-game lead over the Mets on June 16. But the same old problems began to brew. A pulled muscle and a bad knee sidelined Banks. Beckert too was nursing a pulled muscle. The military reserves called Kessinger away to do a two-week stint. And Jenkins, not able to find his form, was struggling with a 3-7 record.

Little wonder that in the third week of June the Swoon began. Twelve losses in a row, one short of the club mark set by the 1944 team, sent the Cubs reeling from first to fourth place, more than three games behind the Mets. Frustration. Durocher. Rookie Joe Decker was fined for a "defiant attitude" because he left the mound before the relief pitcher arrived. Sportswriters began to get Leo's dander up at this point. The Lip let loose. Asked about some of his resultant, highly colorful remarks, Mr. Wrigley came up with a stunning rejoinder: "Well, Mr. Durocher is Mr. Durocher. This is like the cigarette commercial: what do you want, a good manager or good taste?"

More losses. More frustration. After breaking the twelve-game losing streak with a win over the Cardinals on July 1, the Cubs lost three of four to the Pirates at Wrigley Field. On July 5, the Cubs and Pirates got into a dusting match starring pitchers Jim Colborn and Dock Ellis. The umpire called both managers out and ordered them to stop. As Durocher was walking back to the dugout, Ellis yelled something that made Leo turn and start for him. Both dugouts emptied, and the melee was on. Take me out to the brawl game, one reporter punned.

But brawls weren't what the Cubs needed. By July 7, they were 39-40, in third place, four-and-a-half games behind the Mets. Nothing would come together. On July 10, Hundley was reactivated, but two weeks later, Banks went on the disabled list. Jenkins, Holtzman, Hands, and Pappas were pitching well, but the bullpen of Regan, Colborn, and Decker was less than fearsome. Only Williams and Hickman were having impressive years. Hickman even made it into his only All-Star game, where he contributed to the game's drama. It was his single in the twelfth inning that sent Pete Rose crashing into Ray Fosse with the winning run. Game-winning RBIs were not so rare for this unsung hero, but Cub fans were glad to see him gain his moment of fame.

Surprise, Cub fans. In late July, with Banks inactive, the Cubs bought the contract of flamboyant Joe Pepitone from Houston. Joe wasted no time doing his thing. In his first day as a Cub, he singled in the winning run in the first game and drove in a run in the nightcap as the Cubs swept two from the Reds. Along with his solid batting performance, Pepitone brought another special kind of style to the club. Returning from Chicago from the road trip, Pepitone was greeted by a chauffeur in a Cadillac limosine, who called himself "Fabulous Howard." Every day, Joe would be driven to and from Wrigley Field, and his various arrivals were announced by the limosine's horn honking its version of "The Bridge over the River Kwai." Perhaps "Bridge over Troubled Waters" would have been more appropriate. In any case, Durocher, like Queen Victoria, was *not* amused.

Even though Pepitone may have provided the Cubs with some laughs, tensions between Leo and the players were brewing. On August 6, Ron Santo let loose at Leo after learning that he had been demoted to seventh in the batting order. Santo, who had been one of Durocher's strongest supporters, said, "He didn't say a damn thing to me. Not a word. I don't understand him anymore." A few days later, Durocher's contract was extended for another year, and he hired Herman Franks to replace ailing Joe Becker as a coach. Why Herman? Said Leo: "He'll light a fire under those guys." Leo made it clear that Franks would be his right-hand man from now on. In mid-August, Billy Williams announced that after 1,092 consecutive games he wanted to take himself out of the lineup. He said he was simply bushed and he wanted to get his strength back for the stretch drive. Durocher responded that he wasn't going to rest anyone, that all the players wanted to rest. Williams was used as a pinch-hitter that day and started again the next.

As for the pennant race, August was like July. The Pirates, Mets, and Cubs were still in the race simply because no one of them could win often enough to build a lead. On August 28, the Cubs rallied in the late innings for a win. So what? It was the first time since June 3 that they had come from behind to win in the eighth or ninth inning. Would they do the same with the pennant? Finally make a move, and take it all? They hadn't won it when in front; maybe they could do it from behind. On September 1, they were 69-61, in second place, only one game behind the Pirates. With the Mets also in the running, it looked like the race for first place was going to go right to the wire. On September 13, it seemed that fate was making tempting promises to the Cubs. With two out and nobody on in the bottom of the ninth, the Cubs were trailing the Pirates 2-1. Willie Smith hit a routine fly ball to center field. Incredibly, Matty Alou dropped it, and the Cubs were still alive. Kessinger, Beckert, and Williams followed with singles, and the Cubs had a 3-2 win. This victory put them only one game behind the Pirates and one-half game behind the

Mets with seventeen games to play. But events after the game were telling. Remember 1969 and Don Young? Not so with the Pirates. Losing pitcher Steve Blass went immediately to Alou to tell him to forget it and not to let it get him down.

On September 18, Fergie Jenkins won his twentieth game and Billy Williams hit his fortieth home run. The next day the Cubs won again. Then on September 20, leading Montreal 4-1, they lost the game 6-4. They were now two games out with only ten games to go. At this point the hitting simply died (except for the stalwart contributions of Billy Williams). On September 23, the Cardinals took a doubleheader from the Cubs by identical 2-1 scores. A victory the next day was followed by two losses to the Phillies, 5-3 and 7-1. Once again, luck, skill, and time ran out on the Cubs. On September 27, the Pirates clinched the pennant and left it to the Cubs and Mets to battle it out for second place. The Cubs had to split the final four-game series with the Mets to finish second. They did it. On the last day of the season, behind Jenkins at Shea Stadium, the Cubs took the second-place prize. But in the crucial last ten games, the Pirates were 7-3; the Cubs, 4-6.

In the postseason wrap-up, a number of explanations were offered as to why the Cubs didn't make it. As always. Hundley was out half of the season. Banks was out. Callison did not have a great year (.264, 19 HR, 68 RBIs), Leo didn't use enough reserves, and so forth. But the crucial fact was that the bullpen failed. In the latter part of the season, Cub relievers protected leads twenty-two times out of twenty-nine, but they lost fifteen of seventeen games entered with the score tied. Still, there were some fine feats this season, witnessed by some 1,642,705 fans. Santo drove in 114 runs with 26 homers. Jenkins won twenty for the fourth straight year and set another of his Cub strikeout records, this time with 274. Jim Hickman was tremendous with the bat, hitting .315 with 32 HR and

115 RBIs. Newcomers Pappas (10-8, 2.68 ERA) and Pepitone (.268, 12 HR, 44 RBIs in fifty-six games) also did well.

The standout Cub, however, was Billy Williams. His 137 runs scored were the highest in the majors in twenty-three years. His 42 HR, 129 RBIs, and .322 average were personal bests and ranked him among the league-leaders in each offensive category. His 205 hits and 373 total bases were tops in the majors. But, paradoxically, the fans gained a true sense of Williams' accomplishments on September 3, when Billy was rested after 1,117 consecutive games played, a stunningly impressive National League record. Ernie Banks, who had played in 717 consecutive games himself, put into words what many Cub fans had begun to realize: "I think it's [the playing streak] extraordinary, but I don't feel there's much luck in it. Look at the other guys who have played in a lot of games. I didn't know Lou Gehrig but I know Musial. It's not only the case of having a good body and being lucky about not having major injuries. They're the kind that play hard and don't get into situations where they will hurt themselves unnecessarily. Their instincts are good . . . . They are even-tempered, so they don't get upset and lose control of their bodies. They have total self-confidence and they do the right thing automatically. And they don't complain about things like a sore thumb. Billy plays when he's hurt. I can see it, but he never tells anyone." At this point, Billy had completed eleven years of what would be a remarkable seventeen-year tour of duty in professional baseball. Stand up and cheer.

Plaudits aside, the 1970 season was barely over when Ron Santo publicly appealed to the Cub brass not to break up the team by trades. He and the other veterans wanted one more chance to bring home a championship. Apparently the brass agreed because during the off-season John Holland limited himself to reshuffling peripheral players on the roster. Jack Hiatt, Willie Smith, Phil Gagliano, and minor-league prospects Roe Skidmore and Dave Leonards were sent away. And the real price for Joe Pepitone was learned when Roger Metzger was sent to Houston to complete the midseason deal. Coming to the Cubs were infielder Hector Torres, outfielder Jose Ortiz, and catcher Danny Breeden (brother of Hal). And a new crop of rookies, including outfielder Brock Davis and pitchers Earl Stephenson, Bill Bonham, Ray Newman, and Jim Todd, were brought up from the farm system and added to the spring list.

At the annual baseball luncheon in January, Durocher announced that he would give the young players a chance in 1971. Then he proceeded to express disappointment with Johnny Callison, whom he had benched in the stretch as punishment for missing the cut-off man with a throw in a 2-1 loss to the Cardinals. Callison told the press that Leo's criticism was unjust and that Durocher simply put too much pressure on his players. "It got to the point where I even was worried how I looked in batting practice," he said. A small item at the time, but this was a foreshadowing of what was to come.

There were no mineral baths this spring. But there was optimism in camp because both Jose Ortiz and Brock Davis were looking good in center field. If one of them could make it, that would free Pepitone to play first and take the pressure off forty-year-old Ernie Banks, whose knees were telling him that the end was near. Then came bad news. Randy Hundley fell during a rundown play and injured his right knee this time. The word was he would be out for an entire month.

Despite a thrilling opening-day victory with Jenkins beating Bob Gibson of the Cardinals on a tenth-inning homer by Williams, 2-1, the Cubs got off to a slow start. In their first fifteen games, they managed only five victories, scoring an average of only 2.5 runs per game. When Hundley, pinch-hitting on April 12, reinjured his right knee, the physician's report that he would be lost for another month didn't help matters. But something deeper than physical injuries was wrong with the Cubs. They seemed to be just going through the motions. Durocher arranged four locker-room meetings to allow everyone to air his complaints. A number of players spoke out, but underlying tensions remained.

Opening-Day Lineup, 1971

Kessinger, ss
Beckert, 2b
Williams, lf
Santo, 3b
Pepitone, 1b
Callison, rf
Ortiz, cf
Rudolph, c
Jenkins, p

April found the Cubs in fifth place with án 8-13 record. May was not much merrier as they split twenty-eight games for the month. Pepitone was out for two weeks with a bad elbow. Four days after being reactivated, Hundley hurt his knee again and had to undergo surgery. It was now the third time that season that Hundley's knees were injured. Phil Regan was being hit like a batting-practice pitcher. All that could be done, seemingly, was to plug holes and hope. Catcher Chris Cannizarro was acquired from San Diego. Brock Davis and Jose Ortiz were platooned in center. Hope? Well, in previous years when the Cubs got off to a great start, look what happened. Maybe this poor beginning could be a blessing in disguise.

Just maybe. On June 3, Ken Holtzman, 2-6, pitched a 1-0 no-hitter against the Reds and five days later, he threw a twelve-inning one-hit shutout against the Pirates. The whole team began to perk up, and June became an 18-9 month. Brock Davis hit .341 during this stretch, Pepitone had a nineteen-game hitting streak, and Kessinger on June 17 had six hits in six at-bats. By the end of June, the Cubs were up in third place, although eight-and-a-half behind the Pirates.

A 16-13 record in July kept the Cubs in third place, eleven games behind the Pirates. But as Billy Williams said, "We've seen clubs lose big leads before." August would be the time to make something happen, and sure enough, the month opened with a happy surprise. The Cubs called up pitcher Juan Pizarro from Hawaii to start for Holtzman, who was reporting to the National Guard for two weeks. Pizarro made his debut by beating Seaver and the Mets 3-2 and then shutting out the Padres on a one-hitter. The Cubs began to look like they really meant business. By winning twelve of their first eighteen games in August, they pulled into second place, only four-and-a-half games behind the Pirates. On August 20, Jenkins brought his record to 20-9. But then the bubble burst. The next day and the next, the Cubs lost to Houston. On August 23, Durocher called another clubhouse meeting and threw the floor open for comments. Pepitone said that Durocher should stop shouting at the young players and that he should be finding ways to ease rather than create tension. Pappas spoke next and backed up Pepitone. Holtzman told Durocher, in effect, to get off his back. Then Durocher had his say. He criticized individual players one by one until he got to Santo. In front of the team, Durocher accused Santo of demanding from the front office that they designate a Ron Santo day at Wrigley Field. Santo not only denied it but eventually had to be restrained from charging Durocher. Leo took off his uniform and said, "I quit." After he left for his office, several players spoke up and convinced the rest that it would look bad for everyone concerned if Durocher quit after such a blowup. John

Holland was asked to intervene and to convince Leo to stay but also to stop attacking the players. According to Fergie Jenkins, from then on "it was like an armed truce. The unspoken agreement between Leo and the players was to talk to each other only if the situation demanded it. . . . It was like someone had pulled a blanket with 'Death' written on it over the team."

Not surprisingly, the Cubs lost nine of their next thirteen games and dropped out of contention. On September 3, P. K. Wrigley took out an almost full page advertisement in *Chicago Today* to announce his reaction to the situation. The text read:

THIS IS FOR CUB FANS AND ANYONE ELSE WHO IS INTERESTED

It is no secret that in the closing days of the season that held great possibilities the Cub organization is at sixes and sevens and somebody has to do something. So, as head of the corporation, the responsibility falls on me.

By tradition, this would call for a press conference following which there would be as many versions of what I had to say as there were reporters present; and as I have always believed in tackling anything as directly as possible, I am using this paid newspaper space to give you what I have to say direct, and you can do your own analyzing.

I have been in professional baseball a long time. I have served under the only five commissioners we have had to date and four league presidents, and I must have learned something about professional baseball.

Many people seem to have forgotten, but

I have not, that after many years of successful seasons with contesting clubs and five league pennants, the Cubs went into the doldrums and for a quarter of a century were perennial dwellers of the second division in spite of everything we could think of to try and do — experienced managers, inexperienced managers, rotating managers, no manager but re-volving coaches — we were still there in the also-rans.

We figured out what we thought we needed to make a lot of potential talent into a contending team, and we settled on Leo Durocher, who had the baseball knowl-edge to build a contender and win pen-nants, and also knowing that he had been a controversial figure wherever he went, particularly with the press because he just never was cut out to be a diplomat. He accepted the job at less than he was making because he considered it to be a challenge, and Leo thrives on challenges.

In his first year we ended in the cellar, but from then on came steadily up, knocking on the door for the top.

Each near miss has caused more and more criticism, and this year there has been a concerted campaign to dump Durocher that has even affected the players, but just as there has to be someone to make decisions for the corporation, there has to be someone in charge on the field to make the final decisions on the spur of the moment, and right or wrong, that's it.

All this preamble is to say that after careful consideration and consultation with my baseball people, Leo is the team

> manager and the "Dump Durocher
> Clique" might as well give up. He is
> running the team, and if some of the
> players do not like it and lie down on the
> job, during the off season we will see what
> we can do to find them happier homes."
>
> [signed] Phil Wrigley
>
> P. S. If only we could find more team
> players like Ernie Banks.

In effect, the advertisement defended a previously
successful Wrigley decision. His selection of Durocher had
shocked the baseball world, but Leo had gone on to be the
manager when the years of losing were reversed. Rather
than second-guess that decision, Wrigley expressed an
embarrassing lack of confidence in the players (especially
in light of the Banks' reference). What could they say in
response? Much later, Jenkins would remark, "If only Mr.
Wrigley knew what was really going on." At the time,
Kessinger's only comment was, "I just want to finish the
season." The season certainly did get finished; the Cubs
won only eleven of their final twenty-six games and limped
into a third-place tie with the Mets, fourteen games behind
the pennant-winning Pirates. But 1,653,007 fans had come
to Wrigley Field this season and had seen some exception-
ally talented ball players. Glenn Beckert finished third in
the league in batting with a .343 average. Fergie Jenkins
was 24-13, marking the fifth straight season he had won
twenty or more games as a Cub. This time his work gained
the recognition it deserved when Fergie was named
winner of the Cy Young Award. Cub fans had also seen
Ernie Banks wrap up one of the greatest careers in the
history of baseball. Ernie had played in more games,
scoring more runs, with more hits, doubles, total bases,
RBIs, and extra-base hits than any Cub in history. His 512
home runs tied him with Eddie Matthews for ninth on the
all-time career home-run list. Wrigley announced that

Banks would continue to work for the Cubs as long as he wanted to. Last, but not least, there was young Burt Hooton. Called up in September, Hooton struck out fifteen Mets in a 3-2 win at Shea Stadium. (See Chapter 7, "Games to Remember.") In his second start as a Cub, he bested Seaver and the Mets 3-0 on a two-hitter at Wrigley Field. It was enough to make Cub fans dream of what lay ahead.

A word needs to be said here regarding the Cubs of '69, '70, and '71. They were very good teams with a nucleus of regulars often described as the best in either league. A good share of the credit must be given to John Holland. More often than not his trades were good. It is enlightening to note that in 1971, of the fourteen regulars, including pitchers, only four were from the Cub farm system. By comparison, eleven Pirates and eight Cardinals of their top fourteen came up through their own systems.

After the season, Holland, with no minor-league prospects, went back to the trade mart. He sent Brock Davis and pitchers Jim Colborn and Earl Stephenson to Milwaukee for outfielder Jose Cardenal. Johnny Callison was sent to the Yankees for relief hurler Jack Aker. With Hooton now a bona fide starter, the Cubs could afford to separate Holtzman and Durocher. Rick Monday, a highly regarded Oakland centerfielder, was the prize for Holtzman. In acquiring Cardenal and Monday, Holland had apparently filled the gaps in the outfield. What else was needed?

A left-handed starter to replace Holtzman but, most urgently, a new bullpen crew. The Cub relief corps in 1971 totaled eleven saves, a 9-11 won-lost mark, and a 4.26 ERA. Ouch. The Cubs did pick up thirty-five-year-old Steve Hamilton as a free agent, but that was hardly a solution. Would Dan McGinn, a former Notre Dame punter, and Tom Phoebus help?

In spring camp, Leo cracked the whip. He let it be known that this year everyone would be in shape. (Rookie pitcher Rick Reuschel checked in at 249 pounds.) Tension between

Durocher and the players continued to simmer. Holtzman, who had been 74-69 as a Cub, told reporters that he knew six or seven Cubs who didn't want to play for Leo. Peanuts Lowrey, now a coach for the California Angels, responded that the Cubs had too many *prima donnas* and that Holtzman had been the worst of them all. Ron Santo said simply, "I'm going to keep my mouth shut and play ball."

On April Fools' Day, the Players' Association called a strike and demanded increased pension benefits. The strike lasted two weeks and then the season started. Late. The Cubs, however, wasted no time in confounding and delighting the faithful. On opening day, Jose Cardenal made a two-run error with two out in the ninth, costing the Cubs a 4-2 decision to the Phillies. But the very next day Burt Hooton pitched a no-hitter before 9,583 fans on a cold wet day at Wrigley Field. Hooton, making only his fourth major-league start, walked seven and fanned seven in beating the Phillies, 4-0. It was, truly, a chilling and thrilling performance. But it did not inspire a winning streak. In fact, on May 1, the Cubs were 4-10 in last place. Four of their losses had been by one run. At that point, Joe Pepitone decided to quit baseball. He was upset over being benched with a batting average at .125. John Holland, gracious as ever, said Joe would be welcome to come back if he changed his mind.

So first base went to Jim Hickman and third to Carmen Fanzone, filling in for an injured Santo. The Cubs went on a minor tear. Heroics were the order of the day as they won eleven of their next sixteen games. Jose Cardenal's four hits led the way in a 12-1 rout of the Braves. Fanzone homered

---

Opening-Day Lineup, 1972

Cardenal, rf
Beckert, 2b
Williams, lf
Santo, 3b
Pepitone, 1b
Hundley, c
Monday, cf
Kessinger, ss
Jenkins, p

twice and Hickman once as the Cubs beat Houston 6-4. Monday's four hits paced a 7-1 win over the Reds. On May 16, Monday hit three homers and a single against the Phillies. By May 22, the Cubs had moved up to .500 and third place. Cub trades were looking good. Cardenal, Monday, and Aker were doing their part to make Cub fans think pennant again.

Including Joe Pepitone? At the end of May, he announced that he was coming back. His reactivation was scheduled for June 30. Meanwhile the Cubs continued to win. Holland tried to deal for Steve Carlton but failed to land him. Instead Rick Reuschel was recalled from Wichita and got his first win on June 20 with six innings of superb relief pitching. By June 26, Chicago was 34-26, in third place, only five games out. Then, on July 1, Pepitone rejoined the team and Durocher put him in the clean-up spot. Clean-up! Early in July the Cubs slumped, losing seven of nine games on a road trip. By July 10 they were in fourth place, eight games behind the Pirates. More Cub dissension under Leo. When the Cubs beat the Braves 9-8 on July 14, it was only the second time in eighty-three games they had pulled out a win in the ninth inning. Still no bullpen. As July ebbed away, it seemed that the Cubs were headed downward.

Then came a bombshell. On July 25, Holland announced that Durocher had stepped down as manager in favor of Whitey Lockman. Durocher maintained that he was not fired, and the official language used described his action as "stepping aside." Wrigley commented that "the players, in the remainder of the season, [can] find out for themselves if they are pennant contenders." In six-and-a-half seasons, Durocher's Cubs had a 535-526 mark, but that included a 59-103 record in his first year. Since 1948, the Cubs had managed one season better than .500. Under Leo they had given their fans five consecutive years of better than .500 baseball, first-division finishes, and genuine pennant possibilities. An important turnaround in modern Cub history. But in that 1969 season the dream of a pennant had for too long a time been too close to reality. The spectre of failure haunted fans and players alike. Whose fault had it been? Leo's or the players'? Regardless of the answer, as long as Durocher remained, the question also remained. Even Wrigley's comment at Leo's departure demonstrated the pervasive power of the question. Without Leo, different questions could have generated different attitudes. With him, Cub fans saw their Cubs fail to fulfill their longed-for destiny.

After the announcement, Leo paid a brief visit to the dressing room to say good-bye to the Cubs. Then he went to the umpires' dressing room and stayed for twenty minutes. One of the umpires said later, "He isn't such a bad guy — in civilian clothes." A month later the Houston Astros hired Leo to replace Harry Walker as their manager.

Carroll "Whitey" Lockman, the twenty-third manager of the Cubs, had been working for the ball club since 1965 as a manager in the minors, a scout, and most recently, director of player development. He was a shrewd baseball man and enjoyed a reputation for calmness and fairness. The players responded to his style immediately. With the blanket of death removed, Jenkins pitched a no-hitter against the Phillies to give Lockman a successful debut. The Cubs went on to win four of their next six games. On August 7, they were back up to third place. By the end of the month, they had climbed to second, but were still ten games behind the Pirates.

The last five weeks of the season saw so many stellar performances by Cub players the fans got double their pleasure and double their fun. On August 26, Ron Santo got his 2,000th hit and 1,200th RBI as a Cub. Out came the banner from the left-field bleachers: "PIZZA POWER!" On September 2, Milt Pappas pitched a no-hitter that came within one pitch of being a perfect game. (See Chapter 7,

"Games to Remember.") Six days later, Jenkins won his twentieth game for the sixth consecutive year, tying a Cub record set by Mordecai Brown in those glorious years from 1906 to 1911. On September 20, Pappas recorded his 200th major league win as he headed for a 17-7 season, including eleven straight victories. Best of all, Billy Williams, now thirty-four, had a fantastic season. His .333 average was the highest in the major leagues. He was second in the National League in RBIs with 122, and third in home runs (37), hits (191), and doubles (34). Although he finished second to Johnny Bench in the voting for the league's Most Valuable Player (263 points to 211), he received *The Sporting News'* Player of the Year award.

After going 46-44 under Durocher, the Cubs climbed to a 39-26 record under Lockman, good enough for a second-place finish, but never really close to the Pirates. Home attendance was 1,299,163 for the year, down about 300,000 from the previous year. Veterans like Williams, Santo, Hickman, and Jenkins had all done well, and so had the team's young newcomer, Jose Cardenal. Hundley had a disappointing season, and Beckert, hampered by injuries, slipped to .270. Monday at .249 was not an instant success. Second-guessers pointed to Holtzman's nineteen wins for the world champion Oakland A's and said, "I told you so." But one season does not tell the whole story on a trade, and it is doubtful whether Holtzman, openly critical of Durocher, could have pitched that well as a Cub.

Cub players were visibly pleased when Lockman was rehired for 1973. Kessinger summed up their feelings: "If a ballplayer can't play for Whitey, he can't play for anybody." Jack Aker, who had recorded six wins and seventeen saves as a Cub in 1972, said the Cubs would have won the pennant had Lockman been manager all year: "Once he was in charge we had a different type of attitude." Lockman responded in kind to such warm remarks by saying he wouldn't trade his team for the Pirates.

John Holland recognized that this veteran team had perhaps one more shot at the title, and he hustled to supply the missing ingredients. "It is," as Billy Williams said, "now or never for us. We've got an old club. There's no tomorrow for us. We have to win today." Old was true; the average age of the top eight regulars was thirty-two. (During the season when the club celebrated senior citizens' day, someone wagged that he didn't know whether it was for the fans or the players.) Holland heard echoes of Lou Brock when he sent speedy outfielder Bill North to Oakland for relief pitcher Bob Locker. But Locker was a respected and experienced reliever with championship experience. To get a left-handed reliever, Holland gave up pitchers Bill Hands and Joe Decker to the Twins for Dave LaRoche. Hands, now thirty-two, had been a dependable pitcher for the Cubs with a 92-86 record in seven years. But the Cubs now had Jenkins, Pappas, Hooton, and Reuschel for their rotation and no reliable left-hander in the bullpen.

Spring training for the 1973 season found new names in camp — names like LaCock, Hiser, Tyrone, Alexander, and Burris. The most impressive was Ray Burris, who, along with Larry Gura and Bill Bonham, seemed ready to offer strong help to the pitching corps. Disappointingly, LaRoche had to be put on the disabled list before the season because of a sore arm, but everyone else was healthy and ready.

The Cubs opened with a come-from-behind win in the ninth against Montreal and a tenth-inning win the next day, both by 3-2 scores. It signaled a good start, and the Cubs played with enthusiasm. They left April with a 12-8 record, tied for first place with the Mets. Beginning on May 8, the Cubs reeled off seven straight wins to take first place alone with a record of 20-13. Lockman was using all his players, and they responded with their best for him. On May 19, Joe Pepitone's time with the Cubs was up. He was dealt to Atlanta for first baseman Andre Thornton. On the first of June, Chicago was still perched in first, four-and-a-half games ahead of the Mets. Aker and Locker were giving the Cubs their best bullpen in years, figuring in twenty of the first twenty-five wins.

> *Opening-Day Lineup, 1973*
>
> Monday, cf
> Cardenal, rf
> Williams, lf
> Pepitone, 1b
> Santo, 3b
> Beckert, 2b
> Hundley, c
> Kessinger, ss
> Jenkins, p

Unbelievers waited for the June Swoon. Oh, no. Not these Cubs. The Cubs won seventeen of twenty-nine games in June and on June 30 led the league by seven games over Montreal. They were playing as a team. Once after the Cubs wasted a 4-1 lead and lost to the Reds in the ninth, Lockman told his players, "You have to be prepared for adversity. It's part of life." No chewing out, no tension-building pouts. Just a few words saying, in effect, "We'll be all right."

July started out with evidence that the Cubs were serious. On July 1, Hundley hit a three-run homer with two out in the ninth to beat the Mets 6-5. Three days later, Santo homered with a man on and one out in the tenth for a 3-2 win over the Phillies. Such is the stuff of champions! On July 6, Monday grandslammed and singled, driving in six runs in a 8-5 triumph over the Padres in San Diego. This was the first game on an eight-day road trip to the west. The Cubs had invited wives and children to join the entourage. But the ship began to sink. They lost six of the next seven. Man the lifeboats. They came back to the Friendly Confines gingerly holding first by two games over the Cardinals. But it was a serious decline, and the Cubs won only one of six games at home. On the day before the All-Star break, they gave up first place to the Cardinals.

Unfortunately, in the second half of the season, the Cubs were to learn a great deal more about adversity. Age had taken its toll. Jenkins and Pappas were struggling; Santo, Beckert, and Hundley all had injuries; and the team plummeted into a batting slump for the entire month of August. The Cubs averaged fewer than three runs a game that month, winning only nine of nineteen decisions. But all was not lost. On September 18, despite their 64-70 record, the Cubs found themselves in third place, only three-and-a-half games behind the Cardinals. It seemed as though no one wanted to win the pennant. Oh, the cruelty of fate. If the Cubs had put together a season anything like any one of their previous four, they would have won the division championship. As late as September 21, even with a 74-79 record, they were just two-and-a-half games out of first. It came down to the last week. When the Cardinals beat the Cubs in successive days, 1-0 and 2-0, the Cubs dropped behind by four games. The Mets won the flag with a 82-79 mark. The Cubs came in fifth with a record of 77-84, five games out. Last place went to the Phillies.

What happened to the Cubs? Jenkins, Hooton, and Reuschel led the team with fourteen wins each, but each lost more than he won. Pappas went from 17-7 in 1972 to 7-12 for 1973. Only Bob Locker, 10-6 with eighteen saves, had a good year. Hickman, Beckert, Santo, Williams, and Hundley all had their poorest seasons in years, as evidenced by the fact that the Cubs were tenth in hitting in the National League. The 1,351,705 fans who came to Wrigley Field saw many of their familiar favorites for the last time. This once-great team tried but could not limp home to a pennant even when the door was left open. It was time to break up the Cubs and start afresh.

John Holland went to work. Ferguson Jenkins, one of the greatest pitchers in Cub history with a 147-108 record, was sent to the Texas Rangers for infielders Bill Madlock and Vic Harris. Beckert, after nine years and a .284 average as a Cub, went to the Padres for outfielder Jerry Morales. Randy Hundley, once the iron man and sparkplug of the Cubs, was shipped to Minnesota for catcher George Mitterwald. Ron Santo, after fourteen years, 337 home runs, and 1,290 RBIs as a Cub, was traded — of all places — to the White Sox for pitchers Steve Stone and Ken Frailing and catcher Steve Swisher. Veteran manager Gene Mauch once said, "Santo is the best third baseman I've ever seen over a period of time. Billy Cox and Frank Malzone may have been as good for one season, but they can't match Santo over ten years." Mauch was right. Santo was a great Cub, and whatever criticism may be leveled at his emotional style, no one can deny that he was a real competitor.

In another trade, Bob Locker, the Cubs' leading reliever in 1973, went back to Oakland for Horacio Pina, also a reliever. Of the 1969 regulars, only Hickman, Kessinger, and Williams were left. In the spring even Hickman was dealt away, sent to the Cardinals for a pitcher named Scipio Spinks. And if there was any doubt that the Cubs were going all the way with youth, it was dispelled before opening day when veteran Milt Pappas was released despite the fact that he needed only one more win to join Cy Young and Jim Bunning as the only pitchers ever to win 100 or more games in both the American and National leagues. "We couldn't work our pitching staff around a guy trying to win one game," said Lockman.

There were nine rookies on the opening-day roster and the season was still young when it became painfully obvious that this was going to be one of those disasters euphemistically called "a rebuilding year." Cub fans, long on tolerance, may have recalled the early sixties to help them imagine that another great team was being assembled. They had little choice but to endure and hope. There was plenty to endure. For example, on May 24, the Cardinals beat the Cubs 1-0. With one out in the ninth, Ted Simmons was on third and Joe Torre on first. Tim McCarver grounded to Williams at first. Billy fielded the ball and threw quickly to home, catching Simmons in a rundown. Catcher Tom Lundstedt ran Simmons back toward third and flipped the ball to Matt Alexander at third. As soon as Lundstedt let go of the ball Simmons turned and raced past him to score. No one was covering the plate.

> *Opening-Day Lineup, 1974*
>
> Harris, 2b
> Monday, cf
> Morales, lf
> Williams, 1b
> Cardenal, rf
> Madlock, 3b
> Mitterwald, c
> Kessinger, ss
> Bonham, p

On June 1, the Cubs were fifth with an 18-26 record. Things got worse. Gone was the vaunted Cub power. Gone was the array of formidable starting pitchers. Gone, even, was the semblance of a bullpen. But most tragic was the absence of that superb infield defense that for six years had been the hallmark of the Cubs. At the All-Star break, the Cubs remained in fifth, their record immeasurably improved to 41-52. It was like old times in the fifties when the Cubs had to be grateful for some team in the league worse than they. Now, with a six-team division, their chances were less. Even Whitey Lockman got his fill of adversity. He surrendered the managerial post to return to his work as director of player development for the team. His successor was Jim Marshall, who had managed at Wichita and was currently third-base coach with the Cubs.

About the only thing the Cubs didn't lose in the second half of the season was a night game at home. They struggled home with a 25-44 mark under Marshall for a combined season's total of 66-96, and, yes, last place. Ninety-six losses represented the second-worse season in Cub history. Nonetheless, 1,015,378 of the faithful, and I mean *faithful*, came to Wrigley Field. It was like the fifties and early sixties: the Cubs committed 191 errors to lead the major leagues. They were outscored 826 to 669. A silver lining? Well, rookie Madlock had hit .313, and Cardenal and Monday were both over .290. Jerry Morales drove in 82 runs, and Rick Reuschel at 13-12 showed promise. The rest was not encouraging. Vic Harris was no Glenn Beckert, and Steve Swisher was no Randy Hundley. Billy Williams had missed part of the season with injuries, and Bonham, Hooton, Frailing, LaRoche, and Pina had not had the kind of seasons that could bring pleasant winter dreams to Cub fans.

Soon after the season, Holland announced that Billy Williams had agreed to be traded to the Oakland A's after fourteen seasons as a Cub. Billy had scored more runs than any Cub since 1900, 1,312. Williams had 2,510 hits, 402 doubles, 392 homers, and 1,354 RBIs as a Cub. In every way, he was one of the greatest players the Cubs ever had. It would take some getting used to, watching the Cubs without seeing this quietly dignified, wonderfully composed ballplayer. Smooth. Sweet. The Cubs gave him up to get second-baseman Manny Trillo, and relievers Bob Locker and Darold Knowles. Locker had sat out the entire 1974 season with arm trouble and was now coming back to the Cubs.

Fan reaction to the trade was vehemently negative, perhaps in part because they were reluctant to see one of the two remaining survivors of the halcyon days depart.

Now, only Kessinger remained. Holland defended the trade by pointing out that "our primary interest was in getting Trillo, and when you get a young player not known to the public, you don't expect a good reaction." Still, Cub fans were leery. They did not need to be reminded that Lou Brock had stolen a record of 118 bases in 1974 while ex-Cub Bill North had led the American League in thefts with 54. Now, with Williams gone, the Cubs would be without an authentic long ball hitter for the first time in decades. They read with reservations Jim Marshall's statement, "Our theme is improvement." They tended to agree more readily with Burt Hooton's candid remark during spring training for the 1975 season, "We made some mistakes last year and nobody learned from them. That's got to stop."

Spring camp revealed that the Cubs might actually have a pretty fair baseball team. The outfield of Cardenal, Monday, and Morales had both defensive and offensive potential. Reuschel, Bonham, Stone, Hooton, and Burris, backed up by Zamora, Knowles, and Locker figured to do the job.

The season opened with an 8-4 loss to the Pirates. But in their next game, Rick Monday raced home from second after tagging up on a fly deep to right field, and the Cubs had a 2-1 win, the start of a seven-game winning streak, and, eventually, sole possession of first place. By May 5, the surprising Cubs had battled their way to fifteen wins in twenty-one games and opened up a four-game lead over the second-place Mets. Hooton, off to a bad start, was relegated to the bullpen.

Opening-Day Lineup, 1975

> Kessinger, ss
> Cardenal, lf
> Madlock, 3b
> Monday, cf
> Morales, rf
> LaCock, 1b
> Trillo, 2b
> Swisher, c
> Bonham, p

It was clear that he was unhappy and often an unhappy Cub quickly becomes an ex-Cub. So it was with Hooton, who was sent to the Dodgers for pitchers Geoff Zahn and Ed Solomon. In Los Angeles, Burt regained his happiness and his knuckle-curve, while losing much of his excess poundage.

The Cubs held on to first place through May and into the first week of June. And they were doing it without their trademark — power. This Cub team hit singles and doubles and relied on defense and pitching. Alas, when the pitching weakened there were simply not enough Cub runs to bring victories. On June 2, the Cubs were in first place with a 26-20 mark. On June 30, they had plummeted all the way down to fifth place, nine games out, at 36-39. June was not a total loss, however. Cub fans began to recognize a new hero in Bill Madlock, who in one stretch had fourteen hits in eighteen at-bats, including seven straight safeties. But this was tempered somewhat by other events, such as the ten unearned runs the Cubs gave the Expos on June 25 in a 12-6 loss.

Mid-season found the Cubs still in fifth place, five games under .500 and more than eleven behind the Pirates. Marshall trimmed the Cubs' goal to a .500 season, still holding to his theme of improvement. But even that was not to be. Cub pitching simply failed. Even when it was good it was bad. For example, on July 19, Steve Stone allowed only one hit in six-and-two-thirds innings with the Padres, but lost 2-1 when he walked five batters in the sixth inning. But even this two-run game would have looked good a week later when Bill Madlock had a home run and five singles in a 9-8 loss to the Mets. From July 28 through the end of the season, the Cubs won twenty-nine and lost thirty-one. In the stretch, they made things difficult for the contenders, winning two of three from the Cardinals, three of four from the Phillies, and splitting two with the Pirates. But their final 75-87 record tied them with the Expos for fifth and sixth in the standings. Still, the 1,034,819 who came to Wrigley Field had plenty to cheer about. Bill Madlock won the league batting championship with a .354 average. Jose Cardenal hit .317 and stole thirty-four bases, Manny Trillo had 70 RBIs and Jerry Morales 91, as the Cubs finished third in runs scored with 712. The Cubs' hitting was definitely impressive. Their pitching ranked them the worst in the major leagues with 827 runs for a sad team ERA of 4.49.

Before the season had mercifully ended, Mr. Wrigley initiated a general shake-up of the front office. John Holland announced his semiretirement, though he was retained as an advisor. It had been expected that Blake Cullen, Holland's assistant, would succeed him. Instead, E. R. "Salty" Saltwell was named general manager. Saltwell had been manager of park operations, and Wrigley clearly wanted him to exercise a firm hand in the management of the entire Cub operation. Cullen resigned to take a post with the National League office, and Chuck Shriver left his information and services position with the Cubs to take a similar job in California. Buck Peden, coming over from the White Sox, replaced Shriver. Asked to compare the styles of the Sox and the Cubs, Peden commented, "The Cubs are more low key. We don't intend to get into any theatrics."

Saltwell, having studied the Cub player personnel, let it be known that he was ready to trade, but not to be taken. His first deal showed courage at least. He traded popular Don Kessinger, now thirty-three, to the Cardinals for relief pitcher Mike Garman. Kessinger in eleven full seasons as a Cub had been one of the best shortstops in the history of the team. Don had hit .255 in those seasons and been a fine fielder with great range. Fluid. Fluid and graceful. His departure marked the end of an era for the Cubs.

It was time now to look ahead. Dave Rosello and Mick Kelleher, acquired from the Cardinals for Vic Harris, would be competing for Kessinger's job. The rest of the lineup was fairly well set, and on paper at least, it didn't look that bad. The weaknesses were still pitching, the lack of power hitting, and, it must be said, a winning spirit.

Jim Marshall put the Cubs through their paces in Scottsdale, and everyone was eager for the season to open. Unfortunately, Cardinal pitcher Lynn McGlothen was eager too, and he shut out the Cubs in the opener, 5-0. But Bonham and the bullpen trio of Knowles, Garman, and Buddy Schultz led the Cubs to victory in their next four games. For one day, April 14, the Cubs were tied for first place. It was a wonderful day. Randy Hundley who had been traded in 1973 had now been reacquired after his unconditional release from San Diego. He was put into the game against the Mets in the seventh inning, and the crowd gave him an emotional standing ovation. "I had to wipe the tears out of my eyes so I could catch," said Hundley. In the bottom of the seventh, Randy hit a double, igniting a three-run rally that won the game, 6-5. The season should have ended that day. Unfortunately, there were still 157 games to go.

> *Opening-Day Lineup, 1976*
>
> Monday, cf
> Cardenal, lf
> Madlock, 3b
> Morales, rf
> Thornton, 1b
> Trillo, 2b
> Swisher, c
> Rosello, ss
> Burris, p

The Cubs proceeded to lose six straight games, including an incredible display of fallibility when, on April 17, they blew a 13-2 lead and ended up losing to the Phillies, 18-16. In twenty games from April 18 to May 9, the Cubs scored 4.5 runs per game. The problem was that the opposition was scoring an average of 6.4 runs in those games. The fact that the Cubs were in fifth place was due more to pitching failure than anything else, and Saltwell went looking for help. On May 17, he traded Andy Thornton to the Expos for pitcher Steve Renko and first-baseman Larry Biittner.

Three weeks later he bought righthander Joe Coleman from the Tigers for an estimated $100,000 and a player to be named later. Coleman had twice won twenty or more with the Tigers but in his last two seasons he had been struggling. Perhaps he could find his magic again in Chicago. And then again . . .

Renko and Coleman did help improve the pitching at least for a while. But, sure enough, the hitting began to fall off. In the twenty games from May 20 to June 8, Cub pitchers limited the opposition to 3.8 runs a game. However, the Cubs were able to score only 2.6 per game over the same stretch. On June 8, the Cubs were 22-30, in fifth place, fourteen-and-a-half back. With Thornton gone, Marshall tried a series of people at first base: LaCock, Mitterwald, Biittner, Champ Summers, and finally Rick Monday. When Monday had trouble fielding the position the fans had no patience left and they showered him with jeers. Poor Rick. He didn't want to be there to begin with. Meanwhile, his replacement in center field, Joe Wallis, was becoming something of a hero with his astounding catches in the outfield.

Marshall began having private meetings with individual players in an effort to get the team going again, but to no avail. At the All-Star break, the Cubs were 36-48 and mired in fifth place. In the late forties and through most of the fifties this might have been considered a good season. But the powerhouse of the late sixties had reminded Cub fans what it was like to have a good team. In late July, Cub players decided to have a closed-door meeting for players only. One Cub said later that the meeting was wasted because nobody would single anybody else out. "Plenty of guys aren't hustling. We all know who they are but no names were mentioned," said this unnamed player.

The Cubs played .500 ball for the second half of the season, and there were some good omens for the future. Trillo was playing a good second base. Monday, despite back problems, was hitting with power. And Ray Burris, after a bad start, had come back to win twelve of his last fifteen decisions. Bill Madlock was fielding well and was in the thick of the race for a second straight batting title. And a rookie reliever named Bruce Sutter was beginning to baffle hitters with a pitch that dropped a foot on the way to the plate. But overall, the club could mount no real drive. In August, the press began to get on the Cubs as "Marshall's marshmallows" and as a team of complainers. After bouncing back and forth from fourth to fifth, the Cubs finally did edge out the Cardinals for fourth place. Their record was 75-87, twenty-six games behind the Phillies. Madlock, with four hits in the last game of the season, edged out Ken Griffey to win the batting crown at .338. Griffey had asked to sit out the last game to protect his league-leading average but had to change his mind when word of Madlock's tear reached the Reds. But he couldn't get a hit in his two trips. So the good guy won for the second straight year. Madlock seemed certain to be a superstar, and Cub fans rallied their spirits with the certainty that better things lay ahead.

Even though Cub attendance went over the million mark for the ninth straight year, 1976 was the third straight year the operation lost money. It was clear that Mr. Wrigley's patience was worn thin. His comment at the time was, "I've got to shake up the club. I'm just trying to line up everybody I can think of. I don't know what else to do." Predictably, his thoughts would turn to the last time one of his shake-ups had been successful. But this time Durocher would not return as field manager. In fact, Leo's proposition was that he be given a two-year contract as general manager with Maury Wills to be named as his field manager. Additionally, Leo wanted Blake Cullen to return to the Cubs as his assistant and ultimate successor. Had the proposal been accepted, the Cubs might have had the first black manager in the national league, not to mention a man who might have turned them into a running ball club. But the proposal was not accepted, as another former Cub returned to the fold. On November 24, 1976, Bob Kennedy was named vice-president in charge of baseball operations. Jim Marshall was notified that he would not be the Cub manager in 1977, and Salty Saltwell, after only one year as general manager, was given the title of secretary and director of park operations. Lockman was fired as a vice-president, and John Holland was relieved of his remaining duties as a special advisor. Clearly Kennedy was going to be in command of the Cub organization, but as events would develop even he would have to operate under some unusual constraints.

Kennedy began by hiring Herman Franks as the new manager. Franks had managed the Giants to four consecutive second-place finishes in 1965 through 1968. In 1969, he had served briefly as a coach for the Cubs under Leo Durocher. It was felt that Franks would be able to get the most out of the talent available while Kennedy went looking for more. But it soon became apparent that Kennedy's major difficulty would be salary problems with the Cub players. Both Madlock and Monday wanted multiyear contracts with significant pay increases. They had seen what free agents were commanding on the open market, and they requested contract terms that, while not exorbitant, were more than the Cubs were accustomed to paying. Mr. Wrigley reacted strongly and perhaps said more than he intended; "No ball player is worth more than $100,000 and I'm not sure they're worth that much. We'll just have to field the best team we possibly can. We don't expect to win any pennants. All I'm trying to do is survive. You can't give out more than you take in, not forever." Seen from Mr. Wrigley's point of view, the Cubs were a team that had lost money without paying enormous salaries. Logic indicated that the same players making even more money would not change the pennant picture, but would certainly create an even poorer financial structure.

Kennedy had his work cut out for him — he was not working for George Steinbrenner of the Yankees. But he brought a lot of baseball savvy to his job, and he played the market within the limits established by Wrigley. His first deals brought outfielder Greg Gross from Houston for infielder Julio Gonzalez, and outfielder Jim Dwyer from the Mets for Pete LaCock in a three-team deal. In addition, pitcher Willie Hernandez was drafted out of the Phillies' chain for $25,000. Next, Rick Monday was sent to the Dodgers along with Mike Garman for infielders Bill Buckner and Ivan DeJesus and pitcher Jeff Albert. After negotiations with Madlock were unsuccessful, he went to the Giants along with infielder Rob Sperring for Bobby Murcer, Steve Ontiveros, and Andy Muhlstock. In a less sensational deal, Darold Knowles went to Texas for outfielder Gene Clines.

Herman Franks, surveying his new roster, said confidently, "So far as I'm concerned, if everybody can have that one good year, all together, we can win it. Every time I walk on the field I can win." Spoken like a true Cub! Bobby Murcer added his voice to the crescendo of optimism. He promised Cub fans that they wouldn't miss Madlock. "I will hit more home runs, outrun him on the bases and play better on the field. Watching the wind blow in Wrigley Field gets the adrenalin flowing."

Cub fans waited excitedly for the start of the season. They told themselves, as Cub fans had for years, that on paper this was a good squad and what it might lack in superstars was made up for in the quality of the bench. The outfield of Cardenal, Morales, and Murcer would have Clines, Gross, and Wallis in reserve. The infield of Ontiveros, DeJesus, Trillo, and Buckner would be backed up by Kelleher, Rosello, and Biittner. Burris, Rick Reuschel, Renko, Bonham, and rookie Mike Krukow would be supported by Sutter, Paul Reuschel, Jim Todd, and Ken Frailing.

Opening day provided cynics with the opportunity to point out that only the cast of characters had changed; the mistakes were still the same. The Cubs were leading the Mets, 3-1, in the sixth when Murcer and Morales collided trying to catch a flyball. The ball fell safely, enabling the Mets to go on to score four times for a 5-3 win. Though the Cubs came back to split their first four games, it would have been ultimately nicer if they had won all four.

Opening-Day Lineup, 1977

DeJesus, ss
Cardenal, lf
Biittner, 1b
Murcer, rf
Morales, cf
Ontiveros, 3b
Swisher, c
Trillo, 2b
Burris, p

On April 12, 1977, barely a week into his forty-second season with the Cubs, Philip K. Wrigley died at the age of eighty-two. For all of his unique ideas, and for all of the systems, orthodox and unorthodox, that he had used to build the Cubs into a pennant-winning ball club, Mr. Wrigley had made significant contributions to the game of baseball itself. His revolutionary attitude toward television and his insistence that all Cub games be widely broadcast kept the Cubs always available to the average fan. Many times he said that "baseball is for the little man," and that is how he chose to portray himself on those rare occasions when he attended games in the park, shunning his owner's box to sit incognito in the grandstands. It seems also that Wrigley gave to his players the dignity he felt due to working men. No Cub player ever accused him of being unfair or ungenerous. Randy Hundley spoke for generations of Cub teammates when he said, "If all the owners had been as fair to players as Mr. Wrigley was, we wouldn't need a Players' Association." The city of Chicago mourned Mr. Wrigley's death with the respect he had given to it. Flags were flown at half-mast, and tributes came from many persons in and out of the baseball world.

William Wrigley, P. K.'s only son, succeeded his father as chairman of the executive committee of the Cubs. Despite heavy inheritance taxes, the younger Wrigley resisted selling the franchise. And he reaffirmed his late father's stand against night baseball at Wrigley Field.

Wearing black mourning bands in respect, the Cubs returned to the field to play baseball. April finished with ups and downs and a 7-9 record. But then came May, and it proved to be one of the most glorious months in years. Reuschel, Bonham, Burris, and Krukow, backed up by the incredible Bruce Sutter, allowed only 3.7 runs per game in May, while Cub hitters were supplying an average of nearly 6 runs every game. By May 27 the Cubs had second place with a record of 25-14. The stage was set for a three-game confrontation with the league-leading Pirates bringing only a half-game lead into Wrigley Field.

The fans. Cub fans. The fans were so excited that they gave their team a standing ovation before the game even began. It might as well have been the World Series. The north side of Chicago rocked to the chants and cheers emanating from Wrigley Field as the Cubs swept the Pirates and took over first place. Sutter earned saves in all three games, DeJesus made unbelievable plays at shortstop, Trillo moved past Dave Parker as the league's leading hitter, and Mitterwald threw out five of the seven Pirates who tried to steal. Franks was pleased but cautious. "Pennants aren't won in May," he warned. Veteran Cub fans nodded in agreement, grateful for May but knowing full well what June would likely bring.

But the Cubs didn't swoon this June. They just increased their league lead, thank you. When June ended, the Cubs had a 19-8 record for the month, 47-24 for the season, and they were seven-and-a-half games ahead of the second-place Phillies. This was a scrappy, hustling ball club. Cub pitchers weren't hesitating to brush back hitters. Cub hitters were bunching singles and doubles for their runs; as a team they had only forty-four homers by the end of June. One of the opposing players volunteered an explanation for the Cubs' success: "Attitude — that's what's different about the new Cubs . . . . They have the noisiest dugout in the league, they are getting the breaks, and they have about half a dozen guys having their best year — including the one pitcher in baseball who NOBODY can hit — Bruce Sutter." Individual Cubs were beginning to specialize: Buckner in beating the Dodgers, Murcer in beating the Giants, and Sutter in beating everybody. By June 27, Bruce had racked up three wins and twenty saves. On June 25, the Cubs showed how "for real" they were. Trailing the Mets 4-1 with one out in the ninth, the Cubs scored four times to win 5-4. The 33,130 fans were so ecstatic they stayed long after the game, cheering and celebrating the fact that the game is never over.

Early in July Cub fans began to wonder whether a 6-11 stretch was just a slump or the beginning of a full-blown swoon. Strange things were beginning to happen. On July 4, in his fortieth appearance, Sutter was knocked out of a game for the first time. Nine days later, with the Cubs leading 2-1 in the sixth at Shea Stadium, New York suffered a complete blackout and, like everyone else, the Cubs had to find their way home in the dark. Three days after that, Sutter came up with a massive knot beneath his right shoulder. Though selected for the All-Star team, he could not participate.

The All-Star break found the Cubs still clinging to first with a two-game lead over the Phillies. When play resumed on July 21, the Cubs finished the month by winning seven of thirteen games, good enough to retain first place but by less than two games. On July 28, they had demonstrated that they still intended to battle, with a thirteen-inning 16-15 win over the Reds. (See Chapter 7, "Games to Remember.")

But August 4 proved to be their last day at the top of their division. Coincidentally, it was on that day they announced that because of a recurrent strain of the *latissimus dorsi*, Bruce Sutter was now on the twenty-one-day disabled list. Over the years, the Cubs had discovered many ways to slip from first, but a strained *latissimus dorsi* was a new one. It seemed almost as though the Cubs lost their confidence and composure now that they did not have the security of their "enforcer" in the bullpen. Willie Hernandez, Paul Reuschel, and Dave Giusti, purchased from Oakland, simply couldn't do what Sutter had done. Cub woes were compounded when their leading starter, Rick Reuschel, who was having the best season of his career, came down with an ailing back in the first week of August. Reuschel was 14-3 at that point and had hurled thirty-three-and-two-thirds consecutive shutout innings at Wrigley Field. A hitter's park indeed! No fewer than ten Cubs suffered injuries after the All-Star break, but the patched-up lineup continued to battle, though without too much success. A 15-23 record in August took the Cubs into September with a 71-60 mark, in third place, ten games out.

Even with Sutter back in action, the Cubs were unable to mount a stretch drive in September. In fact they managed to win only ten of twenty-nine games during the month and were outscored 134-97. By losing eight of their last nine games, the Cubs settled into a fourth-place finish with an 81-81 mark, twenty games out. Home attendance totaled 1,439,739 for these Cubs who finished sixth in hitting, eighth in pitching, but first in heart.

After the season, Bob Kennedy continued his efforts to build the club. Jose Cardenal, a favorite of Cub fans, was sent to the Phillies for pitcher Manny Seoane. Pitcher Bill Bonham was dispatched to the Reds for pitcher Woody

Fryman, thirty-seven, and young pitcher Bill Caudill. Kennedy knew what he was doing — he wanted Caudill more than Fryman. And the Cubs finally entered the free-agent market to sign slugger Dave Kingman to a five-year contract for an estimated $1.3 million. Jerry Morales went to the Cardinals for catcher Dave Rader and outfielder Hector Cruz. But for one more starting pitcher, the major Cub needs were being attended to. No one could accuse Kennedy of standing pat.

Spring training for the 1978 season began with a somewhat justified optimism. Indicative of the bench strength on the Cubs this year was the four-way battle for the starting assignment in center field between Joe Wallis, Hector Cruz, Gene Clines, and Greg Gross. Gross had led the Cubs in hitting with a .322 mark in 1977. Kingman and Murcer promised power in the other outfield slots. The infield of Ontiveros (.299), DeJesus (.266), Trillo (.280), and Buckner (.284), backed up by Larry Biittner, Mick Kelleher, and the newly acquired Rodney Scott, seemed solid and then some. The catching department, now headed by Dave Rader, was apparently improved. And the pitching staff, led by Reuschel, Burris, Fryman, Lamp, Krukow, and Dave Roberts, with Sutter, Hernandez, and Moore in the bullpen, was solid if unspectacular.

Reports from Arizona fed the optimists' fantasies of flags. But opening day brought a dash of realism to the scenario, as Reuschel was bested 1-0 in a duel with John Candelaria of the Pirates. The next day Sutter walked home the winning run in the tenth inning for a 4-3 Pirate win. Even with weak hitting, unsteady fielding, and poor baserunning, the Cubs managed to win eleven of their first twenty games. Once again, Sutter was the key; he won or saved six of the first eleven Cub wins. May opened with the Cubs losing four of their first five games, but they managed to stay at or near .500 into the third week in May. None of the Eastern Division teams was playing very well so that even with a 16-17 record, the Cubs were in second place, only two games behind the Phillies. The brightest sign was that Dave Kingman had begun to hit. On May 14, he blasted three homers in leading the Cubs to a thrilling fifteen-inning win over the Dodgers. (See Chapter 7, "Games to Remember.")

> **Opening-Day Lineup, 1978**
>
> DeJesus, ss
> Gross, cf
> Buckner, 1b
> Murcer, rf
> Kingman, lf
> Ontiveros, 3b
> Trillo, 2b
> Rader, c
> Burris, p

Beginning on May 19, the Cubs won seven in a row and moved into first place by three-and-a-half games. The heroes began to step forth. On May 24, the day the Cubs took over first, they were trailing 4-2 with two out in the bottom of the eighth. Then Ontiveros and Trillo singled and Rader tripled to tie the game. In the tenth, Kingman was hit by a pitch and Trillo homered for a 6-4 win. Things were looking bright. Dave Roberts won three straight starts and Reuschel, two. Even Cub losing streaks were not catastrophic. After dropping three straight to Montreal, the Cubs were still in first by one-half game, and Herman

Franks was unruffled: "It's not the first time we've lost three in a row." A gift for understatement? But the Cubs rebounded with nine wins in the next eleven games, thanks to two game-winning hits by Trillo, superb pitching by Reuschel and Donnie Moore, and a grand-slammer by Kingman on June 6 against the Astros.

Maybe the right deal could prevent a swoon. By now it was clear that Woody Fryman, 2-4, was not going to be a great help to the Cubs, so he was sent to Montreal for outfielder Jerry White. That left the Cubs without a veteran left-handed starter. In New York the once-great Ken Holtzman was languishing on the bench. Bob Kennedy was able to get Holtzman back with the Cubs along with the guarantee that the Yankees would continue to pick up a large part of his salary. In return, the Yankees acquired minor-league pitcher Ron Davis. Kennedy had gained the edge in the Bonham-for-Fryman deal by also getting minor-leaguer Bill Caudill. But he lost in the Holtzman deal by giving up Davis who would soon develop into a star for the Yankees. Other deals sent Hector Cruz to the Giants for pitcher Lynn McGlothen and brought Mike Vail from Cleveland for Joe Wallis. Give a big plus to Kennedy for those deals.

But not big enough for a pennant. The Cubs led their division through the first three weeks of June, but their 35-26 record allowed them only a three-game lead over the pursuing Phillies. The swoon, when it commenced on June 21, was at least different this year. Instead of losing a round, the Cubs proceeded to lose eight of nine games to the Phillies between June 23 and July 2. When the action began, they were in first place by two games; when it ended, they were in second place by four games. Now relieved of their lofty ambitions, the Cubs began flirting with the .500 mark, which for thirty years or more had been the backup weather vane of success or failure: If you can't finish first, at least win as many as you lose. At the All-Star break, the Cubs were 43-39, in second place, four-and-a-half games out. Bruce Sutter made Cub fans proud as he pitched one-and-two-thirds innings of hitless relief in the All-Star game and was the winning pitcher for the National League.

The second half of the season began with a rash of injuries. No fewer than nine Cubs were out of action at one time or another in July, including Dave Kingman, who went on the twenty-one-day disabled list with a hamstring injury, and Steve Ontiveros, who missed the last eight weeks of the season with a shoulder injury. By August 1, the Cubs were down to .500 but still clung to second place, four games behind the Phillies. This would have been a good year to put together a winning streak in August and open up a sizable lead on the Phillies and Pirates. But it was not to be. Instead, August was one of those win-one, lose-one months, and the monthly tally came to sixteen wins and fifteen losses. At that, the Cubs entered September only five-and-a-half games out. A good stretch drive would do it. Unfortunately, the Cub stretch consisted of thirteen wins in the last thirty-one games, allowing them a season record of 79-83, good enough for a third-place finish, eleven games out. September was just not a good month. The press was openly critical of Herman Franks for misuse of the bullpen, overemphasis on platooning, and making drastic lineup changes after a loss. Things just seemed to fall apart, and the players were clearly not hanging together as a team. As usual, there were some bright spots. The team batting average of .264 was best in the league, with Buckner's .323 tops for the Cubs. Ivan DeJesus hit .278, fielded well, and stole forty-one bases, the most since Kiki Cuyler's forty-three in 1929. Bruce Sutter posted twenty-seven saves, and young Mike Krukow finished with a 9-3 record as the main lights in an otherwise dismal season for Cub hurlers. Attendance at 1,525,311, was encouraging. The fact that even with

Kingman the Cubs hit only seventy-two home runs for the season, was not. Overall, the personnel was not bad but clearly something was missing. Ken Holtzman said that what the Cubs needed most was a real hunger for the pennant, the kind that stops at nothing to win. General manager Bob Kennedy could be counted on to make more beneficial trades, but the winning spirit can't be bought or acquired by trades.

In December, Kennedy sent Rodney Scott and Jerry White to the Expos for outfielder Sam Mejias. Kennedy saved his biggest deal until February when he traded Manny Trillo, Dave Rader, and Greg Gross to the Phillies for Barry Foote, Jerry Martin, Ted Sizemore, and two minor leaguers, Henry Mack and Derek Botelho. On paper it was a good trade for both clubs. The Cubs would be strengthened at both the center-field and catcher positions, both defensively and offensively. Cub fans were sorry to see Trillo go but consoled by the fact that they were not left empty-handed as was often the case in previous seasons. In March, minor deals sent Ed Putman to Detroit for Steve Dillard and Larry Cox to Seattle for Luis Delgado.

The Cubs went to spring training with an improved squad. Reports from Arizona fairly breathed with optimism. And why not? The Cubs had power, depth, steadily improving young pitchers, and a promising young rookie named Scot Thompson. Opening day brought winds gusting up to forty-five miles an hour and a Met victory over the Cubs 10-6. Murcer had trouble with fly balls in right field, and the fans began to ride him. He became the focus of

Opening-Day Lineup, 1979

DeJesus, ss
Sizemore, 2b
Buckner, 1b
Kingman, lf
Murcer, rf
Ontiveros, 3b
Martin, cf
Foote, c
Reuschel, p

fan frustration after his poor season in 1978 when he hit only 9 homers and drove in only 64 runs. He was being accused of lackadaisical play and of not caring. His teammates came to his defense and elected him captain. But Bobby's problems were compounded by the fact that Scot Thompson was hitting well every time he got a chance to play.

Notwithstanding the hoped-for improvement in the 'seventy-nine Cubs, they found the going rough and were not able to get above the .500 mark for the first eight weeks of the season. On April 29, for example, they trailed the Braves 5-0 with two out and nobody on in the ninth. Ho hum? Hardly. They came back with six runs for a miraculous victory. (See Chapter 7, "Games to Remember.") Or what about May 17 when they came back from a fourth-inning 17-6 deficit to tie the game at 22-22 in the eighth? Unfortunately, Mike Schmidt's second homer of the game, a solo shot in the tenth, gave the Phillies a 23-22 win. A record-tying eleven home runs had been hit in the game, three by Dave Kingman. In fact, Kingman was playing like a new man. His strikeouts were down, his average was up, and his fielding was improving steadily. (See Chapter 7, "Games to Remember.")

But the Cubs were still not playing well together, and it was generally conceded that their communications with Herman Franks were not all they could be. After the discouraging 23-22 loss to the Phillies, several players said that the team was dispirited. Franks' reaction was succinct: "That's bull," he said. So much for lack of spirit.

On June 18, the Cubs finally climbed above .500 at 30-29. They were in fifth place but were only five-and-a-half games out. More importantly, they had begun to look like Cubs again. On June 13, they scored in the tenth to beat the Giants, 3-2. The next day they scored twice in the ninth to beat the Giants again, 8-6. And on the third day they scored two in the ninth for a 3-2 decision over the Padres.

In fact, the Cubs won sixteen and lost eight in June and after an 8-3 road trip were greeted by hundreds of fans waiting for them at O'Hare airport. Perhaps it was all coming together. Kennedy had made another shrewd trade in sending Ray Burris to the Yankees for Dick Tidrow and giving the Cubs the best bullpen in the league. Kennedy had also picked up Ken Henderson and Miguel Dilone to add power, experience, and speed to the bench. Cub players were less pleased than their fans when the Cubs let Murcer go to the Yankees on a waiver deal that brought only a minor-league pitcher, Paul Semall, in return. It was clearly a move to cut the payroll as much as to give Scot Thompson or Mike Vail a chance to play.

July started well, and the Cubs won twelve and lost four prior to the All-Star break. On July 16, they were 47-38, in second place and only three games out. Once again, Bruce Sutter was the winning pitcher in the All-Star game. Momentum seemed to be with the Cubs for once. But not all was well. Apparently, Ted Sizemore challenged Franks' authority publicly. Result? He was labeled a troublemaker and sent to the Red Sox, where he made more trouble. Moreover, Kingman was out for twelve days after being hit by pitchers twice in Atlanta. The fact that he had twenty-nine homers and sixty-nine RBIs by mid-July no doubt made him a target.

At the end of July, Chicago had a 54-44 record and was only one-and-a-half games out of first. Fans began to say again, if only we could get some breaks, stay close and then turn it on. . . . On to August.

But first a time-out to celebrate with Jack Brickhouse and all Cub fans the occasion of his 5,000th TV broadcast on August 5. Brickhouse and the Cubs have been inseparable since the first WGN broadcast back in April 1948 (a Cubs/Sox exhibition game in which Bob Kennedy batted cleanup for the Sox). Jack's leisurely, casual, anecdotal approach to the Cubs has come to represent one of the most sensible ways of living with Cub frustration. The game is, above all, fun — even in its disappointments. Brickhouse has always known just how necessary it is to keep this thought ever in front of his fellow fans. Come to the ball park and leave your cares and troubles behind. Atta boy, Jack!

Jack had fairly good news to broadcast for the Cubs in those first two weeks of August. They broke even in fourteen contests. Steve Dillard was the new sparkplug. His four homers in eight games contributed to three wins. Sutter and Tidrow continued to be fantastic, having saved, between them, forty-four of the first sixty-two Cub wins.

On August 13, an old nemesis named Lou Brock got his 3,000th hit in a game against the Cubs. He did it by smashing a drive off Dennis Lamp's pitching hand. When Brock came over to the Cub locker room after the game to make sure that Lamp was not injured, Dennis cracked, "I guess I'd better send my fingers to Cooperstown." And to Brock, "Don't be afraid to pull the ball next time, Lou."

By winning seventeen and losing fifteen in August, the Cubs managed to stay in the race and trailed by only five-and-a-half games going into September. What happened next resembled a collapse more than a swoon. The Cubs started losing games on fielding lapses and mental errors. A number of Cubs, including Foote, Ontiveros, Kingman, and Buckner were out or playing with injuries. By September 17, the Cubs had lost fourteen of their first seventeen September games to slip to fifth place, eleven games out. Lynn McGlothen didn't duck the issue when he was asked what had happened: "The spark is gone; the Cubs killed the Cubs this year." It didn't matter that Kingman led the major leagues with forty-eight home runs or that Bruce Sutter would be named Cy Young Award winner in recognition of his thirty-seven saves. The fold-up was complete and total, not unlike some of the classic Cub swoons in the fifties. For Cub fans of long standing, it was instant replay. But there was a difference. This was not a team that had simply played over its head for a couple of months. This was a team with good hitting (the team batting average was .270, third best in the league), some power, fair pitching (a team ERA of 3.87), and the best bullpen in baseball.

With a week to go in the season, Herman Franks abandoned ship. After his resignation, he attacked several Cub players including Buckner, Foote, Vail, and the departed Sizemore. In the aftermath of Herman's parting shots, it became clear that there had been a serious lack of communication between manager and players all season. These Cubs, like so many of their predecessors in the fifties and sixties, were being accused by their manager and some of the press of being coddled, uninspired, and selfish.

The Cubs finished the season under Joey Amalfitano but could not make it to a .500 season. They came in fifth with an 80-82 mark, a full eighteen games behind the Pirates. It was some consolation that 1,648,587 fans paid their way into Wrigley Field and did not always leave disappointed.

After the season there was a great deal of speculation about who would be named to manage the Cubs in the eighties. Whitey Herzog and Maury Wills were mentioned. Now eighty-one, Charlie Grimm was no longer a possibility. Finally, it was announced that Preston Gomez, former manager of the Padres and Astros, and more recently, a coach with the Dodgers, had accepted the job. It was felt that he was the disciplinarian the Cubs seemed to need.

Chapter Seven:

The Eighties: Building a New Tradition

ON TO THE 1980S. SOCIAL CRITICS HAILED THE NEW YEAR OF 1980 as the end of the Me Decade and the beginning of a time when people would stop looking inward and begin to see themselves as part of the community. The mood of the nation was conservative. The humiliation of American hostages being held in Iran for more than a year and the ability of Arab oil sheiks to affect every facet of our economy made even the liberals bring their flags out of the closet. Inflation. Politics. Remember Ronald Reagan, star of *That Hagen Girl* with Shirley Temple in 1948? He successfully challenged incumbent president Jimmy Carter, and new words entered our vocabulary — *the Moral Majority, supply-side economics*. The decade would not be two years old yet before President Anwar Sadat was assassinated, John Lennon murdered, and assassination attempts made on the lives of President Reagan and Pope John Paul II. Even in sports the scene was out of focus. America boycotted the 1980 Olympics in Moscow; all professional sports were beset by outlandish salaries and a kind of professional detachment that made players more like hired guns than grown-ups having fun doing what most of us would gladly do if only we had the talent. The mood was grim. Politically, economically, and socially grim.

At least the Cubs opened the decade in step with the tempo of the times.

The Cubs approached the 1980 season with relatively few newcomers. Mike Tyson, Lenny Randle, and Miguel Dilone, who had hit .306 in limited service as a Cub after coming over from Oakland in 1979, were touted as the major improvements. But this was not a happy team. Jerry Martin blasted the organization and declared that the Cubs wouldn't win anything unless they changed. One change he recommended was that the Cubs trade him. Bruce Sutter went to arbitration and was awarded $700,000, twice what Kennedy had offered him.

Spring training found the Cubs ailing. Foote had a bad back, Tyson a sore shoulder; Martin was still recovering from knee surgery. The threat of a players' strike began to loom large. Spring exhibition games after April were canceled. Most players stayed in camp to continue conditioning. But some went home until opening day. Vail, Tidrow, McGlothen, Biittner, and Dilone left camp. Dave Kingman stayed and on April 3 doused a sportswriter with a bucket of ice water. Then, a week before the season opened, the Cubs sent Dilone, the fastest man on the team, to Wichita.

Opening day, April 12, the Cubs bowed to the Mets, 5-2. Never mind. The next day Kingman and Martin each homered twice in a 7-5 Cub win. For the next four weeks the Cubs looked good. On April 22, Barry Foote grandslammed in the ninth to give the Cubs a 16-12 win over the Cardinals. In the second game that day, DeJesus hit for the cycle. As late as May 5 the Cubs were in second place with an 11-8 mark. Is it possible to swoon from second place in May? If

Opening-Day Lineup, 1980

Randle, 2b
DeJesus, ss
Buckner, 1b
Kingman, lf
K. Henderson, rf
Ontiveros, 3b
Lezcano, cf
Blackwell, c
Reuschel, p

so, the Cubs did it. The strike threat was settled when the free agent compensation issue was put off until next year. Darn it.

The strike might have been settled, but the Cubs weren't. Gomez switched lineups so often that almost no one felt secure. By June 2, the Cubs were under .500 and in fourth place. Foote went on the disabled list. A week later, Steve Ontiveros announced that he wanted out. Four days after that, Kingman went AWOL for a game and was fined one day's pay; four more days found Dave on the disabled list with a sore shoulder. (Small note: Back in May, Kennedy sold Dilone to Cleveland for $35,000; now his name was striking fear throughout the American League.) Ontiveros got his wish on June 23: The Cubs sold him to the Seibu Indians in Japan. Well, Dave Kingman was reactivated on June 29, and he promptly dropped a fly, giving the Cardinals two runs in their 9-7 win. June ended with the Cubs in fifth place on a 30-39 record. It was not until July 14 that the Cubs took over last place.

On July 25, Preston Gomez was liberated. He had only one lament: "If I had known last winter what I know now, there is no way I would have taken this job." Said Bruce Sutter, "Firing Preston was not the answer. What this club needs is a major overhaul." The Gomez Cubs were 38-52. Perhaps Joey Amalfitano could do better. In his debut as manager, the Cubs led the Dodgers 6-2 in the sixth, only to lose 7-6.

Time to look for the annual bright spots in an otherwise dismal season. Cliff Johnson, obtained from Cleveland for Karl Pagel, won five games with his hitting. Tim Blackwell, taking over for Foote, hit well and shone on defense. Rick Reuschel had his usual August by winning five times. Ivan DeJesus stole forty-four bases, surpassing Kiki Cuyler's forty-three in 1929. And Bill Buckner. All Buckner did was to play hard, at first base and in left field, day in and day out. A "gamer," he had had his fill of teammates dogging it. "Every-one's given up — even the grounds crew," he said. Buckner went into the final game with a five-point lead over Keith Hernandez in the race for the batting title. Instead of sitting out the game to protect his lead, Buckner played and went 0 for 4. Hernandez could only manage one hit, and Billy finished at .324 to .321 for Hernandez. Bruce Sutter, with twenty-eight saves, again led the league in that department, and Dick Tidrow recorded the league high in appearances with eighty-four. But that was all. As a team, the Cubs were tenth in hitting, eleventh in pitching, and dead last in spirit and in the standings. Their 64-98 record was the third worst by a Cub team since 1900. At that, 1,192,070 paid their way in to watch.

After the season, Amalfitano accepted reappointment as manager. "We are going to improve, and I want to be part of it," he said. Cub fans knew Kennedy would back up the truck and haul off the remains. All they could do was hope he would do better than he had with Dilone. For $35,000, Cleveland got a .341 hitter who stole sixty-one bases in less than a full season.

The 1980 season was enough of a disaster that management could not hide the need to send up an SOS. It is an old Cub adage that if you can't cure your problems, you trade them. Over the winter Bob Kennedy dealt Jerry Martin and Jesus Figueroa to the Giants for Joe Strain and Phil Nastu. Larry Biittner and Lenny Randle became free agents; Mike Vail was sent to the Reds for ex-Cub Hector Cruz. Cliff Johnson and Keith Drumright went to Oakland for Mike King. A young catcher named Jody Davis was drafted from the Cardinals' chain.

There were rumors of more trades in the offing. Kingman and Buckner both asked the Cubs to renegotiate their contracts. It is not clear why Kingman expected a raise; a WLS poll had named him "Chicago Sports Flop of the Year." All Buckner asked for was a one-year extension on his present contract, which still had four years to run. Despite his batting championship season, Bill was making less than some benchwarmers on other teams. The Cubs said, "No; it's against our principles." To which Buckner replied, "I'll honor my contract, but I'm not happy about it." So Kingman was rumored to be on the way to the Mets, and Buckner, it was thought, might go to the Giants for Mike Ivie or to the Yankees for Dave Righetti. Reportedly it took William Wrigley himself to veto any trade of Buckner.

An even more important step in planning a balanced budget was the trade that sent Bruce Sutter to the Cardinals for Ken Reitz, Leon Durham, and Tye Waller. In five years with the Cubs, Sutter had accounted for 133 saves. But don't forget, he had won a $700,000 arbitration decision from the Cubs prior to the 1980 season. Amalfitano defended the trade saying it would be difficult to replace Sutter, but the Cubs hadn't played .500 in the past three seasons even with him, so a new direction might be good. Joey pointed out that Reitz had made only eight errors for the Cardinals in 1980 while Cub third basemen committed forty-one errors. Of Durham, Joey said, "I like his handshake. If that's any indication, he's going to do a great job for us."

On February 28, Kennedy sent Kingman to the Mets for outfielder Steve Henderson and $100,000. Kingman had been a pretty fair player for the Cubs. Amalfitano summed it up this way: "He's only a half-inch away from being a superstar. On the other hand, he's only half an inch away from 'See you later.' " Henderson was a better hitter for average than Kingman, slightly better defensively, and greatly superior in attitude. But Kingman's departure took away the Cubs' only real power threat.

Kennedy seemed pleased with his deals. "We got rid of the complainers," he said. Wow. If malcontent could hit, field, or pitch, the Cubs would have won it all in 1980. Presumably wih all the complainers gone, 1981 would be happier at least.

When spring training was over, Kennedy made his final preparation for the season by trading Dennis Lamp to the White Sox for Ken Kravec. The Cub pitching staff for 1981 was the same group that had given up more than 1,500 hits in

1980, except that free agent Rawly Eastwick had replaced Sutter and Kravec was there instead of Lamp. Still, Cub fans were anxious to open the season and to see Durham and Henderson. They were slightly mystified by Amalfitano's candid observation that "we may not have the talent that some of the other teams have, but we do have at least six guys who come to play every day." Six?

The 37,000 fans who showed up on opening day had only a brief moment of cheer in the 2-0 loss to the Mets, and that was to watch Dave Kingman misplay a fly with a triple, this time as a Met. The Cubs won the next day and then went on a losing binge and dropped twelve straight for the second worst start in baseball history. The irony was that this team did want to play, but nothing went right. They had team meetings. They posted insults from sportswriters only to live up to their notices. There was an outbreak of annoying injuries apparently traceable to an easy spring training.

Opening-Day Lineup, 1981
DeJesus, ss
Strain, 2b
Buckner, 1b
Henderson, lf
Durham, rf
Reitz, 3b
Thompson, cf
Blackwell, c
Reuschel, p

Writers started saying that this was the worst team in baseball since World War II, that the whole organization was inept and that Bowie Kuhn should do something about it. Could the Cubs get help from their AAA farm team in Iowa? The Oaks were in last place. How about the AA team in Midland? On April 13, Midland lost to San Antonio, 34-8. Sending Barry Foote to the Yankees for Tim Filer and money was not the answer.

Those fans who continued to come to Wrigley Field took to wearing false noses, eyebrows, and glasses so as not to be recognized. By May 4 the Cubs had managed three wins in eighteen games. Two weeks later they were 5-25.

Bob Kennedy was quoted as saying, "What difference does it make if I finish fourth, fifth, or sixth? I can't put a winner in here this year or next year either." Cub fans will tolerate most anything but not a denial that there was even a chance for the Cubs to come back. On May 22, Wrigley announced that Kennedy had been fired. His five year plan was a flop. And his trades made ex-Cubs out of Madlock, Trillo, Scott, Davis, and Sutter among others. Incredibly enough, Kennedy's replacement was none other than Herman Franks, who had left the Cubs with a bad taste in 1979. Fans appeared wearing T-shirts saying "Cub Fever — Catch It and Die" and carrying signs reading "Double your pleasure, double your fun; sell the Cubs in '81."

Meanwhile on the field, the Cubs kept trying. In their thirty-third game Randy Martz pitched their first complete game of the season — and won. On June 4, Franks acquired Bobby Bonds from Wichita. He broke his little finger in the first inning of his first game as a Cub. A series between the Cubs and the Mets was billed by writer Mike Downey as "a blind date between two ugly people." Couldn't something short of nuclear war wipe the season out, clean the slate, wake the Cubs from this bad dream?

Yes.

On June 12, the Players Union announced that they could not reach agreement with the owners over the matter of compensation to a team losing a player to free agency. The strike was on. A few hours before the strike began, Franks dealt Rich Reuschel to the Yankees for pitcher Doug Bird, $400,000, and a player to be named later (who turned out to be pitcher Mike Griffin). Cub fans were irate. Reuschel, 129-121 in nine years as a Cub, was sad to leave Chicago.

But the surprises were not yet over. On June 16 came the shocking news that William Wrigley had agreed to sell his 81 percent of the Cubs stock to the Tribune Company, the holding company of the *Chicago Tribune* and WGN radio and TV. The news caught everyone by surprise. It meant the end of a sixty-six year association between the Wrigley family and the Cubs, sixty years of which the Wrigley family was majority stockholder. William Wrigley, beset by inheritance tax problems, wanted to sell to a new owner who would keep the Cubs in Chicago and provide the support necessary to make them winners. He did not seek bidders to top the Tribune offer. Negotiations were handled for the Tribune Company by Andrew W. McKenna, a highly respected businessman who had helped save the White Sox for Chicago by inducing Bill Veeck to buy them. As recently as February of 1981, McKenna had been Chairman of the White Sox Board of Directors. Now he was to be Chairman of the Cubs' Board. The sale was big news even if league approval and financial closing would not be achieved for several months. It was material for fantasies. Imagine the Cubs loading their guns with free agents while they improved their farm system!

As the strike dragged on, it looked like the whole season would be lost. As a settlement finally neared, the commissioner's office decreed that the season would be divided into two halves. Each team would start the second half with a clean slate and a chance at a berth in post season playoffs for division titles. A Cub fan's dream! Two chances in one season.

The Cubs opened the second half as they had the first, with the Mets and with a loss. But subsequently, they showed real improvement, especially in pitching. By the end of August they were 11-9, only two games out of first. They stayed within three games of first through September and at season's end were 23-28, six games behind Montreal. They even beat the Pirates out of fifth place by three and one-half games. Of course if one added both halves of the season the Cubs were 38-61, dead last, twenty-one and one-half out. Only Toronto with thirty-seven wins won fewer than the Cubs. Woeful statistics. Team batting poorest in the League at .236. Team pitching, eleventh, with an ERA of 4.01. Attendance of 565,655 in fifty-nine dates, down an average of more

than 5,000 per home date from 1980. Bright spots? Buckner
with a .311 average, seventy-six RBIs, and thirty-five doubles.
Durham at .290; Henderson at .293; Jody Davis showing real
promise.

As Cub fans watched the mini-playoffs, playoffs, and
World Series on TV, they saw nineteen former Cubs in action. Patience wore thin, the fans awaited word from Chairman McKenna that the "World's Greatest Newspaper" had
intentions of fielding the world's greatest baseball team. Even
before the playoffs between the Phillies and Montreal, word
was out that Phillies Manager Dallas Green, who preferred
the front office to the field, was going to be the Cubs' new
general manager. McKenna had set high qualifications for the
job — playing experience, managerial experience, and a
successful record in developing a farm system. According to
one story, McKenna was paging through the Blue Book,
which lists the executives of all major league clubs, when
suddenly he yelled, "Gangbusters! I've found the man for the
job." On October 15, Dallas Green accepted a five-year contract. Green had the reputation of being an incredibly hard-
working, hard-nosed, but fair person.

Dallas Green came aboard with few if any illusions, but he
soon admitted that the situation was even worse than he
imagined. Assessing the front office, he said, "Let's face it,
there is no public relations and no marketing." Evaluating the
team, he commented "there are some decent players here —
not all twenty-five, but some are decent." And he was flabbergasted to find that in the farm system there was no
pitching and no speed. "How much effort does it take to push
a stopwatch?" he wondered aloud.

Green wasted no time cleaning house. He appointed Phillies coach Lee Elia as manager and named Billy Connors,
Gordon McKenzie, and George Vukovich as coaches. Personnel changes throughout the front office and farm system
came swiftly. Veteran writer Dave Condon came away from
Green's first press conference with the feeling that "Dallas

Green would assemble an organization making the old Dick Daley political machine look like an also-ran."

The new general manager also wrote a letter to all Cub players, and he made it clear that henceforth nothing less than all-out effort by every Cub would be acceptable. No more being out of condition, making bonehead plays, or blaming failure on day baseball. He promised to pay well those who play well.

The Cubs were the most active traders at the winter meetings. Green signed reliever Bill Campbell and Cub great Fergie Jenkins as free agents. Then he sent Mike Krukow and a player to be named later to the Phillies for Keith Moreland, Dickie Noles, and Dan Larsen. Later he swapped steady Ivan DeJesus to the Phillies for Larry Bowa and rookie prospect Ryne Sandberg. Observers agreed that the Cubs were considerably strengthened by these moves. The new Cubs leaders will not try to trade and buy themselves into a pennant. Fans can watch the farm system and sing "I'll get by" while the stars develop. In the meantime, the Cubs will be feistier, hungrier, and more peopled with gamers than they have been in a long time.

Green warned that he is not the messiah Cub fans have waited for. Well, maybe not. But his intensity, the freedom he enjoys under Andy McKenna, and the Tribune's willingness to pay the price for talent are enough to change the quality of a Cub fan's optimism from vain hope to realistic expectation. He can't change everything in a year. But I'll bet Ransom Jackson's autograph that the Cubs will win it all in 1984. We are ready. We are ready. Go Cubs!

Chapter Eight:
Games to Remember

Between 1948 and 1979, the Cubs played 5,064 games. Some stand in our memory as thrilling come-from-behind victories, some as painful, blooper-ridden nightmares that are much better left forgotten. But somehow or other, the Cubs have always managed to entertain, to surprise, and to delight the fans, even if the frustration level rises and falls along with the excitement. Of those thirty-two years of ups and downs, the following sixteen games have been selected as the Games to Remember. *The list includes fourteen wins and two losses. OK, OK, it's not representative of their overall won-lost record over the years. But it does represent the kind of excitement the Chicago Cubs have given us. Games to remember — they make up for those to forget.*

The Homer in the Glove

April 30, 1949

Cub pitcher Bob Rush may not remember how many times he went into the last inning or two with a one-run lead and ended up losing a game, thanks to an error by an outfielder. But surely he remembers this game. Perhaps he even wakes from a dream now and then yelling, "Throw the damned thing, Andy!"

On this particular April Saturday, a near-capacity crowd of over 30,000 fans had made their way to Wrigley Field to see the Cubs take on the archrival St. Louis Cardinals. Rush was pitching one of his best games that year and had allowed only two hits up until the sixth inning. In the ninth, with a 3-1 Cub score, Rush opened the inning by fanning Stan the Man Musial. But Enos Slaughter slaughtered the next pitch with a double. Rush threw out Ron Northey at first for the second out of the inning, while Slaughter held at second. But then Eddie Kazak (.304 that season) singled on the next pitch, scoring Slaughter and bringing the score to 3-2. The next batter was twenty-four-year-old rookie, Rocky Nelson, who lined Rush's fastball out to center field. Andy Pafko raced in at full speed and speared the ball as he made a somersault dive. As he rolled himself upright, he lifted the glove high to show the ball to the cheering crowd. Running back to the infield he was suddenly shocked to see the second-base umpire Al Barlick signal *no catch*. The ball was safe and still in play, but Pafko was totally incredulous. While he raced in to argue, Chuck Diering, pinch-running for Kazak, scored, and Nelson was racing around the bases unchallenged. Just before Nelson reached home plate, Pafko desperately threw the ball in, but it popped out of the catcher's glove, and Nelson scored the winning run. The crowd was furious, but no amount of hooting, debris-throwing, or cap-hurling would faze the cool-as-a-cucumber Barlick.

Nelson was credited with a homer in Andy's glove, and when the frazzled Cubs failed to score in the bottom of the ninth, the Cardinals became the 4-3 winners. The next day's sport headlines said, "Umpire Catches It Because He Said Pafko Didn't." Losing pitcher — Bob Rush.

St. Louis	ab	h	o	a	Chicago	ab	h	o	a
Schoendienst, 2b	4	1	2	2	Walker, rf	3	1	1	0
Marion, ss	4	0	1	3	a. Burgess	1	0	0	0
Musial, cf, rf	4	1	2	0	Jeffcoat, rf	1	0	0	0
Slaughter, lf	4	1	3	0	Lowrey, lf	3	1	3	0
Northey, rf	4	0	2	0	Cavarretta, 1b	2	0	15	2
Glaviano, 3b	0	0	1	0	Pafko, cf	3	0	0	0
Kazak, 3b	4	2	0	2	Gustine, 3b	3	2	1	1
Nelson, 1b	4	1	9	1	Scheffing, c	3	1	4	0
Diering, cf	0	0	1	0	Smalley, ss	3	0	0	5
Garagiola, c	4	1	5	1	Verban, 2b	3	0	1	2
Boyer, p	0	0	0	0	Rush, p	3	0	2	6
Hearn, p	3	0	1	2	c. A. Walker	1	0	0	0
b. H. Rice	1	0	0	0					
Wilks, p	0	0	0	0					
Totals	36	7	27	11	Totals	29	5	27	16

```
St. Louis ..................................000  000  013 — 4
Chicago ...................................200  010  000 — 3
```

a. struck out for H. Walker in 6th. b. flied out for Hearn in 8th. c. flied out for Rush in 9th. R — Slaughter, Diering, Garagiola, Nelson, H. Walker, Lowrey 2. E — Smalley. RBI — Lowrey, Gustine 2, Schoendienst, Kazak, Nelson 2. 2B — H. Walker, Lowrey, Garagiola, Slaughter. HR — Nelson. BB — Boyer 3, Hearn 4. SO — Hearn 4, Rush, 4. Winner — Wilks, Loser — Rush. A — 10,228

A Manager's Dream

July 29, 1951

Exactly one week after replacing Frankie Frisch as manager of the Cubs, thirty-four-year-old Phil Cavarretta had a day he would later describe as "my greatest day in baseball." The Cubs were up against the Phillies for a Sunday doubleheader, and things didn't look very promising. Phillies pitchers had just recorded four consecutive shutouts. The Cubs hadn't scored a run themselves over a span of thirty-one innings. And the pitcher for the Phils was Bubba Church, who had beaten the Cubs eight straight times.

But never fear. In the first game Phil put himself in the lineup at first base and drove in three runs with a triple and a sacrifice fly to give the Sunday crowd of 25,840 Wrigley Field patrons a thrilling 5-4 victory. Could they repeat it? Game number 2 (statistics below). Cavarretta let Chuck Connors play first base, and Connors capitalized on the opportunity by making three hits in four trips to the plate, including a double, an RBI, and a stolen base. But the Phillies were also scoring. The Cubs got a rally going in the bottom of the seventh to tie the score at 4-4 with two men on and two out. The Phillies chose to walk Smoky Burgess to get to the pitcher, Dutch Leonard. With the bases loaded and two out, the new Cub manager made his move. Cavarretta had never hit a grand-slam home run in his career. But he did this time. He pulled a Robin Roberts fastball into the right-field bleachers to give the Cubs a lead they would hold for their second victory of the day. The rookie manager had found the player to spark the Cubs' attack. Good show, Phil.

Philadelphia	ab	h	o	a
Waitkus, 1b	5	1	8	1
Ashburn, cf	5	0	1	0
Jones, 3b	3	0	0	3
Ennis, rf, lf	5	2	1	0
Sisler, lf	3	0	0	0
Nicholson, rf	1	0	1	0
Hamner, ss	4	1	1	5
Pellagrini, 2b	2	0	2	0
Cabullero, 2b	1	1	2	2
Wilber, c	3	2	7	1
Thompson, p	3	0	1	0
Church, p	0	0	0	0
Roberts, p	0	0	0	0
Hansen, p	0	0	0	0
c. Brown	1	1	0	0
Totals	36	8	24	12

Chicago	ab	h	o	a
Miksis, 2b	5	1	3	3
Jeffcoat, rf	4	0	1	0
Baumholtz, cf	4	1	1	0
Sauer, lf	4	0	1	0
Jackson, 3b	3	2	1	2
Smalley, ss	4	0	3	3
Connors, 1b	4	3	8	2
Owen, c	2	1	6	1
Burgess, c	0	0	0	0
Rush, p	2	2	1	4
a. Ramazzotti	1	1	0	0
Leonard, p	0	0	1	0
b. Cavarretta	1	1	0	0
Hatten, p	0	0	1	0
Dubiel, p	0	0	0	0
Totals	34	12	27	15

Philadelphia .... 1 0 0   0 0 3   0 1 1 — 6
Chicago .... 0 2 0   0 0 0   6 0 X — 8

Pitchers

Chicago	IP	H	SO	BB
Rush	6	5	5	3
Leonard (W 9-3)	1	0	0	0
Hatten	1⅔	3	0	1
Dubiel	⅓	0	0	0
Philadelphia				
Thompson	6⅓	9	5	4
Church (L 11-6)	⅓	2	1	1
Roberts	⅓	1	0	0
Hansen	1	0	0	0

a. singled for Rush in 6th. b. homered for Leonard in 7th. c. homered for Hansen in 9th. R — Ashburn, Jones, Ennis, Sisler, Hamner, Brown, Baumholtz, Sauer, Jackson, Connors 2, Owen, Burgess, Cavarretta. E — Miksis, Wilber, Thompson, Connors. RBI — Ennis, Owen, Hamner 2, Wilber 2, Jackson, Connors, Cavarretta 4, Brown. 2B — Waitkus, Baumholtz, Connors. HR — Cavarretta, Brown. SB — Connors, Jones. DP — 1 each team. Left on base — Philadelphia 7, Chicago 8. HP — Thompson (Baumholtz). T — 2:28. A — 25,840.

A Solid Gold Toothpick
May 12, 1955

A no-hitter at Wrigley Field? Not over a period of thirty-eight years. Back in 1917, in the famous double no-hitter between Fred Toney of the Reds and Jim "Hippo" Vaughn of the Cubs, Vaughn was finally touched for two hits in the tenth and the Cubs lost, 1-0. But on May 12, 1955, the smallest crowd of the season, 2,918, braved 53° weather to see a game against the Pirates and were gifted with the sight of baseball history.

Sam Jones was a 6'4" fastball pitcher with less than pinpoint control. This season, and the next, he would go on to lead the league in walks, and in strikeouts. He threw hard. "Nervous" might describe an opposing batter stepping into the box to look at this tall, big-nosed black man, chewing on a toothpick, waiting to throw a hummer somewhere near the plate. Shortly before the game, TV announcer Harry Creighton had joked with "Toothpick" about his trademark, promising him a gold tooth-pick if Jones pitched a no-hitter. Seven innings later, Creighton was making phone calls because Jones had been going through the Pirate lineup in good form. He had scattered four walks, but two of those runners had been wiped out in double plays.

Six outs to go. Then, in the eighth, George Freese hit a drive deep to center field, but Eddie Miksis raced back to make a leaping one-handed catch. That should have been drama enough. But the ninth inning was yet to come. Jones, perhaps tightening up from pitching in the cold, completely lost his control. He walked the eighth man in the Pirate lineup, walked a pinch-hitter for the pitcher, and then walked the lead-off man. Cub manager Stan Hack had a tough decision. The Cubs had a four-run lead, but the Pirates were now into the heart of their batting order with no one out. He decided to give Jones one more mistake. But he had to settle Jones down first; when he walked out to the mound he was booed, and when he returned to the bench he was cheered. His advice to Jones? Simple. "Get the ball over. That's all." Jones did. Dick Groat struck out on three pitches. Roberto Clemente, in his rookie year, struck out on five pitches. Frank Thomas on four. Twelve pitches, nine strikes and baseball immortality.

Jones confessed later that he hadn't been aware of the no-hitter until his teammates swarmed out to congratulate him. "I was just out there throwing fastballs and curves. Clyde (McCullough) deserves all the credit. I just kept throwing what he told me." The gold toothpick? Oh yes, in the locker room Creighton kept his promise and presented a gold toothpick to the first black player to pitch a no-hitter in the history of major league baseball.

Pittsburgh	ab	r	h	o	a	e	Chicago	ab	r	h	o	a	e
Saffel, cf	3	0	0	4	0	0	Miksis, cf	4	0	2	3	0	0
Groat, ss	4	0	0	2	0	0	Baker, 2b	3	1	1	2	3	0
Clemente, rf	4	0	0	1	0	0	Speake, lf	5	0	1	1	0	0
Thomas, 1b	4	0	0	2	0	0	King, lf	0	0	0	0	0	0
Long, 1b	0	0	0	5	1	0	Jackson, 3b	4	0	2	3	4	0
G. Freese, 3b	3	0	0	0	1	0	T. Tappe, rf	5	2	2	1	0	0
Atwell, c	2	0	0	4	2	0	Banks, ss	4	0	3	1	3	0
E. Freese, 2b	2	0	0	5	2	0	Fondy, 1b	4	1	2	9	2	0
King, p	0	0	0	0	0	0	McCullough, c	4	0	0	6	1	0
a. Montemayor	1	0	0	0	0	0	Jones, p	4	0	2	1	1	0
Law, p	1	0	0	1	3	0							
b. Ward	0	0	0	0	0	0							
c. Mejias	0	0	0	0	0	0							
Totals	24	0	0	24	9	0	Totals	37	4	15	27	14	0

```
Pittsburgh .............................. 000  000  000 — 0
Chicago    .............................. 110  010  10X — 4
```

a. struck out for King in 3rd. b. walked for Lawin in 9th. c. ran for Ward in 9th. RBI — T. Tappe 2, Miksis, Banks. 2B — T. Tappe. SB — Fondy, Miksis, Baker. SH — Miksis, Baker. DP — Banks, Baker and Fondy, Jackson and Fondy. LOB — Pittsburgh 4, Chicago 13. BB — King 1, Law 1, Jones 7. SO — King 2, Law 2, Jones 6. H — King 5 in 2 innings, Law 10 in 6. R and ER — King 2-2, Law 2-2. WP — Jones, Winner — Jones (4-3). Loser — King (1-1). U — Gore, Donatelli, Dixon, and Conlan. T — 2:38. A — 2,918.

The Day Dick Drott Owned Wrigley Field
May 26, 1957

The Milwaukee Braves were on their way to the 1957 pennant. But on this day, more than 32,000 fans would see them lose twice to the rampaging Cubs and fall into third place. The fans would also be able to see Dick Drott pitch the finest game of his career and set a modern Cub strikeout record in the process. After winning the first game, the Cubs gave their twenty-year-old rookie a quick three-run lead to begin the second game. Another four in the seventh seemed certain to be enough as Drott moved through the Milwaukee lineup. At the end of five innings he had already struck out ten Braves, mixing his fastball with a sharply breaking sidearm curve. Three more strikeouts would be enough to equal the Cub mark of thirteen shared by Lon Warneke and Sam Jones. Seven more would give him a share of the league mark with Dizzy Dean. But things got complicated. After eight innings, the score had moved to 7-3, and the umpires were conferring to discuss calling the game because of darkness. The fans were furious. They got their ninth inning only to see Drott give up two more runs and face the tying run at the plate. When manager Bob Scheffing came out to talk to his young pitcher, it was clear what the fans wanted him to do. He did, slapping Drott on the back and letting him pitch. Four pitches later Billy Bruton had become strikeout victim number fifteen to end the ball game.

It was a stunning performance. Drott managed to strike out every Brave regular at least once and whiffed the eventual MVP, Henry Aaron, as well as Billy Bruton three times each, and Del Crandall twice. Drott went on to a 15-11 season with this .403 Cub team, finishing second with teammate Moe Drabowsky in the strikeout derby. His career was then ruined by arm problems, and this game in this season is how the fans remember him.

Milwaukee	ab	h	o	a		Chicago	ab	h	o	a
Bruton, cf	5	0	4	2		Morgan, 2b	3	0	0	2
Cole, 2b	3	0	5	2		Banks, 3b	4	3	0	0
b. Torre	1	0	0	0		Speake, lf	2	1	3	0
Murff, p	0	0	0	0		Long, 1b	3	2	6	0
Matthews, 3b	4	2	0	2		Moryn, rf	3	2	0	0
Aaron, rf	4	0	2	0		Walls, rf	0	0	0	0
Adcock, 1b	4	0	6	1		Bolger, cf	4	1	2	0
Mantilla, ss,2b	4	0	1	2		Neeman, c	4	1	15	0
Tanner, lf	3	2	0	0		Littrell, ss	4	1	1	1
Crandall, c	4	1	6	1		Drott, p	4	1	0	2
Conley, p	1	0	0	1						
Phillips, p	1	0	0	1						
a. Logan, ss	2	2	0	1						
Totals	36	7	24	13		Totals		31	12	27	5

```
Milwaukee . . . . . . . . . . . . . . . . . . . . . . . . . . . . . . .0 1 0   0 0 0   0 2 2 — 5
Chicago . . . . . . . . . . . . . . . . . . . . . . . . . . . . . .3 0 0   0 0 0   4 0 X — 7
```

Pitchers	IP	H	R	ER	BB	SO
Chicago						
Drott (W 3-4)	9	7	5	4	1	15
Milwaukee						
Conley (L 0-2)	2	5	3	3	3	0
Phillips	5	6	4	4	1	3
Murff	1	1	0	0	0	1

a. tripled for Phillips in 8th. b. grounded out for Cole in 8th. R—Bruton, Tanner 2, Crandall, Logan, Morgan, Banks, Speake, Long 2, Moryn, Littrell. E — Moryn, Mantilla, Aaron, Drott. RBI — Speake, Moryn 3, Tanner, Banks 2, Matthews, Crandall 2. 2B — Banks, Long 2, Tanner. 3B — Logan. HR — Moryn, Tanner, Banks, Crandall. SH — Moryn. SF — Speake. DP — Bruton and Cole. LOB — Milwaukee 5, Chicago 6. T — 2:27. A — 32,127.

Earl Averill's TV Guide
May 12, 1959

Before May of 1959, Earl Averill, Jr., had seen Milwaukee Braves pitcher Lou Burdette in action only during the 1959 World Series telecast. But Averill had a keen eye. Having played at every baseball position (except pitcher) himself, his time with the Pacific Coast League had sharpened his ability to appreciate the subtle qualities that distinguish fine ball players. It was reflected in his play — he was voted Most Valuable Player in that league and the following year had signed with the Cubs. But he kept watching. And studying.

On May 12, the Cubs were in a typical Bert Wilson position in a game with the Braves: the bottom of the ninth, one man out, score 3-2 for Milwaukee. When Burdette hung a curve, Walt Moryn blasted his fourth homer of the season. The Cubs then loaded the bases with two outs, and Averill was ready when manager Bob Scheffing called him to pinch-hit for Don Elston. "I had been watching Burdette from the dugout all through the game," he said. "It looked like everything he was throwing was dropping and only occasionally did he throw a fast one. I hadn't seen him before except on TV during the World Series. I went up there looking for nothing in particular and just swung." Burdette worked a one-ball, two-strike count on Averill, then wound up, pitched, and turned to walk off the field, certain that he had just thrown strike three. Then the plate umpire, Ed Sudol, called it a ball, and Burdette returned, glowering at Sudol. Lew pitched again. And Earl swung one more time, this one connecting for a grand-slam home run over the left-field wall. "It was the most satisfying hit of my career," Averill acknowledged in later years. The Cubs had pulled it out. Final score: 7-3.

Milwaukee	ab	h	o	a		Chicago	ab	h	o	a
Bruton, cf	5	1	3	0		T. Taylor, 2b	3	1	2	3
Matthews, 3b	4	1	0	0		c. Marshall	1	0	0	0
Aaron, rf	5	2	3	0		Goryl, 2b	0	0	0	0
Covington, lf	4	1	3	0		Dark, 3b	4	0	1	6
Torre, 1b	4	0	9	0		Banks, ss	3	0	2	1
Crandall, c	3	1	3	0		Moryn, lf	4	2	2	0
Logan, ss	3	1	1	9		Long, 1b	4	2	9	1
O'Brien, 2b	3	2	3	1		d. King	0	0	0	0
a. Mantilla, 2b	1	0	1	0		Thomson, cf	4	1	3	0
Burdette, p	4	0	0	2		Walls, rf	3	0	3	0
						S. Taylor, c	4	0	4	0
						Anderson, p.	2	1	1	0
						b. Altman	1	0	0	0
						Elston, p	0	0	0	0
						e. Averill	1	1	0	0
Totals	36	9	26	12		Totals	34	8	27	11

```
Milwaukee...............................0 1 0   1 1 0   0 0 0 — 3
Chicago ................................0 0 0   1 0 1   0 0 5 — 7
```

Pitchers	IP	H	R	ER	BB	SO
Milwaukee						
Burdette (L 5-2)	8⅔	8	7	6	2	3
Chicago						
Anderson	8	7	3	3	4	3
Elson (W 1-1)	1	2	0	0	0	1

a. grounded out for O'Brien in 8th. b. popped out for Anderson in 8th. c. flied out for T. Taylor in 8th. d. ran for Long in 9th. e. homered for Elston in 9th. R — Matthews, Crandall, Logan, T. Taylor, Moryn, Thomson, Walls, S. Taylor, Anderson, Averill. E — Logan. RBI — Matthews, Crandall, Logan, T. Taylor, Banks, Moryn, Averill 4. 2B — Anderson, Long. HR — Crandall, Logan, T. Taylor, Matthews, Moryn, Averill. DP — Logan, O'Brien and Torre. LOB — Milwaukee 10, Chicago 3. Balk — Anderson. U — Sudol, Gorman, Boggess, and Landes. T — 2:24. A — 8,288.

Don Cardwell's Debut

May 15, 1960

Welcome to the Cubs, Don Cardwell. On May 6, pitching as a Phillie, Cardwell had hurled six innings of no-hit ball, but the prize had eluded him. Now, as a Cub, with his clothes still stuffed in a Phillies overnight bag, Cardwell would successfully make his claim to fame.

Coach El Tappe might have guessed something was going to happen by the size of his swollen hand after warming up Cardwell before the game. Cub catcher Del Rice had never worked with Cardwell, so they had agreed to work primarily with the fastball while Rice adjusted to the curve. In fact, he didn't throw a slider in the entire game. "Fastballs did it for me. I threw almost all fastballs in the early innings . . . . I just wanted to hum."

Hum he did. The Cardinals' second batter, Alex Grammas, reached on a walk and that was it. Cardwell retired the next twenty-six hitters. But not without plenty of drama for the 33,543 fans at Wrigley Field. By the eighth inning, the tension was tremendous. And when Daryl Spencer led off with a hot smash toward second, everyone held his breath. Jerry Kindall made an excellent play, and people could breathe again. But not for long. In the ninth inning, the fans were on their feet to cheer Cardwell home. The Cards sent up Carl Sawatski to bat for Hal Smith. On a one-ball, two-strike pitch, Sawatski lined a long drive to right field. Altman raced back to grab it with a leaping one-handed catch at the wall. One out. George Crowe, pinch-hitting for Lindy McDaniel, came to the plate. After two pitches missed, Del Rice went to the mound to talk with Cardwell, who then threw a called strike. On the next pitch, Crowe flied to Ashburn in center. Two out. Now the batter was Joe Cunningham. The count went to 3 and 1. Then a called strike made it a full count. Then, bango. Cunningham drilled the next pitch on a line to short left field. It looked like a sure hit, but Moose Moryn came charging like a gazelle and made a sensational one-handed shoestring catch. The crowd's anxiety was relieved. It went wild. Andy Frain, whose ushers had held the crowds in check at Wrigley since 1930, said that what followed was the most tumultuous celebration ever seen at Cubs park. It took Cardwell twenty minutes to make his way through the fans into the clubhouse. "This fame may mean I'll never pitch again because while all the fans were crowding around me they kept standing there beating on my shoulder and pulling on my arm like they wanted a souvenir — me!" he said. "But it was worth it!"

It sure was, Don.

St. Louis	ab	h	o	a	Chicago	ab	h	o	a
Cunningham, rf	4	0	0	0	Ashburn, cf	3	2	2	0
Grammas, ss	1	0	1	4	Altman, rf	4	1	3	0
a. Shannon, 2b	1	0	0	0	Bouchee, 1b	4	0	11	0
White, 1b, cf	3	0	10	0	Banks, ss	4	1	0	3
Boyer, 3b	3	0	2	4	Moryn, lf	3	0	4	0
Spencer, 2b, ss	3	0	2	2	Thomas, 3b	3	1	0	1
Wagner, lf	3	0	1	0	Zimmer, 3b	0	0	0	0
Flood, cf	2	0	1	0	Rice, c	3	1	7	0
b. Musial, 1b	1	0	2	0	Kindall, 2b	3	1	0	4
Smith, c	2	0	5	2	Cardwell, p	3	0	0	2
c. Sawatski	1	0	0	0					
McDaniel, p	2	0	0	2					
d. Crowe	1	0	0	0					
Totals	27	0	24	14	Totals	30	7	27	10

```
St. Louis ...................................0 0 0   0 0 0   0 0 0 — 0
Chicago  ...................................0 0 0   0 1 2   1 0 X — 4
```

Pitchers	IP	H	R	ER	BB	SO
St. Louis						
McDaniel (L 1-2)	8	7	4	4	3	5
Chicago						
Cardwell (W 2-2)	9	0	0	0	1	7

a. flied out for Grammas in 7th. b. struck out for Flood in 8th. c. lined out for Smith in 9th. d. flied out for McDaniel in 9th. R — Ashburn, Banks, Thomas, Kindall. E — none. RBI — Ashburn, Banks 2, Kindall. 2B — Altman. HR — Banks. SB — Kindall. LOB — St. Louis 1, Chicago 4. WP — McDaniel. U — Venzon, Dascoli, Secory, Crawford. T — 1:46. A — 33,543.

Down with the Dodgers
May 23, 1965

The drama was cumulative. It just kept building and building during the four hours it took to play the longest game of the year. It started out simply enough. The Dodgers pounced on Cub starter Bob Buhl for two quick runs in the first inning. And Johnny Podres was pitching well for the Dodgers. A homer by Ron Santo in the sixth was Podres' only mistake over seven innings. But Buhl had settled down, and the zeros began to appear on the scoreboard.

With Santo's blast, the Cubs were only one run down, and it seemed inevitable that they would get it. But they didn't in the seventh, nor in the eighth off Stu Miller, now pitching for Podres, who had been lifted for a pinch-hitter. And all the time, Cub pitching was shutting out the Dodgers. Buhl had been lifted for a pinch-hitter and adequately replaced by Ted Abernathy. Between them, they had held the Dodgers to six hits through nine innings. Now it was the Cubs' ninth. Miller pitched too carefully to Santo and gave him the first Cub walk of the afternoon. Ernie Banks then doubled to move Santo to third and set up Doug Clemens' sacrifice fly. The game was tied but not yet won.

Over the next six innings, the Cubs and Dodgers would have their chance as the tension continued to build. Almost every inning found a base runner, but no run. Lindy McDaniel for the Cubs put five men on over five innings, but kept the Dodgers scoreless by striking out eight. Perranoski and Brewer put five Cubs on during their six shutout innings. One of those Cubs was Roberto Pena, who led off the twelfth. Lindy McDaniel came to bat and everyone in the park knew he would try to bunt Pena to second. Manager Walter Alston was so sure of it that he employed an old Branch Rickey idea and used a five-man infield, bringing his rightfielder Ron Fairly in to play first base to hold Pena close and positioning first-baseman Wes Parker between first and home. The sacrifice failed.

In the sixteenth inning, Banks greeted new Dodger pitcher Howie Reed with a one-out double. Pitching to Clemens, Reed then threw a wild pitch, sending Banks to third. Alston elected to fill the bases to get the force at home and to the bottom of the Cub lineup. Cub manager Bob Kennedy sent George Altman in to bat for Pena, and every pitch became a nightmare of nerves as Altman kept his cool to work Reed for a game-ending walk. A tremendously gutsy pitching duel at Wrigley Field, which saw the Cubs staff hold on for fifteen shutout innings.

Los Angeles	ab	r	h	rbi	Chicago	ab	r	h	rbi
Wills, ss	7	1	2	0	Landrum, cf	7	0	1	0
Parker, 1b	6	0	1	0	Beckert, 2b	7	0	0	0
W. Davis, cf	7	1	3	0	Williams, lf	7	0	1	0
Fairly, rf	6	0	2	1	Santo, 3b	6	2	2	1
Roseboro, c	7	0	1	0	Banks, 1b	6	1	3	0
Lefebvre, 2b	5	0	1	0	Clemens, rf	4	0	0	1
Johnson, lf	7	0	0	0	Bertell, c	3	0	0	0
Tracewski, 3b	5	0	1	0	Stewart, ph	1	0	0	0
Podres, p	2	0	0	0	Roznovsky, c	2	0	0	0
Moon, ph	1	0	0	0	Pena, ss	5	0	2	0
Ferrara, ph	1	0	0	0	Altman, ph	0	0	0	1
Brewer, p	1	0	0	0	Buhl, p	2	0	0	0
Torborg, ph	1	0	0	0	Amalfitano, ph	1	0	0	0
					Gabriel, ph	1	0	0	0
					McDaniel, p	1	0	0	0
					Bright, ph	1	0	0	0
Totals	56	2	11	1	Totals	54	3	9	3

Los Angeles . . . . 2 0 0   0 0 0   0 0 0   0 0 0   0 0 0   0 — 2
Chicago . . . . 0 0 0   0 0 1   0 0 1   0 0 0   0 0 0   1 — 3

Pitching

Los Angeles	IP	H	R	ER	BB	SO
Podres	7	5	1	1	0	2
Miller	2	1	1	1	1	1
Perranoski	2	1	0	0	1	1
Brewer	4	1	0	0	2	3
Reed (L 1-1)	1/3	1	1	1	3	0
Chicago						
Buhl	7	5	2	2	2	1
Abernathy	2	1	0	0	0	3
McDaniel	5	3	0	0	2	8
Ellsworth (W 5-3)	2	2	0	0	1	1

E — Parker, Lefebvre, Wills. DP — Los Angeles 1. LOB — Los Angeles 13, Chicago 13. 2B — Fairly, Davis, Santo, Banks. HR — Santo (9). SB — Wills 2. SH — Podres, Parker. SE — Clemens. WP — McDaniel, Reed. T — 4:09. A — 17,139.

Wonderful Willie Smith

April 8, 1969

Opening day of the year that just might be the year for the Cubs. Things started out normally enough. Fans had been lining up all morning for unreserved grandstand seats. A total of 40,796 would fill the 36,000-seat ball park. Dignitaries on hand included Jimmy Durante, Gov. Richard Ogilvie, and Edgar Munzel, who threw out the first ball. Ernie Banks, with his seventy-three-year-old father up from Dallas for the game, received a standing ovation when he was introduced. He responded with a homer his first time up. And his second. A 500-homer season? Well, not quite, but it did look like the game would be an easy win for Fergie Jenkins. After three, it was Banks 5, Phils 1; after eight, 5-2.

Then things fell apart for a while. Don Money's second homer of the game was a three-run shot that knotted the score in the ninth and brought on Phil Regan for the Cubs. In the eleventh, it was Money again — this time with a double to score Johnny Callison. Cubs' last chance. With one out, Hundley got on, and Durocher played the percentages, letting Willie Smith bat for Hickman against the Phils' Randy Lersch. As Smith stepped to the plate, Durocher kept saying to Bill Hands in the dugout, "Just a dying quail over third, that's all I want." But that wasn't good enough for Hands, who replied, "The hell with that, Skip; he'll hit it out." And so he did. A shot into the right-field bleachers. Twenty-four players and dozens of hysterical fans mobbed Willie at home plate. The right kind of start for the most exciting Cub season since 1945.

Philadelphia	ab	r	h	rbi	Chicago	ab	r	h	rbi
Hisle, cf	5	1	1	0	Kessinger, ss	4	0	1	0
Stone, lf	4	0	0	0	Beckert, 2b	5	1	2	0
Allen, 1b	5	0	0	0	Williams, lf	4	1	1	0
Johnson, 3b	2	0	1	1	Santo, 3b	4	1	1	0
Taylor, 3b	3	0	0	0	Banks, 1b	5	2	3	5
Callison, rf	5	2	3	0	Hundley, c	5	1	1	0
Rojas, 2b	4	1	2	0	Hickman, rf	4	0	0	0
Money, ss	5	2	3	5	W. Smith, ph	1	1	1	2
Ryan, c	5	0	0	0	Young, cf	3	0	0	0
Short, p	1	0	0	0	Jenkins, p	2	0	1	0
Harmon, ph	1	0	1	0	Regan, p	1	0	0	0
Wilson, p	0	0	0	0					
Briggs, ph	1	0	0	0					
Lersch, p	2	0	0	0					
Totals	43	6	11	6	Totals	38	7	11	7

```
Philadelphia.....................1 0 0   0 0 0   1 0 3   0 1 — 6
Chicago..........................3 0 2   0 0 0   0 0 0   0 2 — 7
```

Pitchers	IP	H	R	ER	BB	SO
Philadelphia						
Short	4	6	5	5	2	0
Wilson	2	1	0	0	1	3
Lersch (L 0-1)	4⅓	4	2	2	0	1
Chicago						
Jenkins	8	9	5	5	0	9
Regan (W 1-0)	3	2	1	1	0	2

E — Jenkins, Banks, Johnson, Money. DP — Philadelphia 1. LOB — Philadelphia 6, Chicago 5. 2B — Money. HR — Money 2, Banks 2, W. Smith 1. SH — Stone, Kessinger, Rojas. HPB — By Short (Hundley). U — Venzon, Secory, Pryor and Davidson. T — 2:30. A — 40,796.

Mr. Cub Joins the 500 Club
May 12, 1970

Only 5,264 fans ignored the rain to come to Wrigley Field. They were the smart ones. The rain stopped, the clouds cleared, and in his first trip to the plate, Ernie Banks hit a Pat Jarvis curve into the left-field seats. The greatest Cub of them all had just joined the 500 home run club. Additionally, he had gained his 1,600th RBI.

In the seventh inning, he would drive in his 1,601st run to make the score Braves 3, Cubs 2. Would the Cubs lose on Mr. Cub's day? Not when Ernie's pal Billy Williams hit a Hoyt Wilhelm knuckler into the right-field stands. Two innings later, Kessinger, Beckert, Williams, and Santo would conspire for the winning run.

After the game Banks said, "Cub fans have been an inspiration to me." Of course, the truth is that Ernie had been an inspiration to the fans. He brought to our understanding of the game his integrity as an athlete. Ernie played. He carried his constant enthusiasm through nineteen years of Cub history, through all those losing seasons in the fifties, through the college of coaches, through the Durocher years. How much frustration, pain, disappointment there must have been. But that remained his, while he gave to Cub fans a constant insight into the joy of baseball. "What do you think, Dad, isn't this a great life?" he enthused to his shy, proud seventy-three-year-old father in the locker room after a winning game. The old gent just smiled and nodded.

Atlanta	ab	r	h	rbi	Chicago	ab	r	h	rbi
Jackson, ss	4	1	0	0	Kessinger, ss	5	1	3	0
Millan, 2b	5	1	1	0	Beckert, 2b	5	0	1	0
H. Aaron, rf	4	0	0	0	Williams, lf	4	1	1	1
Carty, lf	3	0	3	0	Santo, 3b	5	1	2	1
Garr, pr	0	0	0	0	Callison, rf	4	0	0	0
Wilhelm, p	0	0	0	0	Banks, 1b	3	1	1	2
King, ph	1	0	0	0	Hickman, cf	3	0	0	0
Priddy, p	0	0	0	0	Martin, c	2	0	0	0
Cepeda, 1b	4	0	0	0	Hall, ph	1	0	0	0
Boyer, 3b	4	1	2	0	Hiatt, c	1	0	1	0
Gonzalez, cf	4	0	0	0	Holtzman, p	2	0	0	0
Lum, ph, lf	1	0	0	0	Abernathy, p	0	0	0	0
Tillman, c	2	0	0	0	Smith, ph	1	0	0	0
Jarvis, p	3	0	0	0	Popovich, ph	1	0	0	0
Didier, c	1	0	0	0	Regan, p	0	0	0	0
Totals	36	3	6	0	Totals	37	4	9	4

```
Atlanta .............................2 0 0   0 0 0   1 0 0   0 0 — 3
Chicago .............................0 1 0   0 0 0   1 0 1   0 1 — 4
```

Pitchers

Atlanta	IP	H	R	ER	BB	SO
Jarvis	8	4	2	2	1	6
Wilhelm	2	2	1	1	0	2
Priddy (L 2-2)	0	3	1	1	1	0
Chicago						
Holtzman	8	5	3	2	3	4
Abernathy	2	1	0	0	0	0
Regan (W 2-0)	1	0	0	0	1	0

E — Martin. DP — Atlanta 1, Chicago 2. LOB — Atlanta 4, Chicago 6. 2B — Boyer, Santo. HR — Banks (3), Williams (12). SF — Banks. WP — Holtzman 3. U — Venzon, Secory, Engel, Wendelstadt. T — 2:45. A — 5,264.

Baffling Burt and the Knuckle Curve
September 15, 1971

The Met hitters had never seen a knuckle curve, and Hooton's was working to perfection. Cub hitters, on the other hand, were looking at Tug McGraw making his first start in over two years. They got to him in the first and third. Given this early lead, the hefty youngster went to work on the Met lineup. With two out in the seventh, the Mets still hadn't touched Hooton for a hit, and he was striking them out in clusters. Then Mike Jorgensen worked Hooton to a 3-1 pitch. End of no-hitter. Ken Singleton did the same except that he hit a homer instead of a single and gave the Mets a 2-2 tie. But Hooton was undaunted. In the eighth and ninth he gave up only one more hit while amassing for the game a total of fifteen strikeouts. Right. Those fifteen strikeouts put him in the company of that other golden-haired Cub rookie, Dick Drott.

Extra innings? Not with Billy Williams taking one of his rare rests. In the ninth Billy batted for Bill North and parked the ball into the stands. A kind of gift, you might say, to this superb young pitcher making Cub history while getting his first major-league victory.

Chicago	ab	r	h	rbi	New York	ab	r	h	rbi
James, cf	4	1	1	0	Martinez, ss	4	0	0	0
Fanzone, lf	4	1	1	0	Garrett, 3b	3	0	0	0
Davis, rf	0	0	0	0	Milner, lf	4	0	1	0
Popovich, 2b	4	0	2	1	Kranepool, 1b	4	0	0	0
Santo, 3b	4	0	2	1	Jorgensen, cf	4	1	1	0
Bourque, 1b	4	0	1	0	Singleton, rf	2	1	1	2
North, rf	3	0	0	0	Dyer, c	3	0	0	0
Williams, ph, lf	1	1	1	1	Foli, 2b	3	0	0	0
Torres, ss	4	0	1	0	McGraw, p	1	0	0	0
Rudolph, c	3	0	1	0	Marshall, ph	1	0	0	0
Hooton, p	4	0	0	0	Rose, p	0	0	0	0
					Jones, ph	1	0	0	0
					Frisella, p	0	0	0	0
Totals	35	3	10	3	Totals	30	2	3	2

```
Chicago ..................................101  000  001 — 3
New York ................................000  000  200 — 2
```

Pitchers

Chicago	IP	H	R	ER	BB	SO
Hooton (W 1-0)	9	3	2	2	2	15
New York						
McGraw	6	6	2	2	1	9
Rose	2	2	0	0	0	1
Frisella (L 7-5)	1	2	1	1	0	2

E — None. LOB — Chicago 6, New York 3. 2B — Fanzone, Rudolph, Torres. HR — Singleton (10), Williams (26). U — Barlick, Pryor, Kibler, Froemming. T — 2:18. A — 21,302.

Pappas Perfect . . . Almost

September 2, 1972

Milt Pappas woke up feeling miserable. He was scheduled to pitch, but the weather was cold and windy (17 mph), and generally 1972 had been a very depressing season for him. In spring training he had broken a finger. All season his elbow had been tight (he had had thirty shots of cortisone for it already). Some days he simply couldn't straighten it out, and today it was bothering him. In addition, he had been out nine days with a bad back earlier in the season, and it still wasn't right. And finally, he had had a nasty cold. He told his wife, Caroline, he was going to call in sick. She talked him out of it. It paid off.

The Cubs were up against the Padres, but perhaps it is better to say the Padres were up against Milt. Cooly and calmly he retired the first twenty-four Padres in order. When Pappas came to bat in the eighth inning, the crowd of 12,979 gave him a standing ovation. The Cubs, meanwhile, had racked up four of the eight runs they would eventually score against Mike Caldwell. The stage was set for the ninth. Pappas got the first two Padres. But against pinch-hitter Larry Stahl the count went to three and two. Milt threw the next pitch low and umpire Bruce Froemming called it that way. Later, Pappas said, "I was hoping he would sympathize with me and give me a call. But they were balls, no question about it." Froemming said, "The pitch was what we call a shoe-shiner." In disappointment, Pappas kicked the rubber and pounded his glove in disgust. He had almost become the twelfth pitcher in the ninety-seven year history of the league to pitch a perfect game. But there was still a no-hitter to worry about. Pappas maintained his cool and retired former Cub Gary Jestadt on a pop-up to end the game. He was mobbed by cheering teammates and fans.

Afterwards, Pappas remarked, "I always said I'd rather be lucky than good, and I was lucky today." Maybe so, but he was also good. Disappointing? No doubt. But also thrilling. As manager Whitey Lockman said after the game: "I've been in professional baseball thirty years, and this is the first time I've been on the winning side of a no-hitter. I couldn't believe the thrill. What a thrill. What a thrill."

San Diego	ab	r	h	rbi	e	Chicago	ab	r	h	rbi	e
Hernandez, ss	3	0	0	0	1	Kessinger, ss	5	1	2	3	0
Jestadt, ph	1	0	0	0	0	Cardenal, rf	4	1	2	1	0
Roberts, lf	3	0	0	0	0	Williams, lf	4	1	2	0	0
Lee, 3b	3	0	0	0	0	Santo, 3b	3	1	0	0	0
Colbert, 1b	3	0	0	0	0	Hickman, 1b	4	1	3	1	0
Gaston, rf	3	0	0	0	0	Fanzone, 2b	3	1	0	1	0
Thomas, 2b	3	0	0	0	0	Hundley, c	4	1	2	0	0
Jeter, cf	3	0	0	0	0	North, cf	4	1	2	1	0
Kendall, c	3	0	0	0	0	Pappas, p.	4	0	0	0	0
Caldwell, p	2	0	0	0	0						
Severinsen, p	0	0	0	0	0						
Stahl, ph	0	0	0	0	0						
Totals	27	0	0	0	1	Totals	35	8	13	7	0

```
San Diego .................................... 0 0 0   0 0 0   0 0 0 — 0
Chicago ...................................... 2 0 2   0 0 0   0 4 X — 8
```

Pitchers

San Diego	IP	H	R	ER	BB	SO
Caldwell (L 6-8)	7⅔	13	8	6	2	4
Severinsen	⅓	0	0	0	0	0
Chicago						
Pappas (W 12-7)	9	0	0	0	1	6

DP — San Diego 3. LOB — San Diego 1, Chicago 6. 2B — Hickman, Kessinger. HPB — By Caldwell (Santo). U — Froemming, Donatelli, Landes and Davidson. T — 2:03. A — 11,144.

Never-Say-Die Cubs

June 25, 1977

A crowd of 33,130 fans showed up at Old-Timers Day to have some fun. Then they watched the new-timers have just as much fun winning like the Cubs of old. Down 4-1 in the ninth, the Cubs decided to make their move. Swisher singled and held up at third when DeJesus doubled with one out. Biittner's double drove them both in and put the Cubs one run away. Buckner then hit a drive into the left-field alley that the wind caught and kept in the park for a Met to catch. But neither Lee Mazzilli nor Steve Henderson, with ten days experience in the majors, were as good as the wind. They caught each other, but not the ball. Buckner said, "When I hit it, I thought it might reach the wall. Then the wind took it in, and I saw both outfielders coming together, and I could only hope that they'd get mixed up." Sitting in the front row of the left-field bleachers leading the crowd in yells of "I got it!" was none other than old-timer Ernie Banks.

Kelleher ran for Buckner and moved to third when Murcer was walked intentionally and Morales unintentionally. Trillo at bat, bases loaded, one out. Manny hit a hot grounder to third-baseman Doug Flynn who bobbled it, stepped on third for one out, and threw to first too late to get Trillo for the final out. Having failed to force the double play allowed Kelleher's score from third to be the winning run. It might not have been pretty, but it was fun. Just ask an old-timer.

New York	ab	r	h	rbi		Chicago	ab	r	h	rbi
Mazzilli, cf	3	1	2	0		DeJesus, ss	4	1	1	0
Harrelson, ss	4	0	1			Biittner, lf	4	2	1	2
Boisclair, rf	4	0	0	0		Buckner, 1b	5	0	3	1
Stearns, c	4	2	3	0		Kelleher, pr	0	1	0	0
Milner, 1b	4	0	0	0		Murcer, rf	3	0	0	0
Kranepool, lf	4	1	1	2		Morales, cf	3	0	2	0
Flynn, 3b	0	0	0	0		Trillo, 2b	5	0	0	1
Youngblood, 3b	3	0	1	0		Ontiveros, 3b	4	0	1	0
H'rson, ph,lf	1	0	0	0		Swisher, c	3	1	1	0
Millan, 2b	4	0	2	0		Burris, p	3	0	1	0
Zachry, p	3	0	0	0		Gross, ph	1	0	0	0
Lockwood, p	1	0	0	0						
Apodaca, p	0	0	0	0						
Totals	35	4	10	2		Totals	35	5	10	4

```
New York ...............................0 2 1   0 0 0   0 1 0 — 4
Chicago .................................0 0 1   0 0 0   0 0 4 — 5
```

Pitchers						
New York	IP	H	R	ER	BB	SO
Zachry	7	6	1	1	5	8
Lockwood	1⅓	3	3	3	0	0
Apodaca (L 2-3)	⅓	1	1	1	2	0
Chicago						
Burris (W 9-6)	9	10	4	3	0	1

E — Burris, Buckner. DP — New York 1, Chicago 1. LOB — New York 5, Chicago 11. 2B — Stearns, Millan, Ontiveros, DeJesus, Biittner, Buckner. HR — Kranepool (8). HBP — By Burris (Mazzilli). Balk — Zachry. U — Weyer, A. Williams, Runge, Montague. T — 2:28. A — 33,130.

Cubs 16, Reds 15

July 2, 1977

Heroes? George Mitterwald, Dave Rosello, Bill Buckner, Rick Reuschel, etc. Records? Eleven home runs in a game, five home runs in the first inning; each tying major league highs. Surprises? Jose Cardenal and Bobby Murcer in the infield; Rick Reuschel in relief.

"It's the greatest game I've ever seen or played in," said Mitterwald, who had just caught his seventh game in five days. Tired? "I hit better when I'm tired." Fortunate for the Cubs. His homer in the twelfth inning, his second of the day, kept the game alive. Without it, Dave Rosello would have been goat instead of hero. In the top of the twelfth, Davey had let a throw get through him at second base enabling George Foster to score. But in the thirteenth he would get the hit to score surprise reliever Rick Reuschel with the winning run. Reuschel had just shut out the Reds on five hits two days before. But with two men on and only one out in the thirteenth, the Cubs went to him again. Tired? "No, I'm not tired from work. I'm tired from being so pumped up." The win pumped Reuschel's record to 15-3.

This crazy baseball game had started with a bang. Five to be exact. Pete Rose hit a lead-off homer. Johnny Bench hit a three-run shot and Mike Lum a two-run version of the same. But before the Cubs made an out, Bill Buckner had them back in the game with a three-run blast, followed immediately by Murcer's solo homer. And so it went. The Cubs had gained the lead and then lost it again to trail 14-10 in the eighth. Herman Franks pulled out all stops to get the Cubs back into the game. Buckner's second home run helped them get three runs in the inning, but they ran out of infielders. Enter Cardenal and Rosello for an inning. An error later, it was Murcer's turn. For the next four innings he switched with Rosello at short and second, depending on which side of the plate the hitter swung from.

And didn't the hitters swing in this game. All the starters got a hit or two or three or five. The teams scored thirty-one runs and still managed to leave thirty-one men on base. Excitement? Ask Rosello: "I've never been happier in my life."

Cincinnati	ab	r	h	rbi	Chicago	ab	r	h	rbi
Rose, 3b	6	1	2	1	DeJesus, ss	5	2	1	0
Griffey, rf	8	2	5	4	Cardenal, ph,				
Morgan, 2b	8	1	2	0	2b,ss,rf	2	0	0	0
Foster, lf	6	2	3	0	Biittner, lf	7	3	3	1
Bench, c	5	2	1	3	Buckner, 1b	8	2	2	5
Geronimo, cf	8	2	2	2	Murcer, rf,2b,ss	8	3	3	2
Concepc'n, ss	6	2	2	2	Morales, cf	6	1	2	1
Lum, 1b	5	3	2	2	Broberg, p	0	0	0	0
Murray, p	1	0	0	0	R. R'schel, p	1	1	1	0
Borbon, p	2	0	0	0	Ontiveros, 3b	6	0	3	2
A'brister, ph	1	0	0	0	Trillo, 2b	3	1	1	1
Sarmiento, p	1	0	0	0	Hernandez, p	0	0	0	0
Hoerner, p	0	0	0	0	Wallis, ph	1	0	0	0
Norman, p	0	0	0	0	Rosello, 2b	3	0	1	1
Summers, ph	1	0	0	0	Mitterwald, c	7	2	3	2
Billingham, p	0	0	0	0	Burris, p	1	1	1	0
					Moore, p	1	0	1	1
					P. R'schel, p	1	0	0	0
					Kelleher, 2b	1	0	0	0
					Gross, ph	0	0	0	0
					Sutter, p	1	0	1	0
					Clines, cf	1	0	1	0
Totals	58	15	19	14	Totals	63	16	24	16

```
Cincinnati . . . . . . . . . . . . . . . . . . . . . 6 0 4   0 0 1   2 1 0   0 0 1   0 — 15
Chicago . . . . . . . . . . . . . . . . . . . . . . 4 3 1   2 0 0   0 3 1   0 0 1   1 — 16
```

Pitchers

Cincinnati	IP	H	R	ER	BB	SO
Murray	1	5	6	6	1	1
Borbon	5	7	4	3	2	6
Sarmiento	2	4	3	3	2	2
Hoerner	$2/3$	1	1	1	0	1
Norman	$2 1/3$	2	0	0	2	3
Billingham (L 8-8)	$1 2/3$	5	2	2	0	0

Chicago	IP	H	R	ER	BB	SO
Burris	2	7	8	8	1	2
Moore	1	5	2	2	1	0
P. Reuschel	$3 1/3$	3	3	3	2	1
Hernandez	$1 2/3$	2	1	1	2	1
Sutter	3	0	0	0	1	6
Broberg	$1 2/3$	2	1	0	3	2
R. R'schel (W 15-3)	$2/3$	0	0	0	0	0

E — Lum, Cardenal, Buckner, Rosello. DP — Chicago 2. LOB — Cincinnati 15, Chicago 16. 2B — Geronimo, Morgan, Griffey 2, Foster, DeJesus, Burris, Mitterwald, Clines. 3B — Moore. HR — Rose (7), Bench (23), Lum (2), Griffey (9), Geronimo (7), Buckner 2 (4), Murcer (15), Mitterwald 2 (8), Morales (8). SB — Concepcion 3, Rose, Lum, Morgan. SH — Rose. U — Harvey, Pryor, Olsen, Crawford. T — 4:50. A — 32,155.

Kong 8, Los Angeles 7
May 14, 1978

It was Mothers Day. It might as well have been Dave Kingman Day. All Kingman did was to hit three homers and drive in eight runs as the Cubs beat the Dodgers 10-7 in fifteen innings. Dave's first four-bagger came in the sixth with one on, bringing the Cubs to within one run of the Dodgers at 3-2. In the ninth, with the Cubs trailing 7-5, Kingman hit another two-run blast to tie the game. It traveled some, this one, 430 feet. The game was tied. Dave waited until the fifteenth to win it. With two out and two on, Dave hit Rick Rhoden's pitch over the wall. It was the second time Kingman had hit three homers in one game at Dodger Stadium, the first time being on June 4, 1976, when he was a Met.

After the game, Kingman was cheered by the fans and interviewed by various members of the press. On his way back to the locker room, he called a Chicago *Tribune* newsman aside and asked if he could use the paper as a greeting card. "Just make it simple: 'Happy Mother's Day, Cappy' . . . .And tell her I love her."

Chicago	ab	r	h	rbi	Los Angeles	ab	r	h	rbi
DeJesus, ss	3	2	1	0	Lopes, 2b	2	1	1	0
Biittner, ph	1	0	0	0	Martinez, 2b	4	2	1	0
Kelleher, ss	1	1	1	0	Russell, ss	8	1	2	0
Ontiveros, 3b	7	0	0	0	Smith, rf	6	1	2	2
Buckner, 1b	8	2	3	1	Cey, 3b	7	1	3	2
Kingman, lf	7	3	4	8	Garvey, 1b	7	0	1	1
Trillo, 2b	7	0	0	0	Monday, cf	7	0	1	1
Murcer, rf	6	1	1	1	Lacy, lf	4	0	1	0
Cruz, cf	3	0	0	0	Garman, p	0	0	0	0
Hernandez, p	0	0	0	0	Dav'lo, ph,lf	3	0	0	0
Moore, p	0	0	0	0	Oates, c	3	0	2	0
Roberts, p	1	0	0	0	Yeager, ph,c	2	0	1	0
Sutter, p	0	0	0	0	Rhoden, p	1	0	0	0
Meoli, ph	0	0	0	0	Rau, p	2	1	1	0
Burris, p	0	0	0	0	Mota, ph	1	0	0	0
P. R'schel, p	1	0	0	0	Hough, p	0	0	0	0
Cox, c	2	0	0	0	Forster, p	0	0	0	0
Rader, c	4	0	0	0	Burke, ph,lf	1	0	0	0
Lamp, p	2	0	1	0	Baker, ph	1	0	0	0
Clines, cf	0	1	0	0	Castillo, p	0	0	0	0
Gross, ph-cf	2	0	0	0	Grote, ph, c	1	0	0	0
Totals	55	10	11	10	Totals	60	7	16	6

```
Chicago.....................0 0 0   0 0 2   2 1 2   0 0 0   0 0 0 — 10
Los Angeles ................1 0 2   0 0 0   2 2 0   0 0 0   0 0 0 —  7
```

Pitchers

Chicago	IP	H	R	ER	BB	SO
Lamp	5⅔	6	3	3	3	3
Hernandez	1	1	2	2	1	0
Moore	0	1	0	0	0	0
Roberts	1	3	2	2	0	2
Sutter	1⅓	1	0	0	1	1
Burris	3	2	0	0	1	3
P. Reuschel (W 1-0)	3	2	0	0	0	1
Los Angeles						
Rau	6	6	2	2	2	1
Hough	⅓	0	2	1	2	0
Foster	⅔	1	0	0	0	0
Garman	2	2	3	3	1	0
Castillo	3	0	0	0	5	2
Rhoden (L 4-2)	3	2	3	3	1	3

E — Cox, Russell, Gross, DeJesus. DP — Chicago 1, Los Angeles 1. LOB
— Chicago 13, Los Angeles 15. 2B — Buckner, Cey, Yeager. HR —
Kingman 3 (7), Murcer (2). SB — Smith. SH — Lopes, Burris, Rader. WP
— Hough. Balk — Lamp. U — Harvey, Olsen, Quick, Crawford. T —
5:02. A — 31,698.

Gone With the Wind

May 1, 1979

Hey! Hey! Put the Cubs and the Phillies in Wrigley Field
with a 20 mph wind blowing out and what do you get?
History. Jack Brickhouse described it as the Cubs' most
exciting game. Larry Bowa allowed as how it "had to be
one of the greatest games ever played." The pitching staffs
buried their heads in shame. Tug McGraw described the
feeling: "It's funny, I mean when you're sitting out there in
the pen and you see the way things are going, you don't
exactly beg to come in the game. And yet, all the time
you're saying to yourself, 'Well, I *know* I could stop all this
foolishness.' So what happens? I get my chance to stop it
and *blowie!*"

Blowie, indeed. In one inning, McGraw's ERA went
from 1.64 to 4.50. Fortunately for Tug, only four of the
seven runs he gave up that inning were earned. At the time
the Cubs were trailing 21-9. No, that wasn't their season
record; that was the score at the half-way point in the ball
game. Six homers had already been hit, two by Kingman
for five runs and four by the Phillies, including Randy
Lerch's first homer. Poor Randy. His blast rounded out his
first inning lead to seven runs, but the excitement must
have been too much. He couldn't get a Cub out until the
score was 7-4 and when that out was followed by a double,
Lerch was sent to the clubhouse. The second inning was
the only inning other than the ninth in which neither team

managed to score. But for the next three innings twenty-four runs would cover the plate.

So McGraw's misfortune made it a five-run ball game, 21-16. Bowa later expressed the concern he felt when he saw that "the Cubs had a field goal kicker warming up on the sidelines for three innings." True enough. In the sixth, the Cubs scored a field goal of runs and did so again in the eighth to finally tie the score at four deuces, 22-22. By now every fan who could was consulting his record book. One more homer would tie the major-league mark already set by the Cubs and Reds in 1977. More importantly, a Cub victory would make them the first National League team ever to overcome a twelve run deficit to win. And if Kingman would hit the homer (what the heck, he already had three), he would tie Schmidt for the league lead. The Phils had already used their bullpen ace, Ron Reed, who'd been the victim of the two field goals. Now it was up to Rawley Eastwick. For the Cubs, Ray Burris had quelled the uprising in the seventh and eighth, and now Bruce Sutter was given the game.

No runs in the ninth. Two out in the tenth and Schmidt worked Sutter to a 3-2 count. After Schmidt's first inning homer, he had been walked in the third, fourth, and fifth innings. But not this time. Sutter's split-fingered fastball dipped but not enough as Schmidt stayed with it and golfed it into the left field seats. The eleventh homer to tie the record, the ninety-seventh total base to set a new major league record. But no Cub win.

Nonetheless, it was an extraordinary game. Every starting player got a hit and all except one scored and drove in at least one run. Bowa had five hits, Maddox was perfect on the day, Kingman and Buckner averaged an RBI an at-bat. Oh, the record for most runs in a game? You guessed it. Cubs and Phillies, August 25, 1922. The Cubs won that one, 26-23.

Philadelphia	ab	r	h	rbi	Chicago	ab	r	h	rbi
McBride, rf	8	2	3	1	DeJesus, ss	6	4	3	1
Bowa, ss	8	4	5	1	Vail, rf	5	2	3	1
Rose, 1b	7	4	3	4	Burris, p	0	0	0	0
Schmidt, 3b	4	3	2	4	Thompson, rf	2	1	1	0
Unser, lf	7	1	1	2	Buckner, 1b	7	2	4	7
Maddox, cf	4	3	4	4	Kingman, lf	6	4	3	6
Gross, cf	2	1	1	1	Ontiveros, 3b	7	2	1	1
Boone, c	4	2	3	5	Martin, cf	6	2	3	3
Meoli, 2b	5	0	1	0	Sutter, p	0	0	0	0
Lerch, p	1	1	1	1	Foote, c	6	1	3	1
Bird, p	1	1	0	0	Sizemore, 2b	4	2	2	1
Luzinski, ph	0	0	0	0	Caudill, p	0	0	0	0
Espinosa, pr	1	1	0	0	Murcer, rf	2	0	1	0
McGraw, p	0	0	0	0	Lamp, p	0	0	0	0
Reed, p	0	0	0	0	Moore, p	1	0	1	1
McCarver, ph	1	0	0	0	Hernandez, p	1	0	0	0
Eastwick, p	0	0	0	0	Dillard, 2b	1	2	1	0
					Biittner, ph	1	0	0	0
					Kelleher, 2b	1	0	0	0
Totals	53	23	24	23	Totals	56	22	26	22

```
Philadelphia ........................7 0 8   2 4 0   1 0 0   1 — 23
Chicago .............................6 0 0   3 7 3   0 3 0   0 — 22
```

Pitchers

Philadelphia	IP	H	R	ER	BB	SO
Lerch	1/3	5	5	5	0	0
Bird	3 2/3	8	4	4	0	2
McGraw	2/3	4	7	4	3	1
Reed	3 1/3	9	6	6	0	0
Eastwick (W 1-0)	2	0	0	0	0	1
Chicago						
Lamp	1/3	6	6	6	0	0
Moore	2	6	7	7	2	1
Hernandez	2 2/3	7	8	6	7	1
Caudill	1 1/3	2	1	1	2	3
Burris	1 2/3	1	0	0	0	0
Sutter (L 1-1)	2	1	1	1	1	1

E — Kingman, DeJesus, Schmidt 2. DP — Philadelphia 2. LOB — Philadelphia 15, Chicago 7. 2B — Bowa 2, Martin, Maddox 2, Rose 2, Foote, DeJesus, Boone, Thompson. 3B — Moore, Gross. HR — Schmidt 2 (14), Boone (2), Lerch (1), Kingman 3 (12), Maddox (6), Ontiveros (1), Buckner (4), Martin (3). SB — Bowa, Meoli. SF — Unser, Gross. HBP — By Hernandez (Boone). T — 4:03. A — 14,952.

The Old and the New
April 29, 1979

OK, Cub fans. Down 5-0 in the ninth, two on, two out
with Ted Sizemore at the plate. Victory is just around the
corner, right? Right. It's easy. Sizemore walks so
Blackwell's single will drive in two. Biittner bats for
DeJesus and singles in another run putting the winning
run in the bat of Bobby Murcer. Perfect. Bobby puts one
into the Atlanta night, and Sutter pitches to hold the lead. If
Bert Wilson were still alive he would have said, "I told you
so."

In honor of Bert and all the Cubs, let's all say it together
— the game *is* never over.

Chicago	ab	r	h	rbi	Atlanta	ab	r	h	rbi
DeJesus, ss	3	0	1	0	Royster, 3b	4	2	3	1
Biittner, ph	1	0	1	1	Matthews, rf	4	1	3	1
Dillard, pr	0	1	0	0	Burroughs, lf	5	0	2	1
Sutter, p	0	0	0	0	Bonnell, pr	0	0	0	0
Murcer, rf	3	1	1	3	Murphy, c	5	1	1	2
Buckner, 1b	5	0	0	0	Lum, 1b	4	0	0	0
Kingman, lf	4	1	1	0	Office, cf	4	0	1	0
Ontiveros, 3b	3	1	1	0	Hubbard, 2b	4	0	0	0
Martin, cf	4	0	0	0	Frias, ss	4	0	1	0
Foote, c	2	0	0	0	McW'liams, p	4	1	1	0
McGlothen, p	1	0	0	0	Garber, p	0	0	0	0
Clines, ph	1	0	0	0					
Kelleher, ss	0	0	0	0					
Sizemore, 2b	3	1	0	0					
Lamp, p	1	0	0	0					
Blackwell, c	2	1	1	2					
Totals	33	6	6	6	Totals	38	5	12	5

Chicago ....0 0 0 0 0 0 0 0 6 — 6
Atlanta ....1 0 2 0 0 1 1 0 0 — 5

Pitchers

Chicago	IP	H	R	ER	BB	SO
Lamp	3⅔	7	3	3	2	1
McGlothen (W 3-2)	4⅓	3	2	2	1	5
Sutter (Save 5)	1	2	0	0	0	0
Atlanta						
McWilliams	8⅔	3	3	3	6	4
Garber (L 1-3)	⅓	3	3	3	0	0

E — None. DP — Chicago 1. LOB — Chicago 6, Atlanta 9. 2B — McWilliams, Matthews, Burroughs. HR — Murphy (9), Murcer (2). SB — DeJesus 2. T — 2:59. A - 5,041.

Cubs Season Statistics, 1948-1981

Abbreviation Key

POS	Fielding Position	DP	Double Plays
AB	At Bats	TC/G	Total Fielding Chances per Game
BA	Batting Average	FA	Fielding Average
HR	Home Runs	G	Games Pitched
RBI	Runs Batted In	IP	Innings Pitched
PO	Put Outs	W	Wins
A	Assists	L	Losses
E	Errors	SV	Saves
	ERA	Earned Run Average	

(Boldfaced type indicates league leader in that position.)

	POS	Cub	AB	BA	HR	RBI	PO	A	E	DP	TC/G	FA
	1B	E. Waitkus	562	.295	7	44	1064	92	9	77	**10.0**	.992
	2B	H. Schenz	337	.261	1	14	184	190	10	45	4.9	.974
	SS	R. Smalley	361	.216	4	36	189	351	**34**	70	4.6	.941
	3B	A. Pafko	548	.312	26	101	125	**314**	29	29	3.4	.938
1948	RF	B. Nicholson	494	.261	19	67	244	7	5	1	1.9	.980
W-64 L-90	CF	H. Jeffcoat	473	.279	4	42	307	12	8	3	2.7	.976
Charlie Grimm	LF	P. Lowrey	435	.294	2	54	225	9	4	2	2.3	.983
8th	C	B. Scheffing	293	.300	5	45	332	36	4	5	4.8	.989
	1B	P. Cavarretta	334	.278	3	40	446	32	3	46		.994
	2B	E. Verban	248	.294	1	16	134	164	11	47	5.5	.964
	OF	C. Maddern	214	.252	4	27	98	6	2	0	1.9	.981
	C	McCullough	172	.209	1	7	225	25	7	5	5.0	.973
	C	R. Walker	171	.275	5	26	178	22	4	3	4.6	.980

Pitcher	G	IP	W	L	SV	ERA
J. Schmitz	34	242	18	13	1	2.64
R. Meyer	29	165	10	10	0	3.66
D. McCall	30	151	4	13	0	4.82
B. Rush	36	133	5	11	0	3.92
H. Borowy	39	127	5	10	1	4.89
R. Hamner	27	111	5	9	0	4.69
C. Chambers	29	104	2	9	0	4.43
D. Lade	19	87	5	6	0	4.02
J. Dobernic	54	86	7	2	1	3.15

	POS	Cub	AB	BA	HR	RBI	PO	A	E	DP	TC/G	FA
	1B	H. Reich	386	.280	3	34	759	**83**	9	57	10.0	.989
	2B	E. Verban	343	.289	0	22	218	249	**17**	60	5.5	.965
	SS	R. Smalley	477	.245	8	35	265	438	**39**	91	**5.6**	.947
	3B	F. Gustine	261	.226	4	27	52	110	12	13	3.2	.931
1949	RF	H. Jeffcoat	363	.245	2	26	250	12	10	2	2.7	.963
W-61 L-93	CF	A. Pafko	519	.281	18	69	217	8	3	2	2.3	.987
Charlie Grimm	LF	H. Sauer	357	.291	27	83	199	10	4	2	2.2	.981
W-19 L-31	C	M. Owen	198	.273	2	18	219	35	8	5	4.4	.969
Frankie Frisch	1B	P. Cavarretta	360	.294	8	49	673	63	5	58	10.6	.993
W-42 L-62	3S	B. Ramazzotti	190	.179	0	6	48	112	3	15		.982
8th	OF	H. Edwards	176	.290	7	21	80	4	1	2	1.7	.988
	C	R. Walker	172	.244	3	22	166	23	7	2	4.6	.964
	OF	F. Baumholtz	164	.226	1	15	67	3	1	3	1.7	.986
	OF	H. Walker	159	.264	1	14	69	3	4	0	1.9	.947

Pitcher	G	IP	W	L	SV	ERA
J. Schmitz	36	207	11	13	3	4.35
B. Rush	35	201	10	18	4	4.07
D. Leonard	33	180	7	16	0	4.15
M. Dubiel	32	148	6	9	4	4.14
D. Lade	36	130	4	5	1	5.00
W. Hacker	30	126	5	8	0	4.23
B. Chipman	38	113	7	8	1	3.97
B. Muncrief	34	75	5	6	2	4.56

	POS	Cub	AB	BA	HR	RBI	PO	A	E	DP	TC/G	FA
	1B	P. Ward	285	.253	6	33	734	73	4	78	10.7	.995
	2B	Terwilliger	480	.242	10	32	314	380	24	80	5.7	.967
	SS	R. Smalley	557	.230	21	85	**332**	**541**	**51**	**115**	**6.0**	.945
	3B	B. Serena	435	.239	17	61	122	274	23	24	3.4	.945
	RF	B. Borkowski	256	.273	4	29	150	3	4	1	2.4	.975
1950	CF	A. Pafko	514	.304	36	92	342	12	8	1	2.5	.978
W-64 L-89	LF	H. Sauer	540	.274	32	103	236	12	9	1	2.1	.965
Frankie Frisch	C	M. Owen	259	.243	2	21	318	39	8	8	4.2	.978
7th	1B	P. Cavarretta	256	.273	10	31	606	47	9	55	9.9	.986
	C	R. Walker	213	.230	6	16	240	34	7	6	4.5	.975
	OF	C. Mauro	185	.227	1	10	86	2	5	0	1.9	.946
	OF	H. Jeffcoat	179	.235	2	18	83	6	3	0	1.7	.967
	OF	R. Northey	114	.281	4	20	38	3	1	2	1.6	.976
	OF	H. Edwards	110	.364	2	21	38	2	1	0	1.4	.976

Pitcher	G	IP	W	L	SV	ERA
B. Rush	39	255	13	**20**	1	3.71
J. Schmitz	39	193	10	16	0	4.99
P. Minner	39	190	8	13	4	4.11
F. Hiller	38	153	12	5	1	3.53
M. Dubiel	39	143	6	10	2	4.16
D. Lade	34	118	5	6	2	4.74
J. Klippstein	33	105	2	9	1	5.25
D. Leonard	35	74	5	1	6	3.77

	POS	Cub	AB	BA	HR	RBI	PO	A	E	DP	TC/G	FA
	1B	C. Connors	201	.239	2	18	452	33	8	41	8.6	.984
	2B	E. Miksis	421	.266	4	35	279	317	19	71	6.0	.969
	SS	R. Smalley	238	.231	8	31	117	190	15	42	4.4	.953
	3B	R. Jackson	557	.275	16	76	198	323	24	32	3.8	.956
1951	RF	H. Jeffcoat	278	.273	4	27	166	1	2	5	2.1	.989
W-62 L-92	CF	F. Baumholtz	560	.284	2	50	307	6	8	2	2.3	.975
Frankie Frisch	LF	H. Sauer	525	.263	30	89	286	19	6	2	2.4	.981
W-35 L-45	C	S. Burgess	219	.251	2	20	210	35	5	6	3.9	.980
Phil Cavarretta	OF	G. Hermanski	231	.281	3	20	134	9	5	1	2.0	.966
W-27 L-47	1B	P. Cavarretta	206	.311	6	28	444	42	3	51	9.2	.994
8th	2B	Terwilliger	192	.214	0	10	136	142	9	37	5.9	.969
	OF	A. Pafko	178	.264	12	35	119	6	1	3	2.6	.992
	1B	D. Fondy	170	.271	3	20	387	27	10	40	9.6	.976
	SS	J. Cusick	164	.177	2	16	78	147	11	25	4.2	.953
	SS	B. Ramazzotti	158	.247	1	15	73	137	11	32	4.3	.950

Pitcher	G	IP	W	L	SV	ERA
B. Rush	37	211	11	12	2	3.83
P. Minner	33	202	6	17	1	3.79
C. McLish	30	146	4	10	0	4.45
F. Hiller	24	141	6	12	1	4.84
T. Lown	31	127	4	9	0	5.46
J. Klippstein	35	124	6	6	2	4.29
B. Kelly	35	124	7	4	0	4.66
D. Leonard	41	82	10	6	3	2.64

	POS	Cub	AB	BA	HR	RBI	PO	A	E	DP	TC/G	FA
	1B	D. Fondy	554	.300	10	67	1257	103	14	92	9.6	.990
	2B	E. Miksis	383	.232	2	19	126	140	14	22	5.2	.950
	SS	R. Smalley	261	.222	5	30	139	200	17	33	4.3	.952
	3B	R. Jackson	379	.232	9	34	91	203	13	13	3.0	.958
1952	RF	F. Baumholtz	409	.325	4	35	248	10	7	3	2.6	.974
W-77 L-77	CF	H. Jeffcoat	297	.219	4	30	218	16	1	2	2.5	.996
Phil Cavarretta	LF	H. Sauer	567	.270	37	121	327	17	6	3	2.3	.983
5th	C	T. Atwell	362	.290	2	31	451	50	12	2	5.1	.977
	32	B. Serena	390	.274	15	61	198	234	8	30		.982
	OF	B. Addis	292	.295	1	20	160	8	2	2	2.2	.988
	OF	G. Hermanski	275	.255	4	34	146	7	3	3	2.1	.981
	SS	T. Brown	200	.320	3	24	58	85	14	17	4.0	.911
	2B	B. Ramazzotti	183	.284	1	12	90	143	5	28	4.8	.979

Pitcher	G	IP	W	L	SV	ERA
B. Rush	34	250	17	13	0	2.70
J. Klippstein	41	203	9	14	3	4.44
W. Hacker	33	185	15	9	1	2.58
P. Minner	28	181	14	9	0	3.74
T. Lown	33	157	4	11	0	4.37
B. Kelly	31	125	4	9	0	3.59
D. Leonard	45	67	2	2	11	2.16

	POS	Cub	AB	BA	HR	RBI	PO	A	E	DP	TC/G	FA
	1B	D. Fondy	595	.309	18	78	1274	115	**18**	105	9.4	.987
	2B	E. Miksis	577	.251	8	39	210	262	**23**	65	5.4	.954
	SS	R. Smalley	253	.249	6	25	153	191	25	39	4.8	.932
	3B	R. Jackson	498	.285	19	66	141	265	22	24	3.2	.949
1953	RF	H. Sauer	395	.263	19	60	221	5	7	1	2.2	.970
W-65 L-89	CF	F. Baumholtz	520	.306	3	25	290	6	6	0	2.3	.980
Phil Cavarretta	LF	R. Kiner	414	.283	28	87	211	6	8	2	1.9	.964
7th	C	McCullough	229	.258	6	23	273	31	4	7	4.2	.987
	23	B. Serena	275	.251	10	52	135	160	7	31		.977
	C	J. Garagiola	228	.272	1	21	296	34	4	2	4.9	.988
	OF	H. Jeffcoat	183	.235	4	22	175	6	5	2	1.9	.973

	Pitcher	G	IP	W	L	SV	ERA
	W. Hacker	39	222	12	**19**	2	4.38
	P. Minner	31	201	12	15	1	4.21
	J. Klippstein	48	168	10	11	6	4.83
	B. Rush	29	167	9	14	0	4.54
	T. Lown	49	148	8	7	3·	5.16
	H. Pollet	25	111	5	6	1	4.12
	B. Church	27	104	4	5	1	5.00
	D. Leonard	45	63	2	3	8	4.60

	POS	Cub	AB	BA	HR	RBI	PO	A	E	DP	TC/G	FA
	1B	D. Fondy	568	.285	9	49	1228	119	9	129	9.8	.993
	2B	G. Baker	541	.275	13	61	355	385	25	102	5.7	.967
	SS	E. Banks	593	.275	19	79	312	475	34	105	5.3	.959
1954	3B	R. Jackson	484	.273	18	67	118	266	18	21	3.2	.955
W-64 L-90	RF	H. Sauer	520	.288	41	103	282	8	11	2	2.1	.963
Stan Hack	CF	D. Talbot	403	.241	1	19	245	10	4	1	2.4	.985
7th	LF	R. Kiner	557	.285	22	73	298	6	9	1	2.1	.971
	C	J. Garagiola	153	.281	5	21	191	23	4	0	4.0	.982
	OF	F. Baumholtz	303	.297	4	28	168	2	2	0	2.4	.988
	C	W. Cooper	158	.310	7	32	190	31	5	4	4.7	.978

	Pitcher	G	IP	W	L	SV	ERA
	B. Rush	33	236	13	15	0	3.77
	P. Minner	32	218	11	11	1	3.96
	W. Hacker	39	159	6	13	2	4.25
	J. Klippstein	36	148	4	11	1	5.29
	H. Pollet	20	128	8	10	0	3.58
	J. Davis	46	128	11	7	4	3.52
	H. Jeffcoat	43	104	5	6	7	5.19
	D. Cole	18	84	3	8	0	5.36

	POS	Cub	AB	BA	HR	RBI	PO	A	E	DP	TC/G	FA
	1B	D. Fondy	574	.265	17	65	1304	**107**	**13**	135	9.7	.991
	2B	G. Baker	609	.268	11	52	**432**	**444**	**30**	114	5.9	.967
	SS	E. Banks	596	.295	44	117	290	482	22	102	5.2	**.972**
	3B	R. Jackson	499	.265	21	70	125	247	20	**26**	2.9	.949
1955	RF	J. King	301	.256	11	45	184	10	2	2	2.1	.990
W-72 L-81	CF	E. Miksis	481	.235	9	41	267	6	3	1	2.5	**.989**
Stan Hack	LF	H. Sauer	261	.211	12	28	122	4	2	1	1.9	.984
6th	C	H. Chiti	338	.231	11	41	495	**69**	9	**10**	5.1	.984
	OF	F. Baumholtz	280	.289	1	27	131	3	1	1	2.1	.993
	OF	B. Speake	261	.218	12	43	90	4	4	1	1.8	.959
	OF	J. Bolger	160	.206	0	7	125	1	6	0	2.6	.955

	Pitcher	G	IP	W	L	SV	ERA
	S. Jones	36	242	14	**20**	0	4.10
	B. Rush	33	234	13	11	0	.350
	W. Hacker	35	213	11	15	3	4.27
	P. Minner	22	158	9	9	0	3.48
	J. Davis	42	134	7	11	3	4.44
	H. Jeffcoat	50	101	8	6	6	2.95
	H. Pollet	24	61	4	3	5	5.61

	POS	Cub	AB	BA	HR	RBI	PO	A	E	DP	TC/G	FA
	1B	D. Fondy	543	.269	9	46	1048	94	17	101	8.7	.985
	2B	G. Baker	546	.258	12	57	362	426	**25**	**99**	**5.8**	.969
	SS	E. Banks	538	.297	28	85	279	357	25	92	4.8	.962
	3B	D. Hoak	424	.215	5	37	122	158	15	16	2.7	.949
1956	RF	W. Moryn	529	.285	23	67	268	**18**	5	2	2.1	.983
W-60 L-94	CF	P. Whisenant	314	.239	11	46	242	6	2	0	2.7	.992
Stan Hack	LF	M. Irvin	339	.271	15	50	216	6	2	0	2.3	.991
8th	C	H. Landrith	312	.221	4	32	483	55	**14**	9	5.6	.975
	UT	E. Miksis	356	.239	9	27	144	151	7	14		.977
	OF	J. King	317	.249	15	54	187	10	2	2	2.4	.990
	OF	S. Drake	215	.256	2	15	142	3	1	1	2.8	.993
	C	H. Chiti	203	.212	4	18	327	35	7	2	5.5	.981

	Pitcher	G	IP	W	L	SV	ERA
	B. Rush	32	240	13	10	0	3.19
	S. Jones	33	189	9	14	0	3.91
	W. Hacker	34	168	3	13	0	4.66
	D. Kaiser	27	150	4	9	0	3.59
	J. Davis	46	120	5	7	2	3.66
	T. Lown	61	111	9	8	13	3.58
	Valentinetti	42	95	6	4	1	3.78
	J. Brosnan	30	95	5	9	1	3.79

	POS	Cub	AB	BA	HR	RBI	PO	A	E	DP	TC/G	FA
1957	1B	D. Long	397	.305	21	62	908	72	5	81	9.5	.995
W-62 L-92	2B	B. Morgan	425	.207	5	27	220	343	14	58	5.0	.976
Bob Scheffing	SS	E. Banks	594	.285	43	102	168	261	11	59	4.4	.975
7th	3B	B. Adams	187	.251	1	10	43	68	6	5	2.5	.949
	RF	W. Moryn	568	.289	19	88	276	13	**12**	3	2.0	.960

	POS	Cub	AB	BA	HR	RBI	PO	A	E	DP	TC/G	FA
	CF	C. Tanner	318	.286	7	42	156	5	2	2	2.0	.988
	LF	L. Walls	366	.240	6	33	174	6	3	0	1.9	.984
	C	C. Neeman	415	.258	10	39	**703**	56	8	**13**	6.5	.990
	01	B. Speake	418	.232	16	50	480	41	7	21		.987
	OF	J. Bolger	273	.275	5	29	152	4	2	1	2.5	.987
	UT	J. Kindall	181	.160	6	12	73	109	15	10		.924

	Pitcher	G	IP	W	L	SV	ERA
	M. Drabowsky	36	240	13	15	0	3.53
	D. Drott	38	229	15	11	0	3.58
	B. Rush	31	205	6	16	0	4.38
	D. Elston	39	144	6	7	8	3.56
	D. Hillman	32	103	6	11	1	4.35
	J. Brosnan	41	99	5	5	0	3.38
	T. Lown	**67**	93	5	7	12	3.77

	POS	Cub	AB	BA	HR	RBI	PO	A	E	DP	TC/G	FA
	1B	D. Long	480	.271	20	75	1173	84	10	130	9.2	.992
	2B	T. Taylor	497	.235	6	27	311	374	23	103	5.2	.968
	SS	E. Banks	**617**	.313	**47**	**129**	292	468	**32**	100	5.1	.960
1958	3B	A. Dark	464	.295	3	43	107	225	18	24	3.2	.949
W-72 L-82	RF	L. Walls	513	.304	24	72	241	10	2	1	1.9	.992
Bob Scheffing	CF	B. Thomson	547	.283	21	82	353	13	4	3	2.5	.989
5th	LF	W. Moryn	512	.264	26	77	265	4	6	1	2.0	.978
	C	S. Taylor	301	.259	6	36	460	23	6	4	5.6	.988
	32	J. Goryl	219	.242	4	14	91	153	16	26		.938
	C	C. Neeman	201	.259	12	29	340	25	3	6	5.2	.992

	Pitcher	G	IP	W	L	SV	ERA
	T. Phillips	39	170	7	10	1	4.76
	G. Hobbie	55	168	10	6	2	3.74
	D. Drott	39	167	7	11	0	5.43
	D. Hillman	31	126	4	8	1	3.15
	M. Drabowsky	22	126	9	11	0	4.51
	D. Elston	**69**	97	9	8	10	2.88
	J. Briggs	20	96	5	5	0	4.52
	B. Henry	44	81	5	4	6	2.88

	POS	Cub	AB	BA	HR	RBI	PO	A	E	DP	TC/G	FA
	1B	D. Long	296	.236	14	37	731	49	12	63	9.3	.985
	2B	T. Taylor	624	.280	8	38	352	**456**	**25**	105	**5.6**	.970
	SS	E. Banks	589	.304	45	**143**	271	**519**	12	95	5.2	**.985**
	3B	A. Dark	477	.264	6	45	111	255	20	20	2.9	.948
1959	RF	L. Walls	354	.257	8	33	203	1	7	0	1.8	.967
W-74 L-80	CF	G. Altman	420	.245	12	47	278	7	3	2	2.4	.990
Bob Scheffing	LF	B. Thomson	374	.259	11	52	223	9	3	4	2.0	.987
5th	C	S. Taylor	353	.269	13	43	497	37	**10**	1	5.0	.982
	OF	W. Moryn	381	.234	14	48	175	9	2	1	1.8	.989
	1B	J. Marshall	294	.252	11	40	558	51	2	52	8.5	.997
	UT	E. Averill	186	.237	10	34	197	49	13	4		.950
	OF	I. Noren	156	.321	4	19	81	4	0	1	2.1	1.000

Pitcher	G	IP	W	L	SV	ERA
B. Anderson	37	235	12	13	0	4.13
G. Hobbie	46	234	16	13	0	3.69
D. Hillman	39	191	8	11	0	3.53
M. Drabowsky	31	142	5	10	0	4.13
B. Henry	65	134	9	8	12	2.68
A. Ceccarelli	18	102	5	5	0	4.76
J. Buzhardt	31	101	4	5	0	4.97
D. Elston	65	98	10	8	13	3.32

	POS	Cub	AB	BA	HR	RBI	PO	A	E	DP	TC/G	FA
	1B	E. Bouchee	299	.237	5	44	709	56	7	56	9.7	.991
1960	2B	J. Kindall	246	.240	2	23	147	218	13	44	4.6	.966
W-60 L-94	SS	E. Banks	597	.271	41	117	283	488	18	94	5.1	.977
Charlie Grimm	3B	R. Santo	347	.251	9	44	78	144	13	6	2.5	.945
W-6 L-11	RF	B. Will	475	.255	6	53	224	10	2	2	2.0	.992
Lou Boudreau	CF	R. Ashburn	547	.291	0	40	317	11	8	2	2.3	.976
W-54 L-83	LF	G. Altman	334	.266	13	51	144	2	1	0	1.9	.993
7th	C	M. Thacker	90	.156	0	6	170	23	4	2	3.9	.980
	UT	F. Thomas	479	.238	21	64	528	92	17	40		.973
	23	D. Zimmer	368	.258	6	35	208	266	16	30		.967

Pitcher	G	IP	W	L	SV	ERA
G. Hobbie	46	259	16	20	1	3.97
B. Anderson	38	204	9	11	1	4.11
D. Cardwell	31	177	8	14	0	4.37
D. Ellsworth	31	177	7	13	0	3.72
D. Elston	60	127	8	9	11	3.40
S. Morehead	45	123	2	9	4	3.94

	POS	Cub	AB	BA	HR	RBI	PO	A	E	DP	TC/G	FA
1961	1B	E. Bouchee	319	.248	12	38	852	76	16	97	8.8	.983
W-64 L-90	2B	D. Zimmer	477	.252	13	40	282	323	17	99	5.4	.973
Vedie Himsl	SS	E. Banks	511	.278	29	80	173	358	19	68	5.3	.965
W-10 L-21	3B	R. Santo	578	.284	23	83	157	307	31	41	3.2	.937
Harry Craft	RF	G. Altman	518	.303	27	96	258	11	6	2	2.1	.978
W-7 L-9	CF	A. Heist	321	.255	7	37	211	9	5	0	2.3	.978
El Tappe	LF	B. Williams	529	.278	25	86	220	9	11	3	1.8	.954
W-42 L-53	C	D. Bertelli	267	.273	2	33	396	49	8	10	5.0	.982
Lou Klein	2S	J. Kindall	310	.242	9	44	206	233	26	61		.944
W-5 L-7	OF	R. Ashburn	307	.257	0	19	131	4	3	0	1.8	.978
7th	C	S. Taylor	235	.238	8	23	319	25	4	5	4.6	.989
	1S	A. Rodgers	214	.266	6	23	404	83	9	44		.982

Pitcher	G	IP	W	L	SV	ERA
D. Cardwell	39	259	15	14	0	3.82
G. Hobbie	36	199	7	13	2	4.26
D. Ellsworth	37	187	10	11	0	3.86
J. Curtis	31	180	10	13	0	4.89
B. Anderson	57	152	7	10	8	4.26
D. Elston	58	93	6	7	8	5.59
B. Schultz	41	67	7	6	7	2.70

	POS	Cub	AB	BA	HR	RBI	PO	A	E	DP	TC/G	FA
1962	1B	E. Banks	610	.269	37	104	**1458**	**106**	11	**134**	**10.6**	.993
W-59 L-103	2B	K. Hubbs	661	.260	5	49	363	489	15	103	5.5	.983
El Tappe	SS	A. Rodgers	461	.278	5	44	239	433	28	91	5.3	.960
W-4 L-16	3B	R. Santo	604	.227	17	83	**161**	**332**	**23**	33	**3.3**	.955
Lou Klein	RF	G. Altman	534	.318	22	74	234	8	7	3	1.9	.972
W-12 L-18	CF	L. Brock	434	.263	9	35	243	7	9	2	2.4	.965
Charlie Metro	LF	B. Williams	618	.298	22	91	273	18	10	4	1.9	.967
W-43 L-69	C	D. Bertell	215	.302	2	18	306	36	5	0	4.6	.986
9th	OF	D. Landrum	238	.282	1	15	122	3	4	3	2.2	.969

Pitcher	G	IP	W	L	SV	ERA
B. Buhl	34	212	12	13	0	3.69
D. Ellsworth	37	209	9	20	1	5.09
D. Cardwell	41	196	7	16	4	4.92
C. Koonce	35	191	10	10	0	3.97
G. Hobbie	42	162	5	14	0	5.22
B. Anderson	57	108	2	7	4	5.02
B. Schultz	57	78	5	5	5	3.82
D. Elston	57	66	4	8	8	2.44

	POS	Cub	AB	BA	HR	RBI	PO	A	E	DP	TC/G	FA
	1B	E. Banks	432	.227	18	64	1178	78	9	97	10.1	.993
	2B	K. Hubbs	566	.235	8	47	338	493	22	96	5.6	.974
	SS	A. Rodgers	516	.229	5	33	**271**	**454**	**35**	**100**	5.1	.954
1963	3B	R. Santo	630	.297	25	99	**136**	**374**	26	25	3.3	.951
W-82 L-80	RF	L. Brock	547	.258	9	37	269	17	8	7	2.1	.973
Bob Kennedy	CF	E. Burton	322	.230	12	41	151	6	4	1	1.8	.975
7th	LF	B. Williams	612	.286	25	95	298	13	4	2	2.0	.987
	C	D. Bertell	322	.233	2	14	549	84	8	15	6.5	.988
	OF	D. Landrum	227	.242	1	10	100	3	3	0	1.9	.972

Pitcher	G	IP	W	L	SV	ERA
D. Ellsworth	37	291	22	10	0	2.11
L. Jackson	37	275	14	18	0	2.55
B. Buhl	37	226	11	14	0	3.38
G. Hobbie	36	165	7	10	0	3.92
P. Toth	27	131	5	9	0	3.10
L. McDaniel	57	88	13	7	**22**	2.86

	POS	Cub	AB	BA	HR	RBI	PO	A	E	DP	TC/G	FA
	1B	E. Banks	591	.264	23	95	**1565**	**132**	10	122	**10.9**	.994
	2B	J. Amalfitano	324	.241	4	27	201	254	17	47	5.5	.964
	SS	A. Rodgers	448	.239	12	46	232	428	24	68	**5.4**	.965
1964	3B	R. Santo	592	.313	30	114	156	**367**	20	**31**	3.4	.963
W-76 L-86	RF	L. Gabrielson	272	.246	5	23	116	5	2	0	1.8	.984
Bob Kennedy	CF	B. Cowan	497	.241	19	50	297	2	10	0	2.3	.968
8th	LF	B. Williams	645	.312	33	98	233	14	13	0	1.6	.950
	C	D. Bertell	353	.238	4	35	531	52	**11**	3	5.4	.981
	2S	J. Stewart	415	.253	3	33	214	307	12	64		.977
	OF	L. Brock	215	.251	2	14	86	8	4	1	1.9	.959

Pitcher	G	IP	W	L	SV	ERA
L. Jackson	40	298	**24**	11	0	3.14
D. Ellsworth	37	257	14	18	0	3.75
B. Buhl	36	228	15	14	0	3.83
L. Burdette	28	131	9	9	0	4.88
E. Broglio	18	100	4	7	1	4.04
L. McDaniel	63	95	1	7	15	3.88

	POS	Cub	AB	BA	HR	RBI	PO	A	E	DP	TC/G	FA
	1B	E. Banks	612	.265	28	106	**1682**	93	15	143	**11.0**	.992
	2B	G. Beckert	614	.239	3	30	326	**494**	23	101	5.5	.973
	SS	D. Kessinger	309	.201	0	14	176	338	**28**	69	5.2	.948
1965	3B	R. Santo	608	.285	33	101	**155**	373	24	27	**3.4**	.957
W-72 L-90	RF	B. Williams	645	.315	34	108	296	10	10	2	1.9	.968
Bob Kennedy	CF	D. Landrum	425	.226	6	34	241	3	3	0	2.1	.988
W-24 L-32	LF	D. Clemens	340	.221	4	26	145	7	3	0	1.5	.981
Lou Klein	C	V. Roznovsky	172	.221	3	15	270	30	5	6	4.8	.984
W-48 L-58	OS	J. Stewart	282	.223	0	19	17	58	8	11		.956
8th	OF	G. Altman	196	.235	4	23	66	0	4	0	1.6	.943
	SS	R. Pena	170	.218	2	12	74	151	17	29	4.8	.930
	C	C. Krug	169	.201	5	24	273	27	6	5	5.3	.980
	C	E. Bailey	150	.253	5	23	237	23	5	3	4.9	.981

Pitcher	G	IP	W	L	SV	ERA
L. Jackson	39	257	14	21	0	3.85
D. Ellsworth	36	222	14	15	1	3.81
B. Buhl	32	184	13	11	0	4.39
C. Koonce	38	173	7	9	0	3.69
T. Abernathy	**84**	136	4	6	**31**	2.57
L. McDaniel	71	129	5	6	2	2.59
B. Faul	17	97	6	6	0	3.54

	POS	Cub	AB	BA	HR	RBI	PO	A	E	DP	TC/G	FA
	1B	E. Banks	511	.272	15	75	1178	81	10	88	9.8	.992
	2B	G. Beckert	656	.287	1	59	373	402	**24**	89	5.3	.970
	SS	D. Kessinger	533	.274	1	43	202	**474**	35	68	4.8	.951
1966	3B	R. Santo	561	.312	30	94	**150**	391	25	**36**	**3.7**	.956
W-59 L-103	RF	B. Williams	648	.276	29	91	319	9	8	3	2.1	.976
Leo Durocher	CF	A. Phillips	416	.262	16	36	258	14	6	2	2.5	.978
10th	LF	B. Browne	419	.243	16	51	200	3	7	0	1.8	.967
	C	R. Hundley	526	.236	19	63	871	**85**	14	8	6.5	.986
	O1	J. Boccabella	206	.228	6	25	230	18	1	13		.996
	OF	G. Altman	185	.222	5	17	42	4	2	0	1.1	.958

Pitcher	G	IP	W	L	SV	ERA
D. Ellsworth	38	269	8	**22**	0	3.98
K. Holtzman	34	221	11	16	0	3.79
F. Jenkins	60	182	6	8	5	3.31
B. Hands	41	159	8	13	2	4.58
C. Koonce	45	109	5	5	2	3.81
B. Hendley	43	90	4	5	7	3.91
C. Simmons	19	77	4	7	0	4.07

	POS	Cub	AB	BA	HR	RBI	PO	A	E	DP	TC/G	FA
	1B	E. Banks	573	.276	23	95	**1383**	91	10	111	10.1	.993
	2B	G. Beckert	597	.280	5	40	327	422	25	89	5.4	.968
1967	SS	D. Kessinger	580	.231	0	42	215	457	19	77	4.8	.973
W-87 L-74	3B	R. Santo	586	.300	31	98	**187**	**393**	26	33	**3.8**	.957
Leo Durocher	RF	T. Savage	225	.218	5	33	133	5	3	1	1.6	.979
3rd	CF	A. Phillips	448	.268	17	70	340	13	7	0	2.6	.981
	LF	B. Williams	634	.278	28	84	271	3	3	1	1.7	.989
	C	R. Hundley	539	.267	14	60	**865**	59	4	7	6.1	.996
	OF	L. Thomas	191	.220	2	23	60	2	2	0	1.5	.969

	Pitcher	G	IP	W	L	SV	ERA
	F. Jenkins	38	289	20	13	0	2.80
	R. Nye	35	205	13	10	0	3.20
	J. Niekro	36	170	10	7	0	3.34
	R. Culp	30	153	8	11	0	3.89
	B. Hands	49	150	7	8	6	2.46
	C. Simmons	17	82	3	7	0	4.94
	Hartenstein	45	73	9	5	10	3.08
	B. Stoneman	28	63	2	4	4	3.29

	POS	Cub	AB	BA	HR	RBI	PO	A	E	DP	TC/G	FA
	1B	E. Banks	552	.246	32	83	1379	88	6	118	10.0	.996
	2B	G. Beckert	643	.294	4	37	356	461	19	107	5.4	.977
	SS	D. Kessinger	655	.240	1	32	263	**573**	33	97	5.5	.962
1968	3B	R. Santo	577	.246	26	98	130	**378**	15	**33**	3.2	**.971**
W-84 L-78	RF	J. Hickman	188	.223	5	23	115	4	3	0	1.8	.975
Leo Durocher	CF	A. Phillips	439	.241	13	33	311	11	7	3	2.3	.979
3rd	LF	B. Williams	642	.288	30	98	261	4	9	0	1.7	.967
	C	R. Hundley	553	.226	7	65	885	81	5	11	6.1	.995
	OF	L. Johnson	205	.244	1	14	97	0	3	0	1.8	.970
	OF	A. Spangler	177	.271	2	18	71	2	2	1	1.6	.973
	OF	W. Smith	142	.275	5	25	42	1	0	0	1.1	1.000

	Pitcher	G	IP	W	L	SV	ERA
	F. Jenkins	40	308	20	15	0	2.63
	B. Hands	38	259	16	10	0	2.89
	K. Holtzman	34	215	11	14	1	3.35
	J. Niekro	34	177	14	10	2	4.31
	R. Nye	27	133	7	12	1	3.80
	P. Regan	68	127	10	5	25	2.20

	POS	Cub	AB	BA	HR	RBI	PO	A	E	DP	TC/G	FA
	1B	E. Banks	565	.253	23	106	**1419**	87	4	116	9.9	**.997**
	2B	G. Beckert	543	.291	1	37	262	401	24	71	5.3	.965
	SS	D. Kessinger	664	.273	4	53	**266**	**542**	20	**101**	5.3	**.976**
1969	3B	R. Santo	575	.289	29	123	**144**	334	27	23	3.2	.947
W-92 L-70	RF	J. Hickman	338	.237	21	54	153	6	3	0	1.3	.981
Leo Durocher	CF	D. Young	272	.239	6	27	191	4	5	0	2.0	.975
2nd	LF	B. Williams	642	.293	21	95	250	15	12	2	1.7	.957
	C	R. Hundley	522	.255	18	64	978	**79**	8	**17**	7.1	.992
	OF	A. Spangler	213	.211	4	23	75	1	4	0	1.4	.950
	O1	W. Smith	195	.246	9	25	185	9	3	14		.985

Pitcher	G	IP	W	L	SV	ERA
F. Jenkins	43	311	21	15	1	3.21
B. Hands	41	300	20	14	0	2.49
K. Holtzman	39	261	17	13	0	3.59
D. Selma	36	169	10	8	1	3.63
P. Regan	71	112	12	6	17	3.70
T. Abernathy	56	85	4	3	3	3.18
R. Nye	34	69	3	5	3	5.09

	POS	Cub	AB	BA	HR	RBI	PO	A	E	DP	TC/G	FA
	1B	J. Hickman	514	.315	32	115	563	60	6	46	8.5	.990
	2B	G. Beckert	591	.288	3	36	302	412	22	88	5.3	.970
	SS	D. Kessinger	631	.266	1	39	257	501	22	86	5.1	.972
	3B	R. Santo	555	.267	26	114	143	320	27	36	3.2	.945
1970	RF	J. Callison	477	.264	19	68	244	8	7	3	1.8	.973
W-84 L-78	CF	C. James	176	.210	3	14	115	5	0	1	1.3	1.000
Leo Durocher	LF	B. Williams	636	.322	42	129	259	13	3	1	1.7	.989
2nd	C	R. Hundley	250	.244	7	36	455	26	5	2	6.7	.990
	1B	E. Banks	222	.252	12	44	528	35	4	53	9.1	.993
	OF	J. Pepitone	213	.268	12	44	121	1	1	0	2.2	.992
	UT	P. Popovich	186	.253	4	20	75	97	4	26		.977
	C	J. Hiatt	178	.242	2	22	380	22	4	1	6.4	.990
	1B	W. Smith	167	.216	5	24	318	11	2	32	7.7	.994

Pitcher	G	IP	W	L	SV	ERA
F. Jenkins	40	313	22	16	0	3.39
K. Holtzman	39	288	17	11	0	3.38
B. Hands	39	265	18	15	1	3.70
M. Pappas	21	145	10	8	0	2.68
J. Decker	24	109	2	7	0	4.62
P. Regan	54	76	5	9	12	4.74

	POS	Cub	AB	BA	HR	RBI	PO	A	E	DP	TC/G	FA
	1B	J. Pepitone	427	.307	16	61	872	64	9	75	9.9	.990
	2B	G. Beckert	530	.342	2	42	275	382	9	76	5.2	.986
	SS	D. Kessinger	617	.258	2	38	263	512	27	97	5.2	.966
	3B	R. Santo	555	.267	21	88	118	274	17	29	2.7	.958
1971	RF	J. Callison	290	.210	8	38	158	3	3	0	1.8	.982
W-83 L-79	CF	B. Davis	301	.256	0	28	213	5	4	1	2.4	.982
Leo Durocher	LF	B. Williams	594	.301	28	93	284	8	7	3	1.9	.977
3rd	C	C. Cannizzaro	197	.213	5	23	311	26	6	2	4.9	.983
	O1	J. Hickman	383	.256	19	60	470	34	3	28		.994
	2B	P. Popovich	226	.217	4	28	74	119	3	26	4.9	.985
	P	F. Jenkins	115	.243	6	20	31	48	7	1	2.2	.919

Pitcher	G	IP	W	L	SV	ERA*
F. Jenkins	39	**325**	**24**	13	0	2.77
M. Pappas	35	261	17	14	0	3.52
B. Hands	36	242	12	18	0	3.42
K. Holtzman	30	195	9	15	0	4.48
J. Pizarro	16	101	7	6	0	3.48
P. Regan	48	73	5	5	6	3.95

	POS	Cub	AB	BA	HR	RBI	PO	A	E	DP	TC/G	FA
	1B	J. Hickman	368	.272	17	64	670	70	6	61	9.7	.992
	2B	G. Beckert	474	.270	3	43	256	396	16	71	5.7	.976
1972	SS	D. Kessinger	577	.274	1	39	259	504	28	90	5.4	.965
W-85 L-70	3B	R. Santo	464	.302	17	74	108	274	21	19	3.1	.948
Leo Durocher	RF	J. Cardenal	533	.291	17	70	223	1	7	1	1.8	.971
W-46 L-44	CF	R. Monday	434	.249	11	42	268	6	1	2	2.1	**.996**
Whitey Lockman	LF	B. Williams	574	**.333**	37	122	233	9	4	0	1.7	.984
W-39 L-26	C	R. Hundley	357	.218	5	30	569	53	3	7	5.5	**.995**
2nd	UT	C. Fanzone	222	.225	8	42	243	115	9	21		.975
	1B	J. Pepitone	214	.262	8	21	552	31	2	51	8.9	.997

Pitcher	G	IP	W	L	SV	ERA
F. Jenkins	36	289	20	12	0	3.21
B. Hooton	33	218	11	14	0	2.80
M. Pappas	29	195	17	7	0	2.77
B. Hands	32	189	11	8	0	2.99
R. Reuschel	21	129	10	8	0	2.93
T. Phoebus	37	83	3	3	6	3.78
J. Aker	48	67	6	6	17	2.96
J. Pizarro	16	59	4	5	1	3.97

	POS	Cub	AB	BA	HR	RBI	PO	A	E	DP	TC/G	FA
	1B	J. Hickman	201	.244	3	20	398	31	5	37	8.5	.988
	2B	G. Beckert	372	.255	0	29	163	262	7	50	4.9	.984
	SS	D. Kessinger	577	.262	0	43	**274**	526	30	**109**	5.3	.964
	3B	R. Santo	536	.267	20	77	107	271	20	17	2.7	.950
1973	RF	J. Cardenal	522	.303	11	68	234	13	5	2	1.8	.980
W-77 L-84	CF	R. Monday	554	.267	26	56	317	9	9	2	2.3	.973
Whitey Lockman	LF	B. Williams	576	.288	20	86	253	14	4	1	2.0	.985
5th	C	R. Hundley	368	.226	10	43	648	59	5	7	5.8	.993
	2B	P. Popovich	280	.236	2	24	171	247	8	53	5.1	.981
	C	K. Rudolph	170	.206	2	17	259	28	9	4	4.6	.970
	UT	C. Fanzone	150	.273	6	22	193	41	8	13		.967
	1B	P. Bourque	139	.209	7	20	327	35	5	32	.97	.986

Pitcher	G	IP	W	L	SV	ERA
F. Jenkins	38	271	14	16	0	3.89
B. Hooton	42	240	14	17	0	3.68
R. Reuschel	36	237	14	15	0	3.00
M. Pappas	30	162	7	12	0	4.28
B. Bonham	44	152	7	5	6	3.02
B. Locker	63	106	10	6	18	2.55
J. Aker	47	64	4	5	12	4.08

	POS	Cub	AB	BA	HR	RBI	PO	A	E	DP	TC/G	FA
1974 W-66 L-96 Whitey Lockman W-41 L-52 Jim Marshall W-25 L-44 6th	1B	A. Thornton	303	.261	10	46	760	70	7	61	9.3	.992
	2B	V. Harris	200	.195	0	11	122	144	16	20	5.0	.943
	SS	D. Kessinger	599	.259	1	42	**259**	476	32	87	5.1	.958
	3B	B. Madlock	453	.313	9	54	84	229	18	14	2.7	.946
	RF	J. Cardenal	542	.293	13	72	262	15	10	4	2.1	.965
	CF	R. Monday	538	.294	20	58	302	10	5	**5**	2.3	.984
	LF	J. Morales	534	.273	15	82	266	5	7	2	1.9	.975
	C	S. Swisher	280	.214	5	27	493	50	7	8	6.1	.987
	1O	B. Williams	404	.280	16	68	635	53	11	50		.984
	C	G. Mitterwald	215	.251	7	28	335	40	10	4	5.7	.974
	UT	C. Fanzone	158	.190	4	22	87	82	15	14		.918

	Pitcher	G	IP	W	L	SV	ERA
	B. Bonham	44	243	11	**22**	1	3.85
	R. Reuschel	41	241	13	12	0	4.29
	B. Hooton	48	176	7	11	1	4.81
	S. Stone	38	170	8	6	0	4.13
	K. Frailing	55	125	6	9	1	3.89
	D. LaRoche	49	92	5	6	5	4.79
	O. Zamora	56	84	3	9	10	3.11
	H. Pina	34	47	3	4	4	4.02

	POS	Cub	AB	BA	HR	RBI	PO	A	E	DP	TC/G	FA
1975 W-75 L-87 Jim Marshall 5th	1B	A. Thornton	372	293	18	60	982	77	13	88	9.5	.988
	2B	M. Trillo	545	.248	7	70	350	**509**	**29**	103	5.8	.967
	SS	D. Kessinger	601	.243	0	46	205	436	22	100	4.7	.967
	3B	B. Madlock	514	**.354**	7	64	79	250	20	14	2.7	.943
	RF	J. Cardenal	574	.317	9	68	313	14	8	3	2.2	.976
	CF	R. Monday	491	.267	17	60	315	6	9	0	2.5	.973
	LF	J. Morales	578	.270	12	91	273	11	6	1	1.9	.979
	C	S. Swisher	254	.213	1	22	426	36	10	5	5.1	.979
	1O	P. LaCock	249	.229	6	30	479	45	6	39		.989
	C	G. Mitterwald	200	.220	5	26	247	32	7	4	4.8	.976
	C	T. Hosley	141	.255	6	20	254	16	9	3	5.3	.968

	Pitcher	G	IP	W	L	SV	ERA
	R. Burris	36	238	15	10	0	4.12
	R. Reuschel	38	234	11	**17**	1	3.73
	B. Bonham	38	229	13	15	0	4.72
	S. Stone	33	214	12	8	0	3.95
	D. Knowles	58	88	6	9	15	5.83
	O. Zamora	52	71	5	2	10	5.07
	G. Zahn	16	63	2	7	1	4.45

	POS	Cub	AB	BA	HR	RBI	PO	A	E	DP	TC/G	FA
	1B	P. LaCock	244	.221	8	28	435	30	12	47	8.8	.975
	2B	M. Trillo	582	.239	4	59	349	**527**	17	103	5.7	.981
	SS	M. Kelleher	337	.228	0	22	147	289	9	52	4.4	.980
1976	3B	B. Madlock	514	**.339**	15	84	107	234	14	21	2.6	.961
W-75 L-87	RF	J. Morales	537	.274	16	67	273	12	5	**6**	2.1	.983
Jim Marshall	CF	R. Monday	534	.272	32	77	278	4	2	0	2.8	.993
4th	LF	J. Cardenal	521	.299	8	47	246	10	5	1	2.0	.981
	C	S. Swisher	377	.236	5	42	574	49	11	6	5.9	.983
	OF	J. Wallis	338	.254	5	21	193	11	5	3	2.3	.976
	C	G. Mitterwald	303	.215	5	28	320	40	7	2	5.7	.981
	SS	D. Rosello	227	.242	1	11	128	217	12	45	4.2	.966

Pitcher	G	IP	W	L	SV	ERA
R. Reuschel	38	260	14	12	1	3.46
R. Burris	37	249	15	13	0	3.11
B. Bonham	32	196	9	13	0	4.27
S. Renko	28	163	8	11	0	3.86
B. Sutter	52	83	6	3	10	2.71
J. Coleman	39	79	2	8	4	4.10
D. Knowles	58	72	5	7	9	2.88
O. Zamora	40	55	5	3	3	5.24

	POS	Cub	AB	BA	HR	RBI	PO	A	E	DP	TC/G	FA
	1B	B. Buckner	426	.284	11	60	966	58	10	75	10.4	.990
	2B	M. Trillo	504	.280	7	57	330	**467**	**25**	81	**5.5**	.970
	SS	I. DeJesus	624	.266	3	40	234	**595**	33	94	5.6	.962
1977	3B	S. Ontiveros	546	.299	10	68	100	324	20	24	2.9	.955
W-81 L-81	RF	B. Murcer	554	.265	27	89	237	11	5	**5**	1.7	.980
Herman Franks	CF	J. Morales	490	.290	11	69	247	8	4	3	2.0	.985
4th	LF	G. Gross	239	.322	5	32	109	3	1	0	1.6	.991
	C	G. Mitterwald	349	.238	9	43	631	78	8	13	**6.6.**	.989
	1O	L. Biittner	493	.298	12	62	792	65	11	51		.987
	OF	G. Clines	239	.293	3	41	68	3	1	0	1.1	.986
	OF	J. Cardenal	226	.239	3	18	85	1	1	0	1.4	.989

Pitcher	G	IP	W	L	SV	ERA
R. Reuschel	39	252	20	10	1	2.79
R. Burris	39	221	14	16	0	4.72
B. Bonham	34	215	10	13	0	4.35
M. Krukow	34	172	8	14	0	4.40
W. Hernandez	67	110	8	7	4	3.03
B. Sutter	62	107	7	3	31	1.35
P. Reuschel	69	107	5	6	4	4.37

	POS	Cub	AB	BA	HR	RBI	PO	A	E	DP	TC/G	FA
	1B	B. Buckner	446	.323	5	74	1075	83	6	85	11.1	.995
1978	2B	M. Trillo	552	.261	4	55	354	**505**	19	**99**	**5.9**	.978
W-79 L-83	SS	I. DeJesus	619	.278	3	35	232	**558**	27	96	5.1	.967
Herman Franks	3B	S. Ontiveros	276	.243	1	22	57	194	9	16	3.4	.965
3rd	RF	B. Murcer	499	.281	9	64	225	8	5	0	1.7	.979
	CF	G. Gross	347	.265	1	39	182	6	4	1	1.7	.979

POS	Cub	AB	BA	HR	RBI	PO	A	E	DP	TC/G	FA
LF	D. Kingman	395	.266	28	79	170	8	4	2	1.8	.978
C	D. Rader	305	.203	3	36	412	51	11	7	4.2	.977
1O	L. Biittner	343	.257	4	50	601	53	9	53		.986
OF	G. Clines	229	.258	0	17	84	6	2	0	1.4	.978
3B	R. Scott	227	.282	0	15	43	101	11	15	2.6	.929

Pitcher	G	IP	W	L	SV	ERA
R. Reuschel	35	243	14	15	0	3.41
D. Lamp	37	224	7	15	0	3.29
R. Burris	40	199	7	13	1	4.75
D. Roberts	35	142	6	8	1	5.26
M. Krukow	27	138	9	3	0	3.91
D. Moore	71	103	9	7	4	4.11
B. Sutter	64	99	8	10	27	3.18
W. Hernandez	54	60	8	2	3	3.75

	POS	Cub	AB	BA	HR	RBI	PO	A	E	DP	TC/G	FA
	1B	B. Buckner	591	.284	14	66	1258	124	7	118	8.8	.995
	2B	T. Sizemore	330	.248	2	24	230	312	15	68	5.8	.973
1979	SS	I. DeJesus	636	.283	5	52	235	507	32	97	4.8	.959
W-80 L-82	3B	S. Ontiveros	519	.285	4	57	98	268	23	27	2.7	.941
Herman Franks	RF	S. Thompson	346	.289	2	29	161	7	5	3	1.7	.971
W-78 L-78	CF	J. Martin	534	.272	19	73	297	11	6	4	2.1	.981
Joey Amalfitano	LF	D. Kingman	532	.288	48	115	240	11	12	3	1.9	.954
W-2 L-4	C	B. Foote	429	.254	16	56	713	63	17	9	6.1	.979
5th	10	L. Biittner	272	.290	3	50	46	3	4	0	1.1	.925
	OF	B. Murcer	190	.258	7		110	4	0	0	2.1	1.000
	OF	M. Vail	179	.335	7	35	51	3	2	0	1.4	.964
	23	S. Dillard	166	.283	5	24	110	4	0	0	1.0	1.000

Pitcher	G	IP	W	L	SV	ERA
R. Reuschel	36	239	18	12	0	3.62
L. McGlothen	42	212	13	14	0	4.12
D. Lamp	38	200	11	10	0	3.51
M. Krukow	28	165	9	9	0	4.20
K. Holtzman	23	118	6	9	0	4.58
D. Tidrow	63	103	11	5	4	2.71
B. Sutter	62	101	6	6	37	2.23

	POS	Cub	AB	BA	HR	RBI	PO	A	E	DP	TC/G	FA
	1B	B. Buckner	578	.324	10	68	826	73	6	67	9.6	.993
	2B	M. Tyson	341	.238	3	23	222	329	18	69	4.9	.968
1980	SS	I. DeJesus	618	.259	3	33	229	529	24	**99**	5.0	.969
W-64 L-98	3B	L. Randle	489	.276	5	39	76	225	**23**	7	2.9	.929
Preston Gomez	RF	M. Vail	312	.298	6	47	126	5	5	1	1.8	.963
W-38 L-53	CF	J. Martin	494	.227	23	73	262	8	6	0	2.1	.978
Joe Amalfitano	LF	D. Kingman	255	.278	18	57	103	8	7	0	1.9	.941
W-26 L-45	C	T. Blackwell	320	.272	5	30	572	93	12	16	6.6	.982
6th	10	L. Biittner	273	.249	1	34	250	19	1	14	6.7	.996
	23	S. Dillard	244	.225	4	27	64	85	3	13	4.0	.980
	OF	S. Thompson	226	.212	2	13	100	4	4	2	1.7	.963
	C	B. Foote	202	.238	6	28	317	36	3	5	6.9	.992

Pitcher	G	IP	W	L	SV	ERA
R. Reuschel	38	257	11	13	0	3.40
M. Krukow	34	205	10	15	0	4.39
D. Lamp	41	203	10	13	0	5.19
L. McGlothen	39	182	12	14	0	4.80
B. Caudill	72	128	4	6	1	2.18
D. Tidrow	**84**	116	6	5	6	2.79
B. Sutter	60	102	5	8	**28**	2.65

	POS	Cub	AB	BA	HR	RBI	PO	A	E	DP	TC/G	FA
	1B	B. Buckner	421	.311	10	75	996	81	**17**	92	10.4	.984
	2B	S. Dillard	119	.218	7	15	54	96	4	21	4.9	.974
1981	SS	I. DeJesus	403	.194	0	13	**221**	343	24	**81**	5.5	.959
W-38 L-65	3B	K. Reitz	260	.215	2	28	57	157	5	11	2.7	**.977**
Joe Amalfitano	RF	L. Durham	328	.290	10	35	159	4	5	1	2.0	.970
6th 1st Half	CF	J. Morales	245	.286	1	25	142	2	2	1	2.0	.986
W-15 L-37	LF	S. Henderson	287	.293	5	35	152	4	8	2	2.1	.951
5th 2nd Half	C	J. Davis	180	.256	4	21	274	44	9	4	5.8	.972
W-23 L-28	CF	B. Bonds	163	.215	6	19	108	2	2	0	2.7	.982
	C	T. Blackwell	158	.234	1	11	268	28	2	1	5.3	.993
	OF	S. Thompson	115	.165	0	8	49	1	1	0	1.7	.980
	OF3	H. Cruz	109	.229	1	11	21	1	0	0	1.4	1.000
	2B	P. Tabler	101	.188	1	5	70	93	3	17	4.7	.982

Pitcher	G	IP	W	L	SV	ERA
M. Krukow	25	144	9	9	0	3.69
R. Martz	33	108	5	7	6	3.67
R. Reuschel	13	86	4	7	0	3.45
K. Kravec	24	78	1	6	0	5.08
D. Bird	12	75	4	5	0	3.60
D. Tidrow	51	75	3	10	9	5.04

Single Season Cub All-Star Team, 1948-1981

Between 1948 and 1980, which Cub players gave to the Cubs a season of baseball that deserves recognition? Jim Hickman, for example, may not be the all-time Cub first baseman, but for one season he was as good as any of them. Listed below are players selections for a Cub All-Star team for this thirty-two year period. Some players, of course, had many distinguished seasons; for them, only their best season was selected (except in those special cases when a player contributed excellent seasons of play at different positions).

Abbreviation Key

Player Statistics

G	Games
AB	At Bats
H	Hits
2B	Doubles
3B	Triples
HR	Home Runs
R	Runs Scored
RBI	Runs Batted In
RP	Runs Produced
BB	Bases on Balls
SO	Strike-outs
SB	Stolen Bases
BA	Batting Average
SA	Slugging Average

Pitcher Statistics

G	Games Pitched
GS	Games Started
CG	Complete Games
IP	Innings Pitched
H	Hits Allowed
BB	Bases on Balls Allowed
ShO	Shutouts
ERA	Earned Run Average
W	Wins
L	Losses
SV	Saves
Pct.	Winning Percentage

(Boldfaced type indicates league leader in that position.)

	G	AB	H	2B	3B	HR	R	RBI	RP	BB	SO	SB	BA	SA
First Base														
Dee Fondy (1953)	150	595	184	24	11	18	79	78	139	44	106	10	.309	.477
Ernie Banks (1962)	154	610	164	20	6	37	87	104	154	30	71	5	.269	.503
Jim Hickman (1970)	149	514	162	33	4	32	102	115	195	93	99	0	.315	.582
Bill Buckner (1980)	145	578	187	41	3	10	69	68	127	30	18	1	**.324**	.487
Second Base														
Ken Hubbs (1962)	160	661	172	24	9	5	90	49	134	35	**129**	3	.260	.346
Glenn Beckert (1971)	131	530	181	18	5	2	80	42	120	24	24	3	.342	.406
Shortstop														
Ernie Banks (1958)	154	**617**	193	23	11	**47**	119	**129**	201	52	87	4	.313	**.614**
Don Kessinger (1969)	158	664	181	38	6	4	109	53	158	61	70	11	.273	.366
Ivan DeJesus (1979)	160	636	180	26	10	5	92	52	139	59	82	24	.283	.379
Third Base														
Andy Pafko (1948)	142	548	171	30	2	26	82	101	157	50	50	3	.312	.516
Ron Santo (1964)	161	592	185	33	**13**	30	94	114	178	**86**	96	3	.313	.564
Bill Madlock (1975)	130	514	182	29	7	7	77	64	134	42	34	9	**.354**	**.479**
Right Field														
F. Baumholtz (1952)	103	409	133	17	4	4	59	35	90	27	27	5	.325	.416
Hank Sauer (1954)	142	520	150	18	1	41	98	103	160	70	68	2	.288	.563
George Altman (1961)	138	518	157	28	**12**	27	77	96	146	40	92	6	.303	.560
Jose Cardenal (1975)	154	574	182	30	2	9	85	68	144	77	50	34	.317	.423
Center Field														
Andy Pafko (1950)	146	514	156	24	8	36	95	92	151	69	32	4	.304	.591
Rick Monday (1976)	137	534	145	20	5	32	107	77	152	60	125	5	.272	.507

	G	AB	H	2B	3B	HR	R	RBI	RP	BB	SO	SB	BA	SA

Left Field

	G	AB	H	2B	3B	HR	R	RBI	RP	BB	SO	SB	BA	SA
Hank Sauer (1952)	151	567	153	31	3	**37**	89	**121**	173	77	92	1	.270	.531
Billy Williams (1972)	150	574	191	34	6	37	95	122	180	62	59	3	**.333**	**.606**
Dave Kingman (1979)	145	532	153	19	5	**48**	97	115	164	45	**131**	4	.288	**.613**

Catcher

	G	AB	H	2B	3B	HR	R	RBI	RP	BB	SO	SB	BA	SA
Randy Hundley (1967)	152	539	144	25	3	14	68	60	114	44	75	2	.267	.403

Pitchers	G	GS	CG	IP	H	BB	SO	ShO	ERA	W	-L	SV	Pct.

Starters

	G	GS	CG	IP	H	BB	SO	ShO	ERA	W	-L	SV	Pct.
Bob Rush (1952)	34	32	17	250.1	205	81	157	4	2.70	17	13	0	.567
Dick Drott (1957)	38	32	7	229	200	**129**	170	3	3.58	15	11	0	.577
Dick Ellsworth (1963)	37	37	19	290.2	223	75	185	4	2.11	22	10	0	.688
Larry Jackson (1964)	40	38	19	297.2	265	58	148	3	3.14	**24**	11	0	.686
Bill Hands (1969)	41	41	18	300	268	73	181	3	2.49	20	14	0	.588
Ken Holtzman (1970)	39	38	15	288	271	94	202	1	3.38	17	11	0	.607
Ferguson Jenkins (1971)	39	**39**	**30**	**325**	**304**	37	263	3	2.77	**24**	13	0	.649
Milt Pappas (1972)	29	28	10	195	187	29	80	3	2.77	17	7	0	.708
Rick Reuschel (1977)	39	37	8	252	233	74	166	4	2.79	20	10	1	.667

Relievers

	G	GS	CG	IP	H	BB	SO	ShO	ERA	W	-L	SV	Pct.
Don Elston (1958)	**69**	0	0	97	75	39	84	0	2.88	9	8	10	.529
Bill Henry (1959)	**65**	0	0	134.1	111	26	115	0	2.68	9	8	12	.529
Lindy McDaniel (1963)	57	0	0	88	82	27	75	0	2.86	13	7	**22**	.650
Ted Abernathy (1965)	**84**	0	0	136.1	113	56	104	0	2.57	4	6	**31**	.400
Phil Regan (1968)	68	0	0	127	109	24	60	0	2.19	10	5	**21**	.667
Bruce Sutter (1979)	62	0	0	101	67	32	110	0	2.23	6	6	**37**	.500

Index of Cub Players, 1948-1981

Coming in September . . .

Take the Cubs one day at a time with . . .

THE CUB FAN'S CALENDAR 1983

If you enjoyed Jim Langford's **The Game Is Never Over,** look forward to this calendar by the same author! Colorful and complete with dozens of classic photos, **The Cub Fan's Calendar 1983** will have all the memorable and all the not-so-memorable events in Cub history printed right on the corresponding dates along with the 1983 team schedule. Add to this the winning combination of Langford's historical knowledge, wit, and loving devotion and you'll have a daily celebration of all the tears and cheers, trades and hopes, fantasies and failures of baseball's most lovable team, the Chicago Cubs! A must for every *tried* and true Cub fan! (September, $7.95)

And on the Southside of town . . .

Watch for Rich Lindberg's WHO'S ON THIRD? THE STORY OF THE CHICAGO WHITE SOX!

Filled with the great days, great people and plays from the 1900s to the 1980s, this is the most comprehensive coverage of the White Sox ever published. With many photos, lots of statistics, index, and chapter on Games to Remember, **Who's On Third?** is a treasury of all the moments and miracles on 35th & Shields. All you Go Go Sox fans, go get this one! (September, $13.95)

Available at your local bookstore or order directly from us (please add $1.50 per order):

Icarus Press
P.O. Box 1225
South Bend, IN 46624